IN THE NAME OF

ALLAH

THE ALL-COMPASSIONATE, ALL-MERCIFUL

FATÂWA

ESSENTIAL RULINGS FOR EVERY MUSLIM WOMAN

- Title: FATÂWA: Essential Rulings for Every Muslim Woman
- Compiled and Translated by: Ibn Maqbool Husain
- English Edition 2 (2005)
- Layout: IIPH, Riyadh, Saudi Arabia
- Filming & Cover Designing: Samo Press Group

FATÂWA

ESSENTIAL RULINGS FOR EVERY MUSLIM WOMAN

فتاوى المرأة المسلمة

By Renowned Scholars of the Twentieth Century
Shaykh Muhammad ibn Ibraheem
Shaykh Abdul-Aziz ibn Bâz
Shaykh Muhammad ibn Sâleh al-Uthaymeen
Shaykh Abdullah ibn Jibreen
Shaykh Sâleh al-Fawzân

Compiled and Translated by:
Ibn Maqbool Husain

الدار العالمية للكتاب الإسلامي

INTERNATIONAL ISLAMIC PUBLISHING HOUSE

King Fahd National Library Cataloging-in-Publication Data

Ibn Maqbool, Husain

Fatâwa: Essential rulings for every Muslim woman. / Husain ibn Maqbool .- Riyadh, 2005

...p ; ...cm

ISBN Hard Cover: 9960-850-79-X
ISBN Soft Cover: 9960-850-80-3

1- Women in Islam I- Title

219.1 dc 1424/6354
1424/6355

ISBN Hard Cover: **9960-850-79-X** Legal Deposit no. **1428/6354**
ISBN Soft Cover: **9960-850-80-3** Legal Deposit no. **1424/6355**

International Islamic Publishing House (IIPH)
P.O.Box 55195 Riyadh 11534, Saudi Arabia
Tel: 966 1 4650818 – 4647213 – Fax: 4633489
E-Mail: iiphiiph.com.sa – iiphsagmail.com
www.iiph.com.sa

LIST OF CONTENTS

PUBLISHER'S NOTE

Allah, the All-Gracious the All-Beneficent, has provided Muslims with many resources that may help them to explore the correct procedures and adopt them in practising the basics of the religion of truth.

First, and foremost, of these resources is the Noble Qur'an, and the honourable Sunnah of the Prophet Muhammad (Blessings and Peace of Allah may be upon him). Next are the companions of the Prophet (may Allah be pleased with them all), the highly knowledgeable followers, the prominent scholars of Islamic jurisprudence and many other qualified authors and writers on various Islamic affairs, may Allah, the All-Glorious, reward them all.

The book in question "Fataawa for Women" is a versatile compilation which presents a large number of religious rulings and verdicts responding to questions addressed by so many women, seeking guidance and knowledge for the proper performance of their worship acts.

The reliable answers of the prominent and competent Shaykhs to those questions have drawn the right path not only for the questioners but also for all readers of this book.

May Allah, the Exalted, have mercy on these renowned Shaykhs, the questioners and all prospective readers, and reward them well.

Muḥammad ibn 'Abdul-Muḥsin Al-Tuwaijri
International Islamic Publishing House
Riyadh, Saudi Arabia
1424 AH / 2003 CE

CHAPTER: PURIFICATION

The ruling on pronouncing the intention with the tongue

Q. What is the ruling on uttering the intention for the prayer and ablution with the tongue?

A. Its ruling is that it is a *bid'ah* (heresy). This is because it was not related by the Messenger of Allah (ﷺ) (Blessings and Peace be upon him) or from his Companions. So, it is obligatory to leave it. The place of the intention is the heart, thus there is no need, whatsoever, to utter it with the tongue. And Allah is the source of success.

Shaykh 'Abdul 'Aziz ibn Baaz.

Ruling concerning a toddler vomiting. on its mother's clothes.

Q. Is it permissible to pray wearing clothes upon which a suckling baby boy has vomited?.

A. The clothes are to be cleaned by sprinkling water on the area that became affected. This ruling applies as long as the boy is still in the breast-feeding stage and has not started eating food yet. This is similar to a baby boy's urine (i.e. the boy is still under breast feeding and has not started eating food yet) that is also to be washed away by sprinkling water upon it and then it is permissible to pray in those clothes. It is not permissible to pray in them before sprinkling them with water. And Allah (ﷻ) 'the Exalted' is the source of success..

Shaykh 'Abdul 'Aziz ibn Baaz

The ruling on the wetness coming out of a woman

Q. I heard from one of the scholars that the wetness that comes out of the vagina of a woman is pure. Since I heard this *fatwa* (legal ruling) I did not use to change my clothes (after seeing wetness) whenever I wanted to pray. Then after the passing of a long time, I heard from another scholar that the wetness is impure. So what is the correct ruling?

A. Everything that comes out of the two private parts, be it water or anything else, breaks the *wuḍoo'* (ablution) and thus whatever has been affected of clothes and body is to be washed. However, if this is on a continued basis, then it takes the ruling of *istiḥaaḍah* (menstruation) and the ruling of continuous flow of urine, in which case, it is to be cleaned with water and a fresh *wuḍoo'* is to be made for each prayer. This is based on the saying of the Messenger of Allah (ﷺ) to a woman with *istiḥaaḍah*:

"...and make *wuḍoo'* for each prayer".

An exception to this is continuous passing of the wind, for which there is no need to clean the clothes with water but rather the person should just make *wuḍoo'* like the *wuḍoo'* for the prayer. The procedure for this is: to wash the face, which includes rinsing the mouth and cleaning the nose, washing the two hands (including the elbows), wiping over the head, and washing the two feet. The ruling is similar for sleep, touching the private parts and eating camel's meat, for which there is no need to clean any clothes with water (as is done say after urinating) but rather, only the *wuḍoo'*, as described above, is obligatory. And with Allah is success.

Shaykh 'Abdul 'Aziz ibn Baaz

Wetness and a woman's body

Q. Is the wetness that comes out of a woman's body pure or impure? May Allah reward you.

A. What is known among the people of knowledge is that everything that comes out of the two private parts is impure except one thing, which is the sperm, for it is pure. Otherwise, all things that come out of the two private parts (from both males and females) are impure and nullify the *wuḍoo'*. So based on this rule, what comes out of a woman, like the water and similar things, is impure and necessitates the performance of *wuḍoo'*. This is what I have reached after research with other scholars and after revision.

However, despite that, I am in a difficult position regarding its ruling because some women have this discharge always and if it is continuous, then it means that it should be dealt with by treating it like the case of continuous urine wherein she would be required to make *wuḍoo'* for each prayer after its time starts and then perform that prayer.

Likewise, I researched with some doctors and it became apparent that if this discharge is from the urinary bladder, then it is as we have said. And if it is from where the baby is born, then it is as we have said regarding making *wuḍoo'* from it. But it is nonetheless pure and does not require washing what has been affected by it.

Shaykh Muhammad ibn 'Uthaymeen

Applying Henna on the head does not negate the purification

Q. A woman made *wuḍoo'* and then applied henna to her hair on the head, then she prayed with the henna still on her head. Is her prayer valid or not? And if her *wuḍoo'* is negated, is she to wipe over the henna or wash her hair then make normal *wuḍoo'* for the prayer?

A. Applying the henna on the head does not nullify a person's *wuḍoo'* so long as she has finished performing the *wuḍoo'*. So if she makes *wuḍoo'* while the henna is on her head or something else similar like a bandage that she has to have on, then it is OK to wipe over it in the smaller purification (i.e. *wuḍoo'*). As for the greater purification (i.e. bathing from state of *janaabah*), then she has to pour water over it three times and wiping is not enough. This is because of an authentic narration recorded by Muslim on the authority of Umm Salamah (رضي الله عنها) (may Allah be pleased with her) that she said: "O' Messenger of Allah, I am a woman who has closely plaited hair on my head; should I undo it for taking a bath resulting from sexual intercourse or menstruation? The Messenger of Allah (ﷺ) said:

> "No, it is enough for you to throw three handfuls of water on your head (making sure that all the hair and the scalp become wet) and then pour water over yourself, and you shall be purified."

However, if she undoes the plaits when washing from menstruation, it is better due to other narrations that have been reported on this issue. And Allah is the source of success.

Shaykh 'Abdul 'Aziz ibn Baaz

Ruling concerning doubts regarding the nullification of *wuḍoo'*

> Q. What is the ruling if a person has a doubt whether the *wuḍoo'* is nullified or not?

A. If a person doubts whether the *wuḍoo'* has nullified or not, then the ruling for this is that the *wuḍoo'* is remaining, unaffected by the doubt. This is based on the saying of the Messenger of Allah (ﷺ) when he was asked about a man who thinks he has nullified his *wuḍoo'* during his prayer:

"Do not leave your prayer until you hear a sound or smell the wind."

The Messenger of Allah (ﷺ) explained to him that the basis is purification until one is sure of nullification. So as long as it is still a doubt (and not reached the level of certainty), then the *wudoo'* is correct and proper and the person is allowed to pray, make *tawaaf* (circumambulation of the Ka'bah) and read from the Qur'an. This is the basis. And all praise is to Allah for the easiness in Islam.

Shaykh 'Abdul 'Aziz ibn Baaz

How does a woman wipe her head for *wuḍoo'*

Q. What is the procedure for a woman to wipe over her head when making *wuḍoo'*? And what is the ruling of wiping only a portion of the head for the woman who has a necessity?

A. The ruling of wiping over the head for the woman is the same as the ruling for a man. She should wipe all of her head from the point where the hair begins including the two ears. However, she does not have to wipe what hangs down from the forelock due to what is established in authentic narrations from the Messenger of Allah (ﷺ) that he used to wipe his head from its front to the back including the two ears. The basis for this is that the men and women have the same ruling in all issues except what has been made a special case or based on proof.

Shaykh 'Abdul 'Aziz ibn Baaz

The procedure for a woman washing herself from *janaabah* and menses

Q. Is there a difference between a man and a woman's washing from *janaabah*? And is it required for the woman to undo her hair or is it enough for her to throw

over her head three handfuls of water based on the
Ḥadith reported on this matter? And what is the
difference between the bathing from *janaabah* and
bathing from menses?

A. There is no difference between a man and a woman's bathing
from *janaabah* and neither of them is required to undo their hair
for washing. Instead, it is enough to throw three handfuls of water
over the head (making sure that all the hair and the scalp become
wet) and then pour water over the rest of the body. This is based
on the Ḥadith of Umm Salamah (؏) wherein she said to the
Messenger of Allah (ﷺ): "I am a woman who has closely plaited
hair on my head; should I undo it for taking a bath because of
sexual intercourse? The Messenger of Allah (ﷺ) said:

> "No, it is enough for you to throw three handfuls of
> water on your head (making sure that all the hair and the
> scalp become wet) and then pour water over yourself,
> and you shall be purified."

Imam Muslim has reported this Ḥadith.

However, if there is something applied to the head of the man or
the woman that prevents the water from reaching the scalp, it is
obligatory to remove it. But if it is thin and does not prevent water
from reaching the scalp, it is not obligatory to remove it.

As for a woman's bathing from menses, the scholars differed as to
whether she has to undo her hair for bathing or not. The correct
opinion is that it is not obligatory for her to undo her hair. This is
based on some narrations of the report from Umm Salamah (؏)
recorded by Imam Muslim, wherein she said to the Messenger of
Allah (ﷺ): "I am a woman who has closely plaited hair on my
head; should I undo it for taking a bath because of sexual
intercourse or menstruation?" The Messenger of Allah (ﷺ) said:

> "No, it is enough for you to throw three handfuls of

water on your head (making sure that all the hair and the scalp become wet) and then pour water over yourself, and you shall be purified."

So, this Ḥadith is clear in that it is not obligatory to undo the hair for bathing from menses and *janaabah.*

However, it is better for her to undo the hair for bathing from menses to be on the safe side and to avoid the difference between the scholars and thus combining all the proofs.

The Permanent Committee for Research and Verdicts

The ruling concerning performing the prayer wearing thin clothes and socks

Q. What is the ruling of a woman's prayer that is performed wearing thin clothes?

A. It is not permissible for a woman to pray in thin outer garments or in thin clothes or the like. The prayer is not valid with these. It is obligatory for her to pray with clothes that cover her completely and nothing of what is underneath the garments should be seen or known in terms of color. This is because the woman is *'awrah** (what has to be covered) and it is obligatory upon her to cover all of her body except the face and two hands whilst in prayer. However, if she covers her hands, it is better. As for the feet, they must be covered with socks that completely cover the feet or with long garments that cover the feet.

Shaykh 'Abdul 'Aziz ibn Baaz

---

* 'awrah: Parts of the body from the navel to the knees for men, and all the body except the face and the hands for women.

The ruling of wiping over thin socks

Q. What is the ruling of wiping over thin socks?

A. Amongst the conditions of wiping over socks is that they should be thick, and cover the feet. Thus if they are thin, it is not allowed to wipe over them because the feet covered with thin socks take the same ruling as that of feet uncovered totally. And Allah is the One who gives success.

Shaykh 'Abdul 'Aziz ibn Baaz

Small holes in the socks are to be overlooked when wiping over them

Q. What is the ruling for one who saw, after the prayer by a long or short period, a medium size hole in one of the socks? Is the prayer to be repeated?

A. If the hole is small, and likewise, if there are small tears in the socks, as defined by what is seen by people as small, then it is to be overlooked and the prayer is valid. It is safer for a male and female believer to take care to have the socks free from tears and holes in order to be on the safe side with respect to his or her religion and in order not to get involved with the difference between the people of knowledge. This general principle is shown in a saying of the Messenger of Allah (ﷺ) wherein he said:

> "Leave what is doubtful for that which is not doubtful."

And also his (ﷺ) saying:

> "Whosoever avoids doubts, then he is free regarding his religion and honor."

And Allah is the source of success.

Shaykh 'Abdul 'Aziz ibn Baaz

Employing a *kaafir* for chores around the house, like cooking and cleaning

Q. We have a non-Muslim maid in our house. So is it permissible for me to leave her to wash the clothes and then I pray in these clothes? And do I eat from what she cooks? And is it permissible for me to find faults with their religion and explain to them the falseness of their religion?

A. It is permissible to get a non-Muslim for cooking and cleaning purposes and the like. Similarly, it is allowed to eat the food they cook, and wear the clothes they sew or wash. This is because a *kaafir's* body is clean and his impurity is abstract. The Companions used to have *kaafir* (disbeliever) slaves, both male and female, and they used to eat from what they obtained from the countries of the disbelievers. This was due to their knowledge that their (i.e. the disbelievers) physical bodies are pure. However, a Ḥadith has been reported that shows the necessity to wash the vessels of the disbelievers before cooking in them if they used them to drink alcohol or used them to cook dead unlawful animals or pigs, and the necessity to wash their clothes which used to touch their *'awrahs*..

As for finding faults with their religion and showing them what is wrong with their religion, then it is permissible, and what is to be intended is the belief that is attributed to their religion currently. It will either be innovated beliefs, such as idol worship, or changed and abrogated beliefs such as with the Christians. The faults are in the changed or innovated religion (and not in what was originally revealed to the respective Prophets). It is upon you to call them to Islam and explain to them its teachings, its benefits, what it is comprised of, as well as explaining to them the difference between Islam and other religions.

Shaykh 'Abdullah ibn Jibreen

Dry impurities do not contaminate other dry things

Q. Does dry urine not make the clothes impure? That is, when a child urinates on the ground, and the urine remains there till it dries and is not cleaned. Then someone comes and sits on the dry urine. So do there clothes become impure?

A. Dry body and clothes are not affected by touching dry impurity. So, similarly, entering barefoot in a toilet that has dried up impurity does not affect dry feet because impurity is transferred with wetness.

Shaykh 'Abdullah ibn Jibreen

Food remains in the teeth and its effect on the *wuḍoo'*

Q. A sister is asking: sometimes I find some food remains in my teeth, so is it obligatory to remove these remains before making *wudoo'*?

A. What is apparent to me is that it is not obligatory to remove them before *wuḍoo'*. However, cleaning the food off the teeth is without a doubt better, cleaner and will keep diseases far away from affecting the teeth. If these remains are not cleaned, they cause the teeth to decay and also cause diseases of the teeth and gums. So what a person should do when he finishes from his food is to clean his teeth till everything that became attached to it is removed. Also, he should use the *miswaak* since food changes the smell of the mouth. The Messenger of Allah (ﷺ) said regarding using miswaak (a short thin stick of a scented tree to clean the teeth):

> "It is a means of cleaning the teeth and a pleasing thing to the Lord."

So this shows that whenever the teeth are in need of cleaning, it is better to be done with a *miswaak*. And Allah knows best.

Shaykh Muḥammad ibn 'Uthaymeen

Cleaning the children does not nullify the *wuḍoo'*

Q. If I am in a state of purity, then I clean my child, does it nullify my *wuḍoo'* or not?

A. Whoever touched the private parts of others with desire then their own *wuḍoo'* would be nullified. There is, however, a difference of opinion regarding touching without desire. The more correct opinion is that touching the private parts of children to clean them does not break the *wuḍoo'* because it is not something expected to raise desires and it is something which is needed by many and thus the nullification of *wuḍoo'* by it would cause a lot of trouble and problem. So if it was something that nullified the *wuḍoo'*, it would have become popular amongst the Companions (aṣ-Ṣaḥaabah) and those after them (at-Taabi'een):

Shaykh 'Abdullah ibn Jibreen

Is oil considered to be a barrier that prevents water from reaching the skin when making *wuḍoo'*

Q. I heard from one of the scholars that oil is considered a barrier that prevents the water from reaching the skin when making *wuḍoo'*. Sometimes when I am cooking, some drops of oil spill on my hair and on the parts of the body that are to be washed in *wuḍoo'*. So, is it a requirement when I am making *wuḍoo'* that I wash these parts with soap or I take a bath such that the water reaches the skin? Similarly, I apply oil to my hair as a treatment. So what do I do? Expecting benefit.

A. Before I answer this question, I would like to explain that Allah, the Glorified and Almighty, said in His book:

﴿يَٰٓأَيُّهَا ٱلَّذِينَ ءَامَنُوٓاْ إِذَا قُمۡتُمۡ إِلَى ٱلصَّلَوٰةِ فَٱغۡسِلُواْ وُجُوهَكُمۡ وَأَيۡدِيَكُمۡ إِلَى ٱلۡمَرَافِقِ وَٱمۡسَحُواْ بِرُءُوسِكُمۡ وَأَرۡجُلَكُمۡ إِلَى ٱلۡكَعۡبَيۡنِۚ...﴿٦﴾﴾ (المائدة : ٦)

"O' you who believe, when you intend to offer prayers, wash your faces and hands up to the elbows, wipe your heads and wash your feet up to the ankles..."

(Qur'an 5: 6)

So the order regarding washing some of these parts and wiping over others, necessitates that anything which prevents the water from reaching them should be removed because if such a thing is present, then it would not be called washing. So based on this, we say that if a person applies oil on the parts that have to be washed during *wuḍoo'*, then if this oil has become solid, it is required to remove it before washing the particular body part. This is because if the oil remains in a solid state, then it will prevent the water from reaching the skin and thus the *wuḍoo'* will be invalid.

On the other hand, if the oil does not become solid and its traces are there on the parts of the body to be washed during *wuḍoo'*, then there is no harm. But in such a situation, the person should make sure of this by passing his hands on these parts during *wuḍoo'* because normally the oil does not mix with water and maybe the water will not reach all the parts of *wuḍoo'* that the water is supposed to clean.

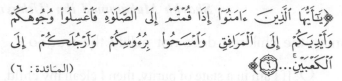

So we say to the questioner that if this particular oil that is on her *wuḍoo'* parts is in a solid state such that it would prevent water from reaching the skin, then she must remove it before making *wuḍoo'*. However, if it does not have a solid state, then there is no blame upon her to make *wuḍoo'* and there is no need to wash it with soap, but she should pass her hand on the part when washing it so that the water does not just slide over it but rather reaches it.

Shaykh Muḥammad ibn 'Uthaymeen

Washing the face and hands with soap when making *wuḍoo'*

Q. What is the ruling on washing the face and hands with soap when making *wuḍoo'*?

A. Washing the face and hands with soap is not legislated. Infact, it is from rigidity and being over-strict and it is established from the Messenger of Allah (ﷺ) that he said:

"Ruined are those who indulge in hair-splitting."

He (the Holy Prophet) repeated this thrice.

But if the situation is such that there is dirt on the hands that can only be removed by using soap or other similar cleaners, then there is no blame in its usage. However, if the matter is normal, then using the soap is considered being over-strict and an innovation and so, do not use it.

Shaykh Muḥammad ibn 'Uthaymeen

Kissing does not break the *wuḍoo'*

Q. My husband always kisses me when he leaves the house, even if he is going out to prayer in the masjid. I feel that sometimes he kisses me with passion, so what is the Islamic ruling regarding my *wuḍoo'*?

A. 'Aa'ishah (رضي الله عنها) reported that the Messenger of Allah (ﷺ) used to kiss some of his wives before going out to prayer and he would not make *wuḍoo'*.

In this Ḥadith is the ruling of touching a woman and kissing her. Does the *wuḍoo'* nullify or does not nullify? The scholars, may Allah have mercy upon them, differed on this issue. There are some among them who said kissing nullifies the *wuḍoo'* in all situations, as soon as a woman is touched. There are others among the scholars who said that the *wuḍoo'* only nullifies if a person touches the woman with desire, and lastly a third opinion of the scholars said that the *wuḍoo'* does not nullify no matter what. This last opinion, which is that the *wuḍoo'* does not nullify even if he kisses, touches or hugs his wife, is the most correct opinion. This is the case so long as he does not ejaculate and no secretions come out. So the *wuḍoo'* of both the man and woman is not nullified. This is because of the rule that the state of the *wuḍoo'* remains upon what it was until there is proof that it has broken. There is no proof in the book of Allah nor in the sunnah of Allah's Messenger (ﷺ) that shows that touching a woman nullifies the *wuḍoo'*. So based on this, touching a woman, even skin to skin contact, and even kissing and hugging with desire, all these do not nullify the *wuḍoo'*. And Allah (ﷻ) knows best.

Shaykh Muḥammad ibn 'Uthaymeen

Penetration necessitates bathing even without ejaculation

Q. Does my wife have to take a bath for *janaabah* even if there was no ejaculation in the uterus, but just penetration? And is there a bath for *janaabah* upon her when she has a loop put in her uterus or is it enough to wash her body and the effected parts only?

A. Yes, she has to have a bath due to mere penetration, even if that is little. This is based on the Ḥadith on the authority of Abu Hurayrah (رضي الله عنه) (may Allah be pleased with him) that the Messenger of Allah (ﷺ) said:

> "When a man sits in between the four parts of a woman and performed the sexual intercourse with her, bath becomes obligatory."

And also the Ḥadith:

> "If the two circumcised parts meet (i.e. the penis and vagina), then a bath is obligatory."

Similarly, she has to bath (*ghusl*) even if she has a loop inside her uterus because penetration and ejaculation has happened most likely.[1] Only *wudoo'* will suffice if there was only touching without penetration.

Shaykh 'Abdullah ibn Jibreen

The woman does not become impure due to menses and post-natal bleeding

Q. After my wife gave birth, one of my friends prohibited her from entering my house on the claim that a woman, whilst in the state of post-natal bleeding, a person is not allowed to eat from what she has cooked with her hands and thinks that her body is impure. This has led me to suspicion in living with her. I hope you can benefit. As far as I know, a post-natal bleeding woman is to stay away from prayer, fasting and reading the Qur'an.

A. A woman does not become impure due to menses or post-natal bleeding, and neither her food becomes forbidden. Similarly, enjoying her in a way except sexual intercourse is also not forbidden. However, it is disliked to enjoy her between the navel

---

[1] It seems that the Shaykh has misunderstood the questioner. The questioner was referring to whether a bath is necessary if a loop is put in. Whereas the Shaykh understood the question to be whether a bath is necessary if sexual intercourse is performed with a woman who has a loop in her vagina.

and knees only. This is based on a Ḥadith recorded by Imam Muslim on the authority of Anas (may Allah be pleased with him) who said that the Jews did not use to eat with a woman who had menses, so the Messenger of Allah (ﷺ) said:

> "Do anything (with a woman while she is in menses) except sexual intercourse."

And also based on what has been recorded by Imams Bukhari and Muslim on the authority of 'Aa'ishah (رضي الله عنها) who said:

> "The Messenger of Allah used to order me to cover myself in a loincloth and then he used to enjoy me whilst I was in menses."

There is no effect of the prohibition of prayer, fasting and reading the Qur'an for the menstruating and post-natal woman on eating with her or eating what she has prepared with her hands. And with Allah is success.

The Permanent Committee for Research and Verdicts

Ruling concerning pills that prevent menses

Q. There are pills that prevent menses or delay it from its normal time. So is it permissible to use them in the time of ḥajj out of fear that the normal time of menses will come during ḥajj?

A. It is permissible for a woman to use these pills during the time of ḥajj fearing that menses might come during the time of ḥajj. However, this has to be after consulting a specialist doctor regarding the safety of the woman (and the effect which the pills may have on her). Similarly, she can take the pills during the month of Ramaḍaan if she desires to fast with the people.

The Permanent Committee for Research and Verdicts

Ruling concerning the abrupt ending of the monthly period

Q. It happens to me during my monthly period, that sometimes it is for 4 days, then it stops for 3 days, and then on the 7th day it comes back with a lighter color. This then changes to a coffee type color till the 12th day. I hope that you, the noble scholars, can guide me to that which is correct?

A. All the days mentioned, the four (the first four days) and six (from the seventh day till the twelfth day), are days of menses (i.e. the menses can sometimes last four days and can also last six days). So you should leave the prayer and fasting during these days and it is not permissible for your husband to have sexual intercourse with you during these days. You should have a bath after the fourth day and pray and you would be allowed for your husband between the two days of menses when you are pure. And there is no objection to you fasting in them also. However, if this is during the month of Ramaḍaan, then you have to fast these days of purity. Then when you become pure again after the six day period (from the seventh day till the twelfth day), which would be the twelfth day, then you should have a bath, pray and fast just like all other women who are not in their menses. This is because the duration of menses increases and decreases, and they come all together and separately also.

May Allah guide us all to what pleases Him, and may He give us, you and all the Muslims, the understanding of the religion and being firm in it.

Shaykh 'Abdul 'Aziz ibn Baaz

Ruling concerning the blood that came after a bath was taken at the end of menses

Q. I noticed that when I am having a bath after my monthly period has ended, and after waiting the normal period for the menses, which is five days, that sometimes some small amount of blood comes out of me. And this is straight after a shower and then after that nothing comes out. I do not know whether to go by my usual monthly period duration of five days and not to consider what exceeds that and to pray and fast and nothing would be upon me. Or do I consider that day also as a day of my menses and I do not pray or fast in it? Please note that this does not happen after every menstrual cycle, but rather after every two or three cycles. I hope that you can benefit me.

A. If what comes out of you after becoming pure is yellowish or blackish, then it is nothing of menses and its ruling is the ruling of urine.

However, if it is clear blood, then it is considered to be menses and you have to repeat the bath due to what is established on the authority of Umm 'Atiyya (رضي الله عنها), who was a female Companion of the Messenger of Allah (ﷺ), that she once said: "We never considered yellowish or blackish discharge as menses after becoming pure."

Shaykh 'Abdul 'Aziz ibn Baaz

If menses finishes before sunset, it is obligatory for the woman to pray *zuhr* and *'asr* prayers

Q. If a woman becomes pure before dawn, is it obligatory upon her to pray *maghrib* (sunset) and *'isha'* (evening) prayers? Likewise, if she becomes pure before sunset, is it obligatory upon her to pray *ẓuhr* (midday) and *'aṣr* (afternoon) prayers?

A. If a menstruating or post-natal bleeding woman becomes pure before sunset, it is obligatory upon her to pray *ẓuhr* and *'aṣr* prayers according to the more correct of the opinions of the scholars. Likewise, if she becomes pure before dawn, it is obligatory upon her to pray *maghrib* and *'isha'* prayers. This has been reported from the two Companions 'Abdur Raḥmaan ibn 'Awf and 'Abdullah ibn 'Abbaas (may Allah be pleased with all of them) and it is also the opinion of most of the scholars. Similarly, if a menstruating or post-natal bleeding woman becomes pure before sunrise, it is obligatory upon her to pray the *fajr* (dawn) prayer also. And with Allah is success.

Shaykh 'Abdul 'Aziz ibn Baaz

A menstruating woman should keep herself clean from urine

Q. When I am in menses, I do not clean myself from urine with water because I fear that the water will harm me. So what is the ruling on this?

A. Instead of water, it will suffice you to clean yourself with clean tissues or any other clean and solid thing that will remove the filth, such as stones, wood or the like. This should be done three times or more until the filth is removed. This is not special to you or the like (i.e. other menstruating women), but instead it is general and applies to all male and female Muslims. This is based on what has been narrated by 'Aa'ishah (﵂) that the Messenger of Allah (ﷺ) said:

> "If any of you goes to the toilet, then let him use three stones, for they will suffice him."

This Ḥadith has been reported by Aḥmed, Nasaa'i, Abu Dawood

and Ad-Daaraquṭni, who said its chain is *ḥasan ṣaheeḥ* (correct, authenticated).

Also it has been reported by Salmaan al-Faarsi (ﷺ) that it was said to him: "Verily, your Prophet (ﷺ) taught you everything, even the manners of toilet." So Salmaan said:

> "Yes he did, he forbade us from facing the *qibla* when passing stool or urine, and from cleaning ourselves after toilet with our right hand, and from cleaning ourselves with less than three stones, and from using manure or bones as a means to clean ourselves."

Muslim, Abu Dawood and Tirmidhi have reported this Ḥadith. And with Allah is success.

Shaykh 'Abdul 'Aziz ibn Baaz

Air that comes out of a woman's vagina and its effect on the prayer

Q. There is a woman, who, when she begins her prayer and goes into the *rukoo'* or *sujood* or sitting positions, air comes out of her vagina. At times, it is such that others around her can even hear it. And at other times, only a small amount comes out and no one can hear it. So does this break the *wuḍoo'* and the prayer?

A. The air that comes out from the front (i.e. the vagina) does not break the *wuḍoo'* (nor the prayer).

The Permanent Committee for Research and Verdicts

Ruling concerning what a woman should do if her menses begins when she is in the mosque

Q. A woman's menses began when she was in the mosque of the Messenger of Allah (ﷺ). However, she waited until her family finished their prayers and then left the mosque with them. Did she sin by that?

A. If the situation was such that she could not leave the mosque by herself, then there is no blame on her. However, if she is able to leave the mosque by herself, then it is obligatory for her to leave quickly because it is not allowed for the menstruating and post-natal bleeding women and the *junub* to stay in the mosque. This is based on the saying of Allah, the Almighty:

﴿يَٰٓأَيُّهَا ٱلَّذِينَ ءَامَنُوا۟ لَا تَقْرَبُوا۟ ٱلصَّلَوٰةَ وَأَنتُمْ سُكَٰرَىٰ حَتَّىٰ تَعْلَمُوا۟ مَا تَقُولُونَ وَلَا جُنُبًا إِلَّا عَابِرِى سَبِيلٍ... ﴿٤٣﴾﴾ (النساء : ٤٣)

"O' you who believe, do not approach the prayer when you are in a drunken state until you know the meaning of what you utter, nor when you in a state of janaabah except when passing through the mosque..."

(Qur'an 4: 43)

Also, it has been reported that the Messenger of Allah (ﷺ) said:

"Verily, I do not permit the mosque for the menstruating women nor the *junub*."

Shaykh 'Abdul 'Aziz ibn Baaz

It is permissible for the menstruating women to read the books of *tafseer*

Q. I read some books of *tafseer* whilst in a state of impurity, such as the monthly period for example. So is there any blame on me for this? And is there any sin upon me for this? Please give me an answer, may Allah reward you with good.

A. There is no blame on a menstruating or post-natal bleeding woman in reading books of *tafseer*. Neither is there any blame in reading the Qur'an without actually touching it. This is the more correct of the two sayings of the scholars on this topic. As for the *junub* person, then he or she is not allowed to read the Qur'an at all until a bath is taken. However, a *junub* person is allowed to read books of *tafseer*, Ḥadith and other topics without reading the verses that are contained within them. This is based on a Ḥadith from the Messenger of Allah (ﷺ) that nothing used to prevent him from the Qur'an except the state of *janaabah*. There is a narration from the Messenger of Allah (ﷺ) that he said:

> "As for the *junub*, then no, not even a verse."

This is part of a Ḥadith recorded by Imams Muslim and Aḥmed with a good chain of narrators.

Shaykh 'Abdul 'Aziz ibn Baaz

It is permissible for a menstruating woman to read the Qur'an and books of supplications

Q. Is it permissible for a menstruating woman to read books of supplications on the day of *'Arafah* even though they contain verses?

A. There is no problem in a menstruating or post-natal bleeding woman reading supplications written in books of ḥajj and also it is OK to read the Qur'an (without touching it) in the more correct of the scholars' opinions. This is because no clear and authentic narration has been reported that prevents them from reading the Qur'an. What has been reported is with respect to the *junub* person that he or she is not permitted to read the Qur'an whilst in the *junub* state. This is based on a Ḥadith reported by 'Ali (رضي الله عنه).

Regarding the menstruating and post-natal bleeding woman, a narration has been reported from Ibn 'Umar (رضي الله عنه) that says: "The menstruating and *junub* are not allowed to read anything of the Qur'an." However, this Ḥadith is weak due to being narrated by a person by the name of Ismaaa'eel ibn 'Ayyash who in turn reported it from the people of Ḥijaz. This person is weak when reporting from them. But she can read, say for example from her memory, without actually touching the Qur'an. However, the *junub* person is not allowed to read even from his or her memory or from the copy of the Qur'an (even without touching it) until a bath is taken.

The difference between the *junub* and the menstruating woman is that the *junub* person is in that state for only a short time and it is possible to take a bath as soon as sexual intercourse is finished. So the period is not long and the matter is in the *junub* person's hands when to have a bath. If it is not possible to use water for whatever (valid) reason, then *tayammum* can be performed and then they can pray and read the Qur'an.

As for the menstruating and the post-natal bleeding woman, then the situation is not in her hands but rather in the Hands of Allah, the Almighty. Both menses and post-natal bleeding require days, for which reason it is permissible for them to read the Qur'an so that they do not forget it and so that they are not deprived of the benefits associated with reading it, such as knowing the shari'ah rulings from the book of Allah.

On the basis of this, it is more so the case that she is allowed to read the books of supplications that contain verses, Ḥadiths and other things. This is the correct opinion and it is the more correct of the two sayings of the scholars (may Allah have mercy upon them) in this issue.

Shaykh 'Abdul 'Aziz ibn Baaz

Ruling concerning the one who is afflicted with the continuous passing of gas

Q. If a Muslim is sick such that it forces gas to be passed out with force from the bottom and is unable to stop this gas, then does this sick person's prayer and purification become invalid when the gas comes out or are they valid based on the ruling concerning one who has the illness wherein urine comes out continuously?

A. This person should try his best to preserve his *wuḍoo'*. If this passing of gas is not continuous, such as say if it comes out sometimes, then this passing will nullify the *wuḍoo'* (and the prayer). However, if it comes out always and never stops, even in the house or bed, or while sitting and moving, and is unable to control it and finds it difficult, then such a person is excused. So the *wuḍoo'* would not nullify and neither the prayer becomes invalid just by the passing of gas because such a person would then take the ruling of one who has continuous discharge. This person should make *wuḍoo'* for each prayer after the time of the prayer starts.

Shaykh 'Abdullah ibn Jibreen

Ruling concerning if there is a doubt as regards the purity of the place of prayer

Q. When we shift from one apartment to another, all or most of these apartments come furnished. So is it permissible for us to pray on the carpet because we do not know who used to live there before us, whether they were Muslims or not?

A. The basis regarding such things is purity, so a judgment (of impurity) should not be made regarding a thing or place except with proof that shows that it is impure. It should also be made sure that the impurity according to shari'ah is present in that thing or place. If these two things are not proven, then a Muslim should pray and that prayer would be valid and correct. And peace and blessings of Allah be upon our Messenger of Allah, his family and Companions.

The Permanent Committee for Research and Verdicts

Ruling concerning the prayer of a woman who bleeds continuously (*mustaḥaaḍah*)

Q. A woman, who has reached the age of fifty-two, has three days of strong bleeding and the rest is light during the month. Should she consider that blood as menses knowing that she is above 50 years of age and also keeping in mind that the blood comes after a month sometimes, and sometimes even after two or three months? Should she pray the obligatory prayers while the blood is still flowing? Similarly, can she pray the voluntary prayers such as the *rawaatib* (the sunnah prayers that are prayed before or after the five obligatory prayers) and the *tahajjud* prayer?

A. A woman, similar to the one mentioned in the question, should consider the blood flow to be bad blood due to her old age and its uneasiness and difficulty for her. It is known from occurrence and also from what has been reported from 'Aa'ishah (رضي الله عنها) that when a woman reaches the age of fifty, pregnancy and menses are ceased. Otherwise, if it continued, it would cause her trouble. So its continuous nature (even at this age) is a proof that it is not menses and thus she can pray and fast. She has to treat that blood as blood of *istiḥaaḍah* (wherein blood flows from a woman continuously even after the monthly normal period ends). In this case, it would not prevent her from the prayers or the fasts. Similarly, it does not prevent her husband from having sexual intercourse with her according to the more correct of the two sayings of the scholars. She should make *wuḍoo'* for each prayer (after the time of the prayer starts) and also put cotton or something similar on the spot from where the blood is coming out. This is based on the saying of the Messenger of Allah (ﷺ) to a woman who was continuously bleeding:

"Make *wuḍoo'* for each prayer."

Reported by Imam Bukhari in his book *Ṣaḥeeḥ*.

Shaykh 'Abdul 'Aziz ibn Baaz

If a post-natal bleeding woman becomes pure before forty days, it becomes obligatory upon her to take a bath, pray and fast

Q. If a post-natal bleeding woman becomes pure before forty days, should she pray and fast or not? And if her menses comes after that, should she break her fast? And if she becomes pure after that for a second time, should she pray and fast or not?

A. If a post-natal bleeding woman becomes pure before the completion of forty days, it becomes obligatory upon her to take a bath, pray and fast Ramaḍaan and she becomes *ḥalaal* for her husband (i.e. it is permissible for her husband to have sexual intercourse with her). Then if the blood comes back within the forty days period, it then becomes obligatory upon her to leave the prayer and fast, and she becomes *ḥaraam* for her husband (i.e. it is not permissible for her husband anymore to have sexual intercourse with her in this state) according to the more correct opinion of the scholars. She then takes on the rulings concerning the post-natal bleeding women until she becomes pure again or completes forty days.

Then if she becomes pure before forty days, or at the forty-day mark, she should take a bath, pray and fast (if it's the month of Ramaḍaan), and she becomes *ḥalaal* for her husband again. However, if the blood continues to flow even after the forty days, then it is false blood and she should not leave the prayer or fast due to that, but rather she should pray and fast in Ramaḍaan, and she becomes *ḥalaal* for her husband, just like a woman who continuously bleeds after menses (*mustaḥaaḍah*). She is then required to clean herself with water and put cotton or something on the spot to reduce the blood flow. She also has to make a fresh *wuḍoo'* for each prayer due to the order of the Messenger of Allah (ﷺ) to a *mustaḥaaḍah* woman. This is the case except if her monthly period comes, i.e. menses, then she should leave the prayer and the fast, and she would be ḥaraam for her husband until she becomes pure from menses again. And with Allah is success.

Shaykh 'Abdul 'Aziz ibn Baaz

Ruling concerning a woman who has an abortion

> Q. There are some pregnant women who decide to have an abortion. In some cases, the creation of the fetus is complete, whilst in other cases it is not complete. Could you please clear how the situation would be regarding the prayer in both cases?

A. If the woman has an abortion and the fetus has the features of a human such as a head or feet or other such things, then she is considered a post-natal bleeding woman and as such takes its rulings and does not pray or fast, and it is not *ḥalaal* for her husband to have sexual intercourse with her until she becomes pure or completes the forty days. Whenever she becomes pure, even within the forty days, it becomes obligatory upon her to take a bath, pray and fast in Ramaḍaan, and she becomes *ḥalaal* for her husband to have sexual intercourse with her.

There is no limit regarding the lowest number of days for post-natal bleeding. Thus if she becomes pure even after the passing of ten days, or more or less, she has to take a bath and she would take on the rulings that any other pure woman would have as has been mentioned earlier. And what she sees after the forty days is false blood and she should fast, pray and it becomes *ḥalaal* for her husband to have sexual intercourse with her. She has to make *wuḍoo'* for each prayer after its time starts, just like a *mustaḥaaḍah* woman (because in this case her blood is continuing even after the forty days). This is based on a saying of the Messenger of Allah (ﷺ) to Faṭimah bint abi Ḥubaish (رضي الله عنها), who was a *mustaḥaaḍah* woman:

> "...and make *wuḍoo'* for each prayer."

Whenever the blood that comes out after the forty-day period coincides with the monthly period, then it has the same rulings as that of menses, which are that it is *ḥaraam* upon her to pray or fast, and it becomes *ḥaraam* for her husband to have sexual intercourse with her.

If the aborted fetus does not have the features of a human being, such as if it were to be just a piece of meat with no features or just a clot of blood, then the woman would by that take on the ruling of a *mustaḥaaḍah* woman and not the rulings of a post-natal bleeding or menstruating woman. She should pray and fast in Ramaḍaan, and it is allowed for her husband to have sexual intercourse with her. Similarly, she should make *wuḍoo'* at the time of each prayer and apply cotton or something similar at the spot from where the blood is coming out. This is to be done till she becomes pure again. It is allowed for her to combine the *ẓuhr* and *'aṣr* prayers, and also the *maghrib* and *'isha'* prayers. A Ḥadith narrated by Ḥamnah bint Jaḥsh shows that in this case, she should take a bath each time she combines the prayers and a separate bath for *fajr* prayer. This is because such a woman is considered to be the same as a *mustaḥaaḍah* woman. And Allah is the source of success.

Shaykh 'Abdul 'Aziz ibn Baaz

Ruling concerning the blood coming out five days prior to the delivery of a baby

Q. Blood came out of a pregnant woman five days before she was set to deliver in the month of Ramaḍaan. So is this blood considered menses or post-natal blood? And what is obligatory upon her?

A. If the situation is as stated wherein she saw blood during her pregnancy five days before delivery, then if she did not see signs of the nearness of the delivery, such as contractions etc, then it is not blood of menses and not post-natal blood either, but rather the correct opinion is that it is false blood. So based on this, she should not leave the acts of worship but she should pray and fast.

However, if she saw signs of the nearness of the delivery, such as contractions etc, then it is post-natal blood and she should leave the prayer and the fast due to it. Then when she becomes pure after the birth, she should make up the missed fasts (if it was the month of Ramaḍaan) and not the missed prayers (as has been reported in Ḥadiths).

The Permanent Committee for Research and Verdicts

A young girl broke her fast due to menses but did not make up the missed fasts due to shyness

Q. When I was thirteen years of age, I fasted the month of Ramaḍaan but left four days due to menses. However, I did not inform anybody about this due to shyness. And since that incident, eight years have passed, so what should I do?

A. Verily, you have erred by leaving the making up of the fasts all this long period because this is a thing that Allah has written upon the daughters of Adam. There is no shame in matters of religion (i.e. if the shame is making a person do something wrong). So now you have to hasten to make up those missed four days and you also have to give *kaffaarah* (atonement) for it, which is to feed a poor person for each of the days missed. The amount to be given (in your situation) is eight handfuls of your country's (normal and average) food. This can all be given to one person or distributed over many poor people.

Shaykh 'Abdullah ibn Jibreen

Ruling concerning menses continuing longer than its normal duration

Q. If a woman's monthly period is normally either eight or seven days, then if continues with her once or twice longer than that, then what is the ruling?

A. If this woman's normal period is six or seven days, then it changes and becomes eight or nine or ten or eleven days, then she should not pray until she becomes pure again. This is because the Messenger of Allah (ﷺ) did not limit the number of days of menses, and Allah, the Almighty, says:

﴿وَيَسْـَٔلُونَكَ عَنِ ٱلْمَحِيضِ ۖ قُلْ هُوَ أَذًى فَٱعْتَزِلُوا۟ ٱلنِّسَآءَ فِى ٱلْمَحِيضِ ۖ وَلَا تَقْرَبُوهُنَّ حَتَّىٰ يَطْهُرْنَ... ﴿٢٢٢﴾﴾ (البقرة: ٢٢٢)

"They ask you concerning menstruation. Say that it is an Adha [a harmful thing for a husband to have sexual intercourse with his wife while she is having her menses], therefore keep away from women during menses and do not go to them until they are purified..."

(Qur'an 2: 222)

So, as long as the blood is remaining, the woman is in menses. After that, when she becomes pure, she has to take a bath and pray. Then if in the next month, the menses comes for a lesser number of days, then she has to take a bath whenever she becomes pure, which is when the blood stops. This is so even if the duration of the second month is not as long as the first month.

The important point here is that, so long as a woman is in menses, she should not pray, whether the menses is according to the norm or more or less. And when she becomes pure, she has to pray.

Shaykh Muḥammad ibn 'Uthaymeen

Ruling concerning a woman if she has an abortion in the third month of the pregnancy

> Q. A year ago, I had an abortion in the third month of my pregnancy. I then did not pray till I became pure (i.e. till the blood stopped). It was said to me that I was supposed to pray. So please tell me what to do now, knowing that I do not know the exact number of days?

A. It is known amongst the people of knowledge that if a woman has an abortion at three months, she should not pray. This is because if a woman aborts a fetus that has the features of a human being, then the blood that comes out is the post-natal blood and thus she should not pray. The scholars have said that it is possible for the features to become apparent when the fetus is eighty-one days old. This figure is less than three months. If she is positive that the abortion was at the three-month mark, then what affected her was menses blood. But if it was before eighty days, then it is false blood and she should not leave prayer due to it.

The woman who asked the question should try to remember the exact number of days of the fetus. Then if the fetus was aborted before eighty days, then she should make up the prayers. And if she does not know how many she left, she should try and estimate and look into it carefully, and then make up the prayers for the number of days she is sure that she did not pray.

Shaykh Muḥammad ibn 'Uthaymeen

Ruling concerning having sexual intercourse before the completion of forty days

Q. Is it permissible for a man to have sexual intercourse with his wife after delivery and before the completion of forty days? And if he did do it with her at thirty days and at thirty-five days when she was pure, but before forty days, then is there anything upon him?

A. It is not permissible to have sexual intercourse with the wife during the duration of the post-natal bleeding after delivery. If she becomes pure before forty days, it is disliked for the husband to have sexual intercourse with her, however it is nonetheless permissible and there is no sin if Allah wills, with the condition that she sees the blood stop completely which would make it obligatory upon her to pray, fast (if its the month of Ramadaan) and do other things (that are binding upon her when she is pure).

Shaykh 'Abdullah ibn Jibreen

Ruling concerning the supplications made by a menstruating woman

Q. Will Allah, the Almighty, accept the supplication and seeking of forgiveness of a menstruating woman?

A. Yes (Allah will accept). It is permissible for her to make supplications and infact, it is desirable for a menstruating woman to increase the supplications, the seeking of forgiveness, remembrances and invocations, especially during the blessed times. So whenever the reasons for acceptance are fulfilled, then Allah will accept, from both the menstruating woman and others.

Shaykh 'Abdullah ibn Jibreen

Ruling concerning the prayer of the menstruating woman

Q. My monthly period started when I was in prayer, so what should I have done? Also, should I make up for the prayers during the time of the menses?

A. If the menses starts after the time of prayer started, for example, the menses starts after the time of *ẓuhr* prayer starts, then you have to make up that particular prayer once you become pure. This is based on the saying of Allah, the Almighty:

﴿...إِنَّ ٱلصَّلَوٰةَ كَانَتْ عَلَى ٱلْمُؤْمِنِينَ كِتَٰبًا مَّوْقُوتًا ﴿١٠٣﴾﴾

(النساء : ١٠٣)

"...*Verily, the prayer is enjoined upon the believers at fixed hours.*" *(Qur'an 4: 103)*

However, you do not have to make up for the prayers that occur during the menses because the Messenger of Allah (ﷺ) said in a long Ḥadith:

"A woman, when she has menses, she doesn't pray and doesn't fast."

There is a consensus among the people of knowledge that she does not have to make up for the prayers missed during the period of menses.

But if she becomes pure and there is still enough time for one *rak'ah* (unit of prayer) of a particular prayer left, then she has to pray that prayer also because the Messenger of Allah (ﷺ) said:

"Whoever is able to pray a *rak'ah* of the *'aṣr* prayer before the sun sets, then he has caught the *'aṣr* prayer (i.e. he did not miss it)."

So if she becomes pure during the time of *'aṣr* prayer or before sunrise and there is enough time left for sunset or sunrise to pray one *rak'ah*, then she has to pray *'aṣr* before sunset and *fajr* before sunrise (depending on what time she became pure).

Shaykh Muḥammad ibn 'Uthaymeen

Ruling concerning writing the Qur'an by a menstruating woman

Q. Is it permissible for a menstruating woman to read the Qur'an with a view to following the guidance in it or to getting proof for a matter from it? And is it permitted for her to write the verses of the Qur'an or the noble Ḥadiths?

A. There is no problem in a menstruating woman reading books that contain verses of the Qur'an or that contain the explanations of the verses (but not the Qur'an itself). Similarly, there is no problem if she includes them in something she is writing, as an example. Also, it is permissible for her to use them as proof for a particular ruling or to read them such as in a supplication. This is because all these actions are not called reciting the Qur'an. She is also allowed to carry books of *tafseer* or similar books if there is a necessity.

Shaykh 'Abdullah ibn Jibreen

A woman should not be hasty in deciding the end of her menses

Q. My monthly periods fluctuate between seven and eight days. In some instances, I do not see blood or purity on the seventh day. So what is the ruling regarding prayer, fasting and sexual intercourse?

A. Do not be hasty until you see the white substance that the women know as a sign of purity (i.e. that marks the ending of menses). The stopping of the blood is not a sign of purity but rather, seeing the signs of purity and the ending of the normal duration of menses are to be considered.

Shaykh 'Abdullah ibn Jibreen

The blood that comes out before the normal time of menses is false blood and thus the prayer should not be left due to it

Q. Before the normal time of menses by about three or four days, some blood comes that leaves only a trace, the color of which is brown. I do not know what its ruling is, whether it is clean or impure, and thus I become confused and very worried as to whether I should pray or not?

A. If a woman knows her normal time of menses each month, either by its color, or number of days, then she should leave the prayer only during that time. Then she should take a bath and pray (at the end of menses). So the blood that comes before the normal time is considered false blood and she should not leave the prayer or fasting due to it. Instead, she should clean the blood off herself at the time of each prayer and apply cotton to the spot and make a fresh *wuḍoo'* for each prayer and then pray even if the blood continues to flow. This is because a woman with such a situation would be considered as *mustaḥaaḍah*. So if she has already left the prayer due to this before, then to be on the safe side, she should make up for those prayers, and if Allah wills, there is no trouble in that.

Shaykh 'Abdullah ibn Jibreen

A child urinating on a mother during her prayer

Q. I made *wudoo'* for the prayer. Then I held my baby when I was praying and while I was praying, he urinated on my clothes. I washed the affected area and then prayed without making another *wudoo'*. So is my prayer correct?

A. Yes, your prayer is correct because what affected you of the baby's urine does not break the *wuḍoo'* but rather, as you did, you only needed to wash what the urine fell on.

The Permanent Committee for Research and Verdicts

A doctor's clothes becoming dirty with the water that comes out of a woman during childbirth

Q. If the clothes of a doctor become polluted with the liquid that comes out of a woman during delivery, is the doctor allowed to pray in those clothes knowing that it is difficult to change the clothes for every prayer due to the nature of the work?

A. The doctor must have with him or her spare clean clothes in which to perform the prayer instead of the unclean clothes. And doing this would not be difficult.

The Permanent Committee for Research and Verdicts

Manner of wiping over the head during *wuḍoo'*

Q. Is it prescribed for a woman, when wiping over the head during *wuḍoo'*, to begin from the front of the head and then go towards the back, and then finally to come back to the front, as is prescribed for a man?

A. Yes, this is the case because the basis concerning Islamic rulings is that whatever is established for men is also established for women and vice versa, except if there is a specific proof that shows that a ruling only applies to men and not women or vice versa. In this issue, I do not know of any proof that is specific to a woman and thus she should also, like a man, wipe over the head from the front to the back. If the hair is long, it will not be affected by this since the purpose is not to press hard on the hair till they become soaked or to reach the scalp, rather the wiping should be done with calmness and tranquility.

Shaykh Muhammad ibn 'Uthaymeen

Making *wuḍoo'* with nail polish on is not permissible

Q. What is the ruling concerning *wuḍoo'* of a woman who has nail polish on?

A. It is not permissible for a woman to wear nail polish during times when she is praying (i.e. not in her menses) because it prevents water from reaching the nails, which is a must when making *wuḍoo'*. And anything that prevents the water from reaching the skin or nails is not allowed to be used by a person making *wuḍoo'* or taking a shower because Allah, the Glorified and Almighty, said:

﴿...فَٱغۡسِلُواْ وُجُوهَكُمۡ وَأَيۡدِيَكُمۡ ...﴾ (المائدة : ٦)

"*...And wash your faces and hands...*" *(Qur'an 5: 6)*

So if this questioner has nail polish on, it will prevent water from reaching the nails and thus it could not be said that she has washed her hands. If this happens, then she would have left out one of the obligatory acts of *wuḍoo'* or bathing.

However, regarding a woman who is not praying, say due to menses, there is no problem in her using nail polish except if this action is among the characteristics of the *kaafir* women in which case it would not be allowed because it would be considered imitating them (which is *ḥaraam*).

Shaykh Muḥammad ibn 'Uthaymeen

Ruling concerning *wuḍoo'* for a woman who washes her child

Q. What is the ruling concerning a woman, who has made *wuḍoo'*, and then her child passed urine and stool. She then washed and cleaned the child from the impurity. So does this break her *wuḍoo'*?

A. If the woman touched one of the child's private parts (either the front of the back), the *wuḍoo'* breaks due to it. Otherwise, the *wuḍoo'* does not break just by cleaning the child, even if she happened to actually touch the child's stool or urine. She should, however, make sure that she properly cleans her hands afterwards and also make sure that she protects herself properly from the impurity such that it does not get on her body or clothes.

Shaykh Muḥammad ibn Ibraheem

Ruling concerning touching the private parts of a child

Q. Does touching a child's private parts when changing her diaper or her clothes break the *wuḍoo'*?

A. Touching the private parts without anything in between (i.e. skin to skin) breaks the *wuḍoo'*, whether the person being touched is a child or a grown up person. This is based on the saying of the Messenger of Allah (ﷺ):

> "Whoever touches his private parts should make *wuḍoo'*."

So, touching the private parts of someone else is like touching ones own private parts.

The Permanent Committee for Research and Verdicts

Air that comes out of a woman's vagina and its effect on the *wuḍoo'*

Q. Does the coming out of air from a woman's vagina break the *wuḍoo'* or not?

A. No, this does not break the *wuḍoo'* because it did not come out of an impure part, such as the gas that comes out of the anus.

Shaykh Muḥammad ibn 'Uthaymeen

Ruling concerning touching a woman and its effect on the *wuḍoo'*

Q. Does touching a woman nullify one's *wuḍoo'*?

A. The correct opinion is that touching a woman does not nullify the *wuḍoo'* except if something comes out of the private part. The proof of this is an authentic Ḥadith that the Messenger of Allah (ﷺ) used to kiss some of his wives and then go out to pray without making *wuḍoo'* after the kiss. Also, the bases is that the *wuḍoo'* does not nullify until something happens for which there is proof in the Qur'an and Sunnah. So in such a situation, a man has made *wuḍoo'* based on proofs from the Qur'an and Sunnah. So now his *wuḍoo'* does not break until something happens for which there is proof in the Qur'an and Sunnah. As regards the saying of Allah, the Exalted:

﴿...أَوْ لَـٰمَسْتُمُ ٱلنِّسَآءَ...﴿٦﴾﴾ (المائدة: ٦)

"*...or you have been in contact with women...*"
(Qur'an 5: 6),

— it means sexual intercourse, as has been authentically reported from Ibn 'Abbaas (رضي الله عنه).

Shaykh Muḥammad ibn 'Uthaymeen

Ruling concerning touching a strange woman (i.e. a woman for whom the man is not a *maḥram*) and its effect on the *wuḍoo'*

Q. Does touching or shaking hands with a strange woman for whom the man is not a *maḥram* nullify the *wuḍoo'*?[2] We have found in some books of jurisprudence things that indicate that touching a woman does not nullify the *wuḍoo'* but it was general. So is there any specific ruling concerning a woman for whom a man is not a *maḥram*?

A. The correct opinion among the sayings of the scholars is that shaking hands or touching a woman does not nullify the *wuḍoo'*,

---

[2] One should note that it is not permissible for a man to touch or shake hands with a woman who is not his *maḥram*.

whether she is a strange woman (a woman for whom the man is not a *maḥram*, in which case it is *ḥaraam* to touch her) or ones wife or ones *maḥram* relatives. This is because, once a person performs *wuḍoo'*, it remains and is not nullified until there is some proof to indicate that a certain action nullifies the *wuḍoo'*. In this case, there is no proof. As for the contact mentioned in the following saying of Allah, the Exalted:

﴿يَٰٓأَيُّهَا ٱلَّذِينَ ءَامَنُوٓاْ إِذَا قُمْتُمْ إِلَى ٱلصَّلَوٰةِ فَٱغْسِلُواْ وُجُوهَكُمْ وَأَيْدِيَكُمْ إِلَى ٱلْمَرَافِقِ وَٱمْسَحُواْ بِرُءُوسِكُمْ وَأَرْجُلَكُمْ إِلَى ٱلْكَعْبَيْنِ وَإِن كُنتُمْ جُنُبًا فَٱطَّهَّرُواْ وَإِن كُنتُم مَّرْضَىٰٓ أَوْ عَلَىٰ سَفَرٍ أَوْ جَآءَ أَحَدٌ مِّنكُم مِّنَ ٱلْغَآئِطِ أَوْ لَٰمَسْتُمُ ٱلنِّسَآءَ فَلَمْ تَجِدُواْ مَآءً فَتَيَمَّمُواْ صَعِيدًا طَيِّبًا فَٱمْسَحُواْ بِوُجُوهِكُمْ وَأَيْدِيكُم مِّنْهُ...﴿٦﴾﴾

(المائدة: ٦)

"*O' you who believe, when you intend to offer the prayer, wash your faces and your hands up to the elbows, wipe over your heads and wash your feet up to the ankles. If you are in a state of janaabah, purify yourselves [i.e. take a bath]. But if you are ill or on a journey, or any of you comes after answering the call of nature, or you have been in contact with women, and you find no water, then perform tayammum with clean earth and rub therewith your faces and hands...*"

(Qur'an 5: 6),

— the intent here is sexual intercourse according to the correct opinion of the scholars.

The Permanent Committee for Research and Verdicts

Ruling concerning looking at a naked woman or man (i.e. one's wife or husband) and its effect on the *wuḍoo'*

Q. Is the *wuḍoo'* nullified just by looking at a naked man or woman?[3] And is the *wuḍoo'* nullified if a person looks at his own *'awrah*?

A. No, the *wuḍoo'* does not nullify by just looking at a naked man or woman.[4] Similarly, the *wuḍoo'* does not nullify just by looking at ones own *'awrah* because there are no proofs from either the Qur'an or Sunnah that show this.

The Permanent Committee for Research and Verdicts

Ruling concerning the *wuḍoo'* of the nurse who performs the delivery of babies

Q. Does the nurse or doctor who performs the delivery have to take a bath or it is enough to make *wuḍoo'*?

A. The nurse or doctor does not have to take a bath nor do they have to make *wuḍoo'* due to delivering the baby. Rather, if they are going to pray, what is obligatory upon them is to clean whatever impurity, such as blood or anything else that affected their body or clothes as a result of the delivery. If, however, a nurse or a doctor happened to touch the private parts of the woman who delivered the baby, they then have to make *wuḍoo'*.

The Permanent Committee for Research and Verdicts

---

[3] This is referring to looking at one's wife or husband naked. As for looking at other naked people, even if they are *maḥram*, that is not permissible at all.

[4] However, if as a result of looking some fluid came out, then that nullifies the *wuḍoo'*.

The manner of washing from *janaabah* and whether there is any difference between it and washing from menses

Q. Is there any difference between a man and a woman washing from *janaabah*? And is a woman required to undo the plaiting of her hair or is it enough to pour three handfuls of water over the head as has come in the Ḥadith? And what is the difference between washing from *janaabah* and menses?

A. There is no difference between a man and a woman washing from *janaabah* and neither of them is required to undo the plaiting of the hair for the bath. Rather, it is enough to throw three handfuls of water over the head (making sure that all the hair and the scalp become wet) and then to pour water over the rest of the body. This is based on a Ḥadith on the authority of Umm Salamah (رضي الله عنها) who said to the Messenger of Allah (ﷺ): "I am a woman who has closely plaited hair on my head; should I undo it for taking a bath resulting from sexual intercourse"? The Messenger of Allah (ﷺ) said:

> "No, it is enough for you to throw three handfuls of water on your head (making sure that all the hair and the scalp become wet) and then pour water over yourself, and you shall be purified."

Imam Muslim reported this Ḥadith.

If the man or woman has applied something to the hair that prevents the water from reaching the scalp, it has to be removed. But if it will not prevent the water from reaching the scalp, it does not have to be removed (since the purpose of the water reaching the scalp is achieved).

As for a woman bathing from menses, the scholars have differed as to whether she has to undo the plaits or not. However, the correct opinion is that the plaits do not have to be undone (i.e. it is not obligatory). This is based on some other narrations of the incident of Umm Salamah (ɢ) wherein she said: "I am a woman who has closely plaited hair on my head; should I undo it for taking a bath resulting from sexual intercourse and menses"? The Messenger of Allah (ﷺ) said:

> "No, it is enough for you to throw three handfuls of
> water on your head (making sure that all the hair and the
> scalp become wet) and then pour water over yourself,
> and you shall be purified."

So in this particular narration, the word menses has been used thus showing clearly that the plaits do not have to be undone for the bath of menses and for the bath of *janaabah*. However, it is better if a woman does undo the plaits for the bath of menses to be on the safe side and not to get into the differences of the scholars. Also, doing this would be like acting by the combination of all the proofs.

The Permanent Committee for Research and Verdicts

Ruling concerning the obligation of making the water reach the scalp when bathing from *janaabah*

Q. If a woman is in a state of *janaabah* and she has a bath, does she have to wash the hair such that the water reaches the scalp?

A. The bath from *janaabah* and other such obligatory baths must be performed such that the water reaches the scalp. The ruling is the same for both men and women based on the saying of Allah, the Exalted:

$$﴿...وَإِن كُنتُمْ جُنُبًا فَٱطَّهَّرُوا۟...۝﴾ \quad (المائدة: ٦)$$

"...*If you are in a state of janaabah, purify
yourselves...*"   *(Qur'an 5: 6)*

It is not allowed for her to just wash the tips of the hair. Rather, the water has to reach the skin and the scalp. However, if the hair is plaited, then it is not obligatory to undo the plaits but the obligation is that the water should reach each and every hair by pouring water and then pressing the hair such that the water reaches all the hair (and the scalp).

Shaykh Muḥammad ibn 'Uthaymeen

Ruling concerning a wet dream for a woman

Q. Does a woman have a wet dream? And if she has one, is it obligatory to take a bath due to it? And if someone had a wet dream but did not take a bath, what is upon them now?

A. Yes, it is possible for a woman to have a wet dream because the women are like men (i.e. they are like their sisters). So just like a man has a wet dream, a woman also has a wet dream.

If a man or a woman has a wet dream but when they wake up, do not find any traces of water, then they do not have to take a bath. But if they see some water, it then becomes obligatory to take a bath. This is based on a Ḥadith reported by Umm Sulaym (رضي الله عنها) who said to the Messenger of Allah (صلى الله عليه وسلم): "O' Messenger of Allah, does a woman have to take a bath if she has a wet dream?" The Messenger of Allah (صلى الله عليه وسلم) replied to her:

"Yes, if she sees water (after waking up)."

Thus based on this Ḥadith, if a woman sees water (after waking up), it becomes obligatory to take a bath.

As for a woman who had a wet dream in the past, if she did not see any water (after waking up), then there is nothing upon her now. But if she did see traces of water after waking up, she should then try to estimate how many prayers she prayed without having a bath and then pray them again.

Shaykh Muḥammad ibn 'Uthaymeen

Ruling concerning a woman seeing herself having sexual intercourse with a man in a dream

Q. What is upon a woman if she sees herself having sexual intercourse with a man in her dream?

A. If a man sees in his dream that he is having sexual intercourse with a woman or a woman sees in her dream that she is having sexual intercourse with a man, there is no sin upon them for that because they are not responsible for what they see in a dream and they are not responsible for what happens when they are asleep. This is because Allah, the Exalted, does not burden a person beyond his or her scope and also it is established that the Messenger of Allah (ﷺ) said:

> "The pen has been raised from three types of people: from a sleeping person till he wakes up, from an insane person till he regains sanity and from a child till he reaches maturity."

Imams Aḥmed, Abu Dawood, Nasaa'i and Al-Ḥaakim reported this Ḥadith. Al-Ḥaakim said that this Ḥadith is upon the condition of Bukhari and Muslim. However, if a person has such a dream and then as a result of it ejaculates (i.e. semen comes out), then a bath becomes obligatory.

The Permanent Committee for Research and Verdicts

Ruling concerning a doctor or a woman who puts her hand in the vagina

Q. What is the ruling if a woman puts her hand in the vagina (accidentally) while washing herself after answering the call of nature? Or what if the doctor puts her hand or some machine for a checkup or medicine for curing a disease? Does all this necessitate a bath? And if this happens to be during the daytime in the month of Ramaḍaan, does the fast break and does the person have to make up for it?

A. If what has been mentioned in the question happens, then the bath of *janaabah* does not have to be taken. And similarly, it does not break the fast.

The Permanent Committee for Research and Verdicts

Ruling concerning doubting if one is in a state of *janaabah*

Q. A woman doubts a lot during the night whether she is in a state of *janaabah* or not, without her husband touching her. It is just a doubt that she has. It has reached a level that these doubts come to her even when she is awake. This has left her confused. So what should she do?

A. If a woman doubts that she is in a state of *janaabah*, then she does not have to take a bath because of mere doubts. The norm is that a person is not in *janaabah* and that a person is free from having to take a bath (until something sure happens which changes this state).

The Permanent Committee for Research and Verdicts

Permissibility of delaying the bath of *janaabah* and menses till the time of *fajr* prayer

Q. Is it permissible to delay the bath of *janaabah* till the time of *fajr* prayer? And are women permitted to delay the bath of menses and post-natal bleeding till the time of *fajr* prayer?

A. If a woman sees that she has become pure (after menses or post-natal bleeding) before *fajr*, she then has to fast that day and there is no problem in her delaying the bath till after the *fajr* time starts, but should not postpone it till sunrise (in which case the time of *fajr* prayer would be finished). Rather, it is obligatory upon her to have a bath and pray before sunrise.

Likewise, a person in the state of *janaabah* is not allowed to delay the bath till after sunrise (since the time of the *fajr* prayer would be finished) but rather it is obligatory upon that person to have a bath and pray before sunrise. With regards to a man, he should hasten his bath (and not leave it late during the *fajr* time) such that he can pray in congregation in the mosque.

Shaykh 'Abdul 'Aziz ibn Baaz

Ruling concerning a person in the state of *janaabah* sleeping before making *wuḍoo'*

Q. Is a person in the state of *janaabah* allowed to sleep before making *wuḍoo'*?

A. There is no sin if a *junub* person sleeps before making *wuḍoo'*. However, it is better to perform *wuḍoo'* before sleeping because the Messenger of Allah (ﷺ) performed *wuḍoo'* and told others to do it.

The Permanent Committee for Research and Verdicts

Ruling concerning whether the bath of *janaabah* will suffice the baths of Friday and menses

Q. Will the bath of *janaabah* suffice the bath of Friday or the bath of menses and post-natal bleeding?

A. Whosoever has to take more than one bath, it is sufficient for him to take a bath once if he intended all of them by that one bath and if he intended that it would make it permissible for him to pray or perform *ṭawaaf* (circumambulation around the Ka'bah) or other deeds. This is based on the saying of the Messenger of Allah (ﷺ):

> "Verily all actions are by intentions and a person will have what he intended."

Imams Bukhari and Muslim reported this Ḥadith.

Also, this is the case because if a person has a bath of *janaabah* on Friday, then the purpose of taking a bath on Friday is achieved by it.

The Permanent Committee for Research and Verdicts

Ruling concerning using henna during menses and whether that has any effect on the bath

Q. Does the usage of henna during the days of menses have any effect on the correctness of the bath (taken at the end of menses)?

A. Using henna does not have any effect on the bath nor on the *wuḍoo'* because it does not have any thickness or density that prevents the water from reaching the skin and scalp underneath. However, if it becomes hard, such that water will not get through it to the scalp, then it is obligatory to remove it before taking the bath.

The Permanent Committee for Research and Verdicts

Ruling concerning the impurity of the body of a person in the state of *janaabah*

Q. If a husband and wife have sexual intercourse, are they permitted to touch anything before they take a bath? And if they do touch something, does that thing also become impure?

A. It is permissible for a *junub* person to touch anything, whether clothes, pots or whatever else, before taking a bath. This ruling is the same for a man and woman. Nothing becomes impure just by them touching it. Similarly, if a woman in her menses or in her postnatal bleeding period touches something, it does not become impure. This is because their bodies and sweat are clean but the blood that comes out is impure.

The Permanent Committee for Research and Verdicts

Ruling concerning *tayammum* (earth ablution) and whether it is only for men or for women also

Q. Is the *tayammum* specific for men only or for both men and women when there is no water to make *wudoo'* for the prayer?

A. The bases for all rulings is that they apply to both men and women equally except what has been specified as being applicable to only one and not the other. So Allah, the Exalted, said with regards to *tayammum*:

﴿يَٰٓأَيُّهَا ٱلَّذِينَ ءَامَنُوٓاْ إِذَا قُمۡتُمۡ إِلَى ٱلصَّلَوٰةِ فَٱغۡسِلُواْ وُجُوهَكُمۡ
وَأَيۡدِيَكُمۡ إِلَى ٱلۡمَرَافِقِ وَٱمۡسَحُواْ بِرُءُوسِكُمۡ وَأَرۡجُلَكُمۡ إِلَى
ٱلۡكَعۡبَيۡنِۚ وَإِن كُنتُمۡ جُنُبٗا فَٱطَّهَّرُواْۚ وَإِن كُنتُم مَّرۡضَىٰٓ أَوۡ عَلَىٰ سَفَرٍ أَوۡ
جَآءَ أَحَدٞ مِّنكُم مِّنَ ٱلۡغَآئِطِ أَوۡ لَٰمَسۡتُمُ ٱلنِّسَآءَ فَلَمۡ تَجِدُواْ مَآءٗ فَتَيَمَّمُواْ
صَعِيدٗا طَيِّبٗا فَٱمۡسَحُواْ بِوُجُوهِكُمۡ وَأَيۡدِيكُم مِّنۡهُۚ مَا يُرِيدُ ٱللَّهُ
لِيَجۡعَلَ عَلَيۡكُم مِّنۡ حَرَجٖ وَلَٰكِن يُرِيدُ لِيُطَهِّرَكُمۡ وَلِيُتِمَّ نِعۡمَتَهُۥ
عَلَيۡكُمۡ لَعَلَّكُمۡ تَشۡكُرُونَ ٦﴾ (المائدة: ٦)

"*O' you who believe, when you intend to offer the prayer, wash your faces and you hands up to the elbows, wipe your heads and wash your feet up to the ankles. If you are in a state of janaabah, purify yourselves. But if you are ill or on a journey, or any of you comes after answering the call of nature, or you have been in contact with women [i.e. had sexual intercourse], and you find no water, then perform tayammum with clean earth and wipe your faces and hands. Allah does not want to place you in difficulty, but He wants to purify you and to complete His favor upon you that you may be thankful."* *(Qur'an 5: 6)*

So the order in the verse concerning the *tayammum* is general and encompasses both men and women. Thus *tayammum* applies to women just like it applies to men according to the consensus of the scholars.

The Permanent Committee for Rescarch and Verdicts

Ruling concerning *tayammum* during winter

Q. My mother is old and because our house is in a place where the weather is very cold, she is unable to use water to perform *wuḍoo'*, especially for *fajr* prayer. So is it allowed for her to make *tayammum* in such a case? Currently, when she makes *tayammum* and prays, she believes that her prayer is not complete and correct, thus she repeats it after sunrise (when the weather warms up a little).

A. It is obligatory to use water for the purification for prayer (i.e. *wuḍoo'* and not tayammum) during winter if there is something by which you can heat up the water. In such a case, doing *tayammum* is not allowed.

The Permanent Committee for Research and Verdicts

Lower and upper limits regarding the duration of menses

Q. Is there any limit on the lowest and highest possible days of menses?

A. No, there is no lower limit nor any upper limit to menses according to the correct opinion of the scholars. This is based on the saying of Allah, the Exalted:

﴿وَيَسْـَٔلُونَكَ عَنِ ٱلْمَحِيضِ قُلْ هُوَ أَذًى فَٱعْتَزِلُوا۟ ٱلنِّسَآءَ فِى ٱلْمَحِيضِ وَلَا تَقْرَبُوهُنَّ حَتَّىٰ يَطْهُرْنَ...﴿٢٢٢﴾﴾ (البقرة: ٢٢٢)

"They ask you concerning menstruation. Say that it is an Adha [i.e. a harmful thing for a husband to have a sexual intercourse with his wife while she is having her menses], therefore keep away from women during menses and do not go to them till they are purified [from menses and have taken a bath]..." (Qur'an 2: 222)

So Allah did not specify any limits with days for how long to stay away but rather made the limit based on the time the woman becomes purified from menses. This shows that it is the criteria by which to base the rulings and thus whenever menses is present, the rulings apply and when the woman is pure again, the rulings concerning menses no longer apply.

Also, there is no proof showing any limits to menses even though there is a need for knowing such information (if it existed). So if there were any such limits with days or age in Islam, it would have been made clear in either the Book of Allah or the Sunnah of His Messenger (ﷺ).

So based on this, whenever a woman sees blood that has characteristics of menstrual blood according to women, then it is menses and has no limits on its duration. An exception to this is if the blood continues to flow from a woman and does not stop at all or stops for a short time, say a day or two each month, then that blood would be considered blood of *istiḥaaḍah*.

Shaykh Muḥammad ibn 'Uthaymeen

Presence of menstrual blood at the age of seventy

Q. If a woman reaches the age of seventy and has blood flowing with characteristics of menstrual blood, should she leave the prayer and fast?

A. If a woman has reached the age of seventy and has blood flowing from her with the characteristics of menstrual blood, she should then not pray or fast because there is no lower or upper limit to the age of having menses. So this blood takes the rulings of menstrual blood (and thus whatever is allowed in menses is allowed now and whatever is prohibited in menses is prohibited now since it is considered to be menses).

Shaykh Sa'di

Ruling concerning menses if it increases by two days or so

Q. A woman's menstrual period increased over its normal duration by two days. So what is the ruling concerning these two days?

A. Firstly, it is obligatory for us to know that menses is natural blood that Allah, the Glorified and Almighty, creates in a woman when she is ready to be pregnant. This is because the menses is what the fetus uses as nourishment from its mother's uterus. For this reason, a pregnant woman does not have menses because the blood goes to nourish the fetus by the will of Allah.

So even though it is natural blood, Allah described it in the Qur'an as *Adha*:

﴿وَيَسْـَٔلُونَكَ عَنِ ٱلْمَحِيضِ قُلْ هُوَ أَذًى ... ﴿٢٢٢﴾﴾ (البقرة: ٢٢٢)

"They ask you concerning menses, say that it is an Adha [a harmful thing for a husband to have sexual intercourse with his wife while she is having her menses]..." *(Qur'an 2: 222)*

This is because it is impure. So whenever menses is present, its rulings apply. Even if that is more than the normal period, its rulings still apply. So for example, if the normal period of a woman was six days and it increased by two days, then these extra two days follow the other six and she does not have to pray or fast, and it is not allowed for her husband to have sexual intercourse with her.

This is the case because Allah, the Glorified and Almighty, did not specify a limit to the length of menses and likewise, the Sunnah of the Messenger of Allah (ﷺ) has not specified anything. So as long as menses is remaining, its rulings remain and apply. Then when a woman becomes pure, the rulings concerning menses do not apply anymore (whether the normal period has increased or not).

A similar situation to this is if a post-natal bleeding woman becomes pure before the completion of forty days, does she start to pray again or wait for the full forty days to finish? The answer is that she should pray because she has become pure from the blood. Then should she fast or not? Yes, she should fast if it is in the month of Ramaḍaan. And is her husband allowed to have sexual intercourse with her or not? Yes, he is allowed to have sexual intercourse with her without any dislike. If the prayer becomes allowed for her and it is a much greater matter than sexual intercourse, then it is more so that sexual intercourse should also be allowed.

Shaykh Muḥammad ibn 'Uthaymeen

Period of menses changing from beginning of a month to the end of a month

Q. A woman used to have her menses at the start of every month. It then changed and now it came at the end of the month, so what is the ruling?

A. If the menses becomes delayed from its normal period, such as in this case wherein the menses used to be at the start of the month and then she saw it at the end of the month, then the correct opinion is that whenever she sees blood, it is to be regarded as menstrual blood. And then whenever she becomes pure from that, she will be pure again from menses due to what was just mentioned above.

Shaykh Muḥammad ibn 'Uthaymeen

Ruling concerning menses in old age

Q. A woman's normal menstrual period is five days. Then when she becomes forty-eight years old, her menses would not come for a number of months and then comes back. Sometimes it reaches four months and ten days before the menses returns. But when it returns, it comes back for fourteen days. So what is the ruling concerning the rest of the days?

A. The normal state for a woman is to have her menses and then becomes pure from it every month. But this woman, with the Will of Allah, is in a situation wherein she does not have menses for four months and then has menses the whole fifth month. It is as if her menses gathers up during the four months and then comes all at once during the fifth month. So we say to this aged woman whose menses has begun to delay considerably and then comes back, that all these days, when the blood is present, are her menstrual period (thus all rulings concerning menses apply).

Shaykh Muḥammad ibn 'Uthaymeen

Continuous menses with small breaks in between

Q. Some women have continuous menses wherein the blood only stops for a day or two and then returns. So what is the ruling in this case concerning the prayer, fast and all other acts of worship?

A. It is a common belief among the scholars that if a woman has a normal period of her menses, then when this period finishes, she has to take a bath and then pray and fast (if it is the month of Ramaḍaan). Whatever she sees after the stopping of the blood by a day or two or three, then it is not menses. This is the view of some scholars who have the opinion that the least number of days between two menses (periods) is thirteen days. Other scholars say that whenever she sees blood, it is to be considered menses. And whenever she sees that she has become pure again, then she is pure (and rulings for a pure woman apply to her) even if the duration between two menses is not thirteen days.

Shaykh Muḥammad ibn 'Uthaymeen

Menses coming and going in the same month

Q. If a woman has her menses, then she becomes pure and takes a bath, then she starts to pray and after nine days, blood comes out again. Then she stays like that (as if in menses) for three days without praying. Then she becomes pure and prays for eleven days after which her normal menses period comes. So should she repeat the prayers of the three days or consider it as menses?

A. Whenever the menses comes, it is to be considered menses whether or not the duration between two menses is long or short. So if she has her menses, then becomes pure, then after five or six or ten days her menses returns for a second time, then she should not pray because that blood is menses. Likewise, whenever she becomes pure and then her menses comes, she should not pray. However, if her blood continues with her always and does not stop except very little, then she becomes *mustaḥaaḍah* (i.e. a woman with false blood flowing out continuously). In such a case, she should not pray only during her normal duration of menses (and then apart from that time, she would not be considered to be in menses).

Shaykh Muḥammad ibn 'Uthaymeen

Increase in the menses duration and change in its color

Q. A woman's normal duration of menses is ten days. Then in the month of Ramaḍaan, it came for fourteen days without her becoming pure. It then started to come out black and yellow for a period of eight days in which she prayed and fasted. So, are her prayers and fasts in these eight days correct? What is obligatory upon her now?

A. Menses is something that is well known among women and they are more knowledgeable concerning it than men. So if this woman whose menses increased from its normal duration knows that extra blood to be her normal blood of menses, then it is obligatory upon her to treat it as menses and not pray or fast. However, if the blood continues for most of the month, it would be considered *istiḥaaḍah* and she should not leave her prayer after that except whenever her normal menses would have been.

So based on this rule, we say to this woman that the days in which she fasted after she became pure and then saw the blood that she knows is not her normal menses blood, but rather it was yellow or brown or black sometimes, then it is not to be considered menses and her fasts kept in those eight days are correct and she does not have to repeat them. Likewise, her prayers that she performed during those days are not *ḥaraam* (illegal, prohibited) for her.

Shaykh Muḥammad ibn 'Uthaymeen

Blood stopped for a long time then some drops came out

Q. A woman's menses stopped for six months. Now she is doing *I'tikaaf* (seclusion) for five days. A small amount of blood came out on the fifth day of *I'tikaaf* so should she leave her *I'tikaaf*?

A. She should not leave her *I'tikaaf* since this blood that came out is a small amount whereas the menstrual blood is well known to the woman by its color and characteristics.

Shaykh Muḥammad ibn 'Uthaymeen

Not being able to distinguish between menstrual blood and other blood

Q. If a woman is not able to distinguish between the blood that comes out of her, whether it is menstrual blood or *istiḥaaḍah* or something else, so what should she consider it to be?

A. The norm and the basis is that the blood that comes out of a woman is menstrual blood until it becomes apparent that it is *istiḥaaḍah*. So in this case, it is to be considered menses as long as it is not known that it is *istiḥaaḍah*.

Shaykh Muḥammad ibn 'Uthaymeen

Ruling concerning whether a woman becomes pure just by not seeing blood anymore

Q. In the last days of menses and just before becoming pure again, a woman does not see any signs of blood. So, should she fast that day even if she has not seen the whitish discharge (which is a sign of purity) or what should she do?

A. If it is from her habit that she does not see the white discharge, as is the case with some women, she should keep the fast. However, if it is from her habit to see the white discharge, she should not fast until she sees the white discharge.

Shaykh Muḥammad ibn 'Uthaymeen

Ruling concerning continuous yellowish discharge after becoming pure

Q. What is the ruling concerning a woman who sees yellow liquid, and not white discharge, after she becomes pure from menses?

A. If a woman does not see the white discharge that is a sign of purity, then the yellow discharge takes it place. This is because the white discharge is one sign of purity but not the only sign since there are other signs also. So the sign of purity with most women is the white discharge but the sign can also be something else. It may also be the case that a woman does not have white or yellow discharge at all but rather dryness until her next menses comes. So every woman has a ruling depending on her situation.

Shaykh Muḥammad ibn 'Uthaymeen

Ruling concerning the discharge of blood during pregnancy

Q. What is the ruling concerning the blood that comes out during pregnancy?

A. A pregnant woman does not have menses, as has been mentioned by Imam Aḥmed. Women know that pregnancy has started when their menses stops. Allah, the Glorified, created the menses as nourishment for the fetus in the uterus of the mother. So if pregnancy starts, menses stops. However, with some women, menses continues during pregnancy just like it was before pregnancy and thus it is to be regarded as menses because the pregnancy did not have any effect on it. So this menses takes the same rulings as normal menses (outside of pregnancy).

The blood that comes out of a pregnant woman is of two types:

First: This type is considered to be menses because it continued with the woman just like it was before she became pregnant. It is a proof that her pregnancy did not affect her menses.

Second: Blood that comes out of a pregnant woman either due to an incident, or if she carried something heavy, or if she herself fell down from some high place or the like. So this is not menses and thus the woman is not prevented from praying or fasting. She takes the rulings of pure, non-menstruating women.

Shaykh Muḥammad ibn 'Uthaymeen

Ruling concerning sexual intercourse during menses

Q. What is the ruling concerning a man having sexual intercourse with his wife during her menses?

A. A man having sexual intercourse with his wife when she is having her menses is ḥaraam based on clear texts from the Quran and Sunnah. Allah, the Glorified, says:

﴿وَيَسْـَٔلُونَكَ عَنِ ٱلْمَحِيضِ قُلْ هُوَ أَذًى فَٱعْتَزِلُوا۟ ٱلنِّسَآءَ فِى ٱلْمَحِيضِ...﴾ (البقرة: ٢٢٢)

"*They ask you concerning menstruation. Say that is an Adha [a harmful thing for a husband to have sexual intercourse with his wife while she is having her menses], therefore keep away from women during menses...*" *(Qur'an 2: 222)*

So what is meant is the prohibition of having sexual intercourse during menses because sexual intercourse is done where the menses comes out of, which is the vagina. If however someone dared and had sexual intercourse with his wife, he should repent and never commit such a sin again. He also has to expiate for this sin which is to give either a *dinaar* (monetary unit) or half a *dinaar* in charity based on a Ḥadith by Ibn 'Abbaas (ﷺ) that the Messenger of Allah (ﷺ) said about such a person:

"Give a *dinaar* or half a *dinaar* in charity."

Imams Aḥmed, Abu Dawood, Tirmidhi and Nasaa'i reported this Ḥadith. The meaning of *dinaar* is a *mithqaal* (4.68 gram) of gold. If someone cannot find that, it will suffice him to give in charity its amount in silver. And Allah knows best.

Shaykh Muḥammad ibn Ibraheem

Ruling concerning reciting the Qur'an by a *junub* person

Q. What is the ruling concerning reciting the Qur'an, from the *muṣḥaf* (Qur'an) or from memory, by a person who is in *janaabah*?

A. It is not permitted for a *junub* person to recite the Qur'an until they take a bath. The ruling is the same whether they are reciting by looking in a *muṣḥaf* or from their memory. Also, it is not permitted to recite from the *muṣḥaf* unless a person is clean from both major and minor impurities (i.e. has had a bath from *janaabah* if needed and has made *wuḍoo'* also).

The Permanent Committee for Research and Verdicts

Ruling concerning a menstruating woman touching books and magazines that have verses of the Qur'an in them

Q. Is it *ḥaraam* for a menstruating woman or a *junub* person to touch books and magazines that contain Qur'anic verses?

A. It is not *ḥaraam* for a *junub* person, or a menstruating woman or a person who does not have *wuḍoo'* to touch books or magazines that have some verses of the Qur'an in them because these things are not considered to be *muṣḥaf*.

Shaykh Muḥammad ibn 'Uthaymeen

Is it permissible for a menstruating woman to enter the mosque?

Q. Is it permissible for a menstruating woman to enter the mosque? What is the proof for the answer?

A. It is not permissible for a menstruating woman to enter the mosque except in a situation where she is just passing through the mosque, in which case it is permissible, similar to the case of a *junub* person. This is based on the saying of Allah, the Glorified:

﴿يَٰٓأَيُّهَا ٱلَّذِينَ ءَامَنُواْ لَا تَقۡرَبُواْ ٱلصَّلَوٰةَ وَأَنتُمۡ سُكَٰرَىٰ حَتَّىٰ تَعۡلَمُواْ مَا تَقُولُونَ وَلَا جُنُبًا إِلَّا عَابِرِي سَبِيلٍ حَتَّىٰ تَغۡتَسِلُواْۚ ... ﴿٤٣﴾﴾

(النساء: ٤٣)

"O' you who believe, do not approach the prayer when you are in a drunken state until you know [the meaning] of what you utter, nor when you are in a state of janaabah [i.e. in a state of sexual impurity and have not yet taken a bath] except when just passing through the mosque till you wash your whole body..."

(Qur'an 4: 43).

The Permanent Committee for Research and Verdicts

Ruling concerning a menstruating woman washing her head

Q. What is the ruling concerning a woman washing her head during her menses? Some people say that it is not permissible for her to do that.

A. There is nothing wrong in a menstruating woman washing her head. As for the saying of the people that it is not permissible, there is no truth to their saying and she is allowed to wash her head and body.

Shaykh Muḥammad ibn 'Uthaymeen

Ruling concerning acts of worship upon a woman who becomes purified from post-natal bleeding before forty days

Q. Is it obligatory upon a post-natal bleeding woman to fast and pray before the forty days?

A. Yes, whenever a woman with post-natal bleeding becomes pure before the forty days, it becomes obligatory upon her to fast if it is the month of Ramaḍaan. Similarly, it is obligatory upon her to pray and it is permissible for her husband to have sexual intercourse with her. This is because she is pure (as a result of the blood stopping and she has had the bath) and there is nothing to prevent her from fasting, praying or the permissibility of having sexual intercourse.

Shaykh Muḥammad ibn 'Uthaymeen

Continuation of blood flow after forty days

Q. What is the ruling concerning a woman whose postnatal blood continues to flow even after the forty days have finished? Should she fast and pray?

A. If a post-natal bleeding woman has blood flowing from her even after the forty days, and this blood is the same as the blood before the forty days, then there are two situations. If this extra blood-flow after the forty days coincides with her normal menses time, then she has to treat it as menses and takes on all rulings concerning menses. But if the blood flow after the forty days does not coincide with her normal menses time, then the scholars have differed on this issue and have the following two sayings:

Some of them said that she should take a bath and then pray even if the blood flow continues from her because she would then be like a *mustaḥaaḍah* woman (and thus takes its rulings).

Some other scholars said that she should wait till sixty days because there have been real cases wherein some women have remained in their post-natal bleeding period for sixty days due to that being their normal post-natal duration. So based on this, a woman should wait till sixty days. Then if the blood continues to flow from her and if it is during her normal menses time, she has to treat it as menses. Otherwise, if it continues to flow from her and is not during her normal menses time, she should wash herself and pray since she would then be *mustaḥaaḍah*.

Shaykh Muḥammad ibn 'Uthaymeen

Ruling concerning a woman who does not have post-natal bleeding

Q. If a woman does not have any blood that comes out of her after delivery, is she permissible for her husband to have sexual intercourse with and does she have to pray and fast or not?

A. If a woman does not have any blood coming out of her after delivery, it is obligatory upon her to have a bath, and then pray and fast (if it is the month of Ramaḍaan). Also, it is allowed for her husband to have sexual intercourse with her after she has taken a bath. However, the normal and most common situation is for a woman to have the bleeding during the delivery or just after it, even if it is a small amount.

The Permanent Committee for Research and Verdicts

CHAPTER: PRAYER

The ruling concerning one who does not pray

Q. What is the ruling regarding a person who died while he did not use to pray? The person knew that his parents were Muslims. How are we to be with him regarding the following issues: cleaning his body, shrouding him, the funeral prayer, the burial, supplication for him and seeking forgiveness for him?

A. A person is a *kaafir* (disbeliever) if the prayer was obligatory upon him and he did not pray despite knowing the Islamic ruling on the issue, did not pray. He should not be washed, or prayed upon, or buried in the graveyard of the Muslims and he is not to be inherited by his close Muslim relatives. Instead, his property and wealth now belong to the Muslim treasury according to the more correct opinion of the two sayings of the scholars. This is based on the saying of the Prophet (ﷺ) reported in a *ṣaḥeeḥ* ḥadith:

> "Between a man and disbelief and *shirk* (polytheism) is the prayer."

Imam Muslim reported this Ḥadith.

Similarly, the saying of the Prophet (ﷺ):

> "The covenant between us and them is the prayer. The one who leaves it has disbelieved."

Imam Aḥmed and the authors of the *Sunan* recorded this ḥadith with an authentic chain of narrators from Buraydah (رضي الله عنه).

The famous *Tabi'ee* (follower of ṣaḥaabah) 'Abdullah ibn

Shaqeeq al-'Uqailee (may Allah have mercy upon him) said: "The Companions of the Prophet (ﷺ) did not use to see any act, the abandonment of which would be disbelief, except the prayer." The ḥadiths and narrations with this meaning are numerous.

This is regarding one who left the prayer out of laziness and did not deny the obligatory nature of the prayer. As for a person who denies the obligatory nature of the prayer, then he is a *kaafir*, out of the fold of Islam, with the consensus of the scholars.

We ask Allah to improve the situation of the Muslims and make them tread the straight path. Verily, He is the Hearer and the One Who answers.

Shaykh 'Abdul 'Aziz ibn Baaz

There is no *Adhaan* or *Iqaamah* for women

Q. There is a mosque in the department where the female students pray the *ẓuhr* prayer. One of the students gives the *iqaamah* for the prayer. Is this prescribed for women?

A. There is no *adhaan* or *iqaamah* for women, rather, that is something only legislated for men. And with Allah is success.

Shaykh 'Abdul 'Aziz ibn Baaz

The ruling of a woman's prayer without a *ḥijaab* (Islamic dress)

Q. If a woman is in such a situation that she has to pray without *ḥijaab* or her clothes do not satisfy the Islamic dress code requirement, such as some hair or the shin visible for whatever reason, then what is the ruling?

A. Firstly, it should be known at the onset that the *ḥijaab* is obligatory for the woman. Thus it is not allowed for her to leave that or to have an easy and relaxed attitude towards it. If the prayer time comes and a Muslim woman is not covered with the proper Islamic *ḥijaab*, then the ruling takes on the following details.

If the improper dressing or the improper *ḥijaab* is due to a necessity or compulsion, then she should pray according to her situation and her prayer will be valid and there will not be any sin upon her. This is based on the saying of Allah, the Almightly:

﴿لَا يُكَلِّفُ ٱللَّهُ نَفْسًا إِلَّا وُسْعَهَا...﴿٢٨٦﴾﴾ (البقرة: ٢٨٦)

"Allah does not burden a soul more than it can bear..."

(Qur'an 2: 286)

And also:

﴿فَٱتَّقُوا۟ ٱللَّهَ مَا ٱسْتَطَعْتُمْ...﴿١٦﴾﴾ (التغابن: ١٦)

"*...And fear Allah as much as you can...*"

(Qur'an 64: 16)

If the improper dressing and *ḥijaab* is due to the woman's choice and actions, such as following the customs and imitation or similar, and if the clothes are such that only her face and hands are not covered, then she can pray in that situation (i.e. in those clothes) and her prayer will be valid and correct. However, if there are males around her who are not her *maḥram* (unmarriageable close relative), then she will be sinning for that (as it is obligatory for a woman to be completely covered when in presence of non-*maḥram* men).

But if the *ḥijaab* is not covering the shin, the forearms, the head or the like, then it is not allowed for her to pray in such a situation and if she prays, then her prayer will be invalid. She will be sinning in two ways: one due to uncovering and the other due to her praying in such a state (with respect to clothes).

Shaykh 'Abdul 'Aziz ibn Baaz

Is a woman suffering from continuous urine allowed to leave the prayer

Q. A pregnant woman who, in her ninth month, suffered from continuous discharge of urine at all times, stopped praying in the last month. So is this considered leaving the prayer? And what is upon her to do now?

A. It is not allowed for such a woman or others to stop the prayer. Instead, she should pray according to her situation and make a fresh *wuḍoo'* at the time of each prayer, like a woman with *istiḥaaḍah* is required to do. She should apply cotton or something similar to her private part to stop or reduce the flow of urine and then pray each prayer in its proper time. It is prescribed for her to pray the voluntary prayer in due time also. She is allowed to combine the *ẓuhr* and *'aṣr* prayers and pray them together, and similarly, combine the *maghrib* and *'isha'* prayers and pray them together, just like a *mustaḥaaḍah* woman is permitted to do. Allah, the Almighty, says:

﴿فَاتَّقُوا اللَّهَ مَا اسْتَطَعْتُمْ... ﴿١٦﴾﴾ (التغابن: ١٦)

"*...And fear Allah as much as you can...*" *(Qur'an 64: 16)*

This woman has now to make up for the missed prayers and also do sincere repentance to Allah, the Glorified. Repentance is to be done by first regretting what she has done and then by making a firm resolution to never do that again. This is based on the saying of Allah, the Almighty:

﴿...وَتُوبُوا إِلَى اللَّهِ جَمِيعًا أَيُّهَ الْمُؤْمِنُونَ لَعَلَّكُمْ تُفْلِحُونَ ﴿٣١﴾﴾

(النور: ٣١)

"*...And repent all of you to Allah, O' believers, that you may be successful.*" *(Qur'an 24: 31)*

Shaykh 'Abdul 'Aziz ibn Baaz

The ruling concerning a woman covering her hands and feet during prayer

Q. What is the ruling concerning covering the hands and feet during prayer? Is it obligatory upon a woman or is it allowed for her to uncover these parts, especially if there are no non-*maḥram* men around her or if she is praying with other women?

A. As for the face, the Sunnah is to uncover it if there are no non-*maḥram* men around. As for the feet, it is obligatory to cover them according to the opinion of most of the scholars. Some scholars have the opinion that it is allowed to uncover the feet, but most of the scholars say that it is forbidden to uncover them and it is obligatory to cover them.

For this reason, Abu Dawood reported on the authority of Umm Salamah (رضي الله عنها) that she was asked about a woman who prays in a *khimaar* (veil covering head and face) and *qamees* (dress or gown). Umm Salamah replied: "There is no problem as long as her outer garment covers her feet." So the covering of the feet is better and safer at all times.

As for the hands (i.e. palms, up to the wrists), then there is a choice in it. There is no problem in uncovering them nor in covering them. Some of the people of knowledge have the opinion that it is better to cover the hands. And Allah is the source of success.

Shaykh 'Abdul 'Aziz ibn Baaz

Ruling concerning a woman praying with gloves

Q. What is the ruling on praying with gloves?

A. There is nothing wrong with a woman praying with gloves on because she has been ordered to cover herself while praying, except the face if there are no non-*maḥram* men around her. Wearing the gloves will cover the hands but if she covers her hands with something else, like a *jilbaab* (garment, gown) or similar, that will suffice. However, if there are non-*maḥram* men around her, she should cover her face also just like the rest of the body. As for a man, it is not prescribed for him to cover his hands, not with gloves or anything else. In fact, for a man, it is Sunnah to touch the place of prayer with the skin of his face and hands (i.e. in the prostration position) as the Messenger of Allah (ﷺ) used to do and likewise his Companions (may Allah be pleased with them).

Shaykh 'Abdul 'Aziz ibn Baaz

The times when the hands should be raised during the prayer

Q. What are the times when the hands should be raised to the shoulder or ear level during prayer? And is this raising of the hands to be done all throughout the prayer or just in the first *rak'ah*?

A. It is desired to raise the hands up to the shoulder or ear level at the following times: the first *takbeer* [saying Allah is Greatest (when beginning the prayer)], when going to and coming back from *rukoo'* (of every *rak'ah*) and when standing up for the third *rak'ah* after the *tashahhud* (testifying that there is no god except Allah, Alone, and Muhammad is His Prophet) of the second *rak'ah* in the *ẓuhr*, *'aṣr*, *maghrib* and *'isha'* prayers. These are based on narrations from the Prophet (ﷺ) wherein he did just that. And Allah is the source of success.

Shaykh 'Abdul 'Aziz ibn Baaz

The placement of the hands during prayer

Q. Where are the hands to be placed during the prayer just before and after *rukoo'* (bowing)?

A. Placing the hands together, one on top of another, is Sunnah both before the *rukoo'* and after rising from *rukoo'*. It is established in an authentic Ḥadith on the authority of Waail ibn Ḥajr (ﷺ) who said: "I saw the Messenger of Allah (ﷺ) when he was standing (during prayer) that he had placed his right hand on the back of the left palm, wrist and forearm." Abu Dawood and Nasaa'i have reported this ḥadith with an authentic chain of narrators.

Similarly, Imam Aḥmed reported with a good chain of narrators the following ḥadith: "That the Prophet (ﷺ) used to put his right hand on his left hand and placing them on the chest when he stood during prayer." Imam Bukhari reported a similar ḥadith in his *Ṣaheeḥ*, on the authority of Sahl ibn Sa'ad who narrated from Abu Ḥaazim, who said: "The people used to order a man when he prayed to put his right hand on the left arm during prayer." Abu Ḥaazim said: "I do not know this, except that it must have reached the Prophet (ﷺ).

So these show that a person in the standing position in the prayer is to put his right hand on the left one. And this ruling is the same for both before and after the *rukoo'*.

Shaykh 'Abdul 'Aziz ibn Baaz

Which is to be preceded to the ground when prostrating, the knees or the hands?

Q. Which is the more correct: to put the hands on the ground first or the knees when the person is going down for prostration?

A. The more correct is to go down with the knees then the hands then the face based on a ḥadith reported by Haail and other reports with the same meaning.

Shaykh 'Abdul 'Aziz ibn Baaz

Satanic whisperings and doubts during prayer

Q. I often have doubts during my prayer regarding the number of *rak'ahs* I have prayed. Despite the fact that I read out in a loud voice during prayer, I still get doubts. Then when I finish the prayer, I feel as if I have left out a *rak'ah* or two, or the sitting for *tashahhud*. Even though I take much care not to have doubts during prayer, I still have them. I hope you can guide me as to what I should do regarding the situation as described above? Is it obligatory upon me to repeat the prayer due to the doubts? And is there any supplication I can make at the beginning of the prayer to remove these doubts?

A. It is obligatory upon you to fight these satanic whisperings and be careful of them. You should increase the seeking of refuge with Allah from the accursed *Shayṭaan* (Satan) based on the saying of Allah, the Glorified:

﴿قُلْ أَعُوذُ بِرَبِّ ٱلنَّاسِ ① مَلِكِ ٱلنَّاسِ ② إِلَٰهِ ٱلنَّاسِ ③ مِن شَرِّ ٱلْوَسْوَاسِ ٱلْخَنَّاسِ ④ ٱلَّذِى يُوَسْوِسُ فِى صُدُورِ ٱلنَّاسِ ⑤ مِنَ ٱلْجِنَّةِ وَٱلنَّاسِ ⑥﴾ (الناس: ١-٦)

"Say: 'I seek refuge with [Allah] the Lord of mankind, The King of mankind, The God of mankind. From the evil of the whisperer, who whispers in the hearts of mankind. From among the Jinn and mankind."

(Qur'an 114: 1-6)

And also the saying of Allah, the Glorified:

﴿وَإِمَّا يَنزَغَنَّكَ مِنَ ٱلشَّيْطَٰنِ نَزْغٌ فَٱسْتَعِذْ بِٱللَّهِ ۚ إِنَّهُۥ سَمِيعٌ عَلِيمٌ ۝٢٠٠﴾ (الأعراف: ٢٠٠)

"And if an evil whisper comes to you from Shayṭaan [Satan], then seek refuge with Allah. Verily, He is All-Hearer, All-Knower." *(Qur'an 7: 200)*

If you get these doubts after you finish from your prayer or *wuḍoo'*, then do not turn to them and do not consider them as anything. Consider that your prayer is correct and your *wuḍoo'* is correct also. And if a doubt comes during your prayer as to whether you have prayed three or four *rak'ahs*, then assume it is three *rak'ahs* and finish the prayer based on this. Then you should do the two prostrations for forgetfulness before the *salaam* (i.e. just before the ending of the prayer). This ruling is based on an order from the Prophet (ﷺ) to anyone who has this situation, wherein he forgets, that such a person should do as we have just mentioned. May Allah protect us from the *Shayṭaan.*

Shaykh 'Abdul 'Aziz ibn Baaz

Hearing a knock on the door during prayer

Q. If someone knocks on the door when I am praying, and there is no one else in the house, what should I do?

A. If you are praying a voluntary prayer, then the matter is easier. There is no objection in breaking the prayer and answering the door. However, if you are praying a *farḍ* (obligatory) prayer, then you should not hasten the prayer (nor break it) except if there is some important matter that you fear will be lost or gone by not answering immediately. If you can signal to the person at the door, which would be in the form of saying *Subḥaanallah* (glorified is Allah) out loud by the men and clapping the hands by the women, to let the person at the door know that you are in the house and busy with the prayer, then that will suffice. The Prophet (ﷺ) said:

> "When something happens during the prayer, the men should glorify Allah (i.e. say *Subḥaanallah*) and the women should clap their hands."

So, if it is possible to indicate to the person at the door, with the men saying out loud *Subhaanallah* and the women clapping their hands, then that should be done. But if this will not benefit, say due to long distance and the person knocking not being able to hear, then there is no harm in breaking the prayer, especially the *nafl* (optional) prayer. As for the *fard* prayer, if there is a concern that the person is knocking due to an important and urgent matter (which will be lost or gone by not answering immediately), then there is no problem in breaking the prayer and then repeating the prayer right from the beginning (and not where it was left off). And all praises are for Allah.

Shaykh 'Abdul 'Aziz ibn Baaz

A woman in her house is not allowed to follow the Imam in the masjid

Q. My mother lives next to a mosque and the only thing between her house and the mosque is a small street. She can hear the *adhaan* (call to prayer) and the prayer. She then prays with the Imam from the house. Is this allowed? And if it is not allowed, then what should she do about the prayers she has prayed like this (i.e. prayed in her house by following the Imam from the mosque)? I hope you can benefit me, may Allah reward you with good.

A. If the situation is as has been mentioned in the question, then it is not allowed for her to follow the Imam with her prayer except if she can see the Imam or some of the followers. But if she cannot see any of them, then the more correct opinion of the people of knowledge is that she cannot follow the Imam in the prayer.

As for what has passed of her prayers when she followed the Imam from her house, then she does not have to repeat them, if Allah wills, because there is no clear proof to say that her prayers were invalid. This matter is one of those requiring *ijtihaad* (legal judgement) from the people of knowledge. The safest and more correct thing is what we have mentioned. And Allah is the source of success.

Shaykh 'Abdul 'Aziz ibn Baaz

There is no problem in reading the Qur'an from the *muṣḥaf* in the *tahajjud* (night prayers)

Q. Is it allowed to read the Qur'an from the *muṣḥaf* during the night prayer knowing that I have memorized very little and I desire to finish the Qur'an in the night prayers?

A. There is no problem in doing that. Dhakwaan, the slave of 'Aa'ishah (رضي الله عنها) used to pray with her in the month of Ramaḍaan from the *muṣḥaf*, which has been reported by Bukhari in his *Ṣaḥeeḥ* as a *ta'leeq* ḥadith (unconnected to the Prophet). This is also the saying of many people of knowledge. Those who prohibit it do not have proof. This is because not everybody memorizes the Qur'an and there is a severe need for its recitation from the *muṣḥaf*, both during the prayer and when a person is not praying, especially the night prayer and during Ramaḍaan for those who have not memorized the Qur'an. And with Allah is success.

Shaykh 'Abdul 'Aziz ibn Baaz

The ruling concerning raising the hands during the supplication of *witr* prayer

Q. What is the ruling regarding raising the hands during the (supplication of the) *witr* (odd number of rak'ahs after evening prayer) prayer?

A. It is permitted to raise the hands during the *qunoot* (humility, devoutness) of the *witr* prayer because it is of the same type as the *qunoot* of the voluntary prayers. It is established from the Prophet (ﷺ) that he raised his hands during the *qunoot* of the voluntary prayers. Al-Bayhaqi reported this ḥadith with an authentic chain of narrators.

Shaykh 'Abdul 'Aziz ibn Baaz

A person prayed *witr* during the first part of the night, and then was able to wake up at the end of the night (for *tahajjud*)

Q. If I pray the *witr* prayer during the first part of the night, and then I wake up at the end of the night, how should I pray (i.e. the *tahajjud* and *witr* prayers)?

A. If you prayed *witr* during the first part of the night, then if Allah makes it easy for you to wake up at the end of the night, then pray what Allah has made easy for you to pray (in *tahajjud*) in odd number of *rak'ahs*, but do not pray the *witr* prayer at the end. This is based on the saying of the Prophet (ﷺ) wherein he said:

"There are no two *witr* prayers in one night."

And also, it is established on the authority of 'Aa'ishah (رضي الله عنها) that the Prophet (ﷺ) used to pray two *rak'ahs* after the *witr* in a sitting position. The wisdom in this act, and only Allah truly knows the wisdom, could be to show the people that it is allowed to pray after one has prayed *witr*.

Shaykh 'Abdul 'Aziz ibn Baaz

The end time for the *witr* prayer

Q. What is the end time in which it is possible to pray the *witr* prayer?

A. The last time is the end of the night, before the dawn of *(fajr)* prayer due to the saying of the Prophet (ﷺ):

"The night prayer is two *rak'ah* followed by two *rak'ah* and so on, and when you apprehend the approaching of dawn, offer one *rak'ah* as *witr*."

Bukhari and Muslim reported this ḥadith.

Shaykh 'Abdul 'Aziz ibn Baaz

Calculating the last one third of the night according to hours

Q. I would like to know when the last one third of the night begins, in terms of hours?

A. It is not possible to estimate that with exact and limited hours. However it is possible for every person to know this by dividing the night into three parts. The night is from the sunset to the dawn or *fajr*. Then if the first two thirds pass, then what is remaining is the last third. It is reported by Bukhari and Muslim on the authority of Abu Hurayrah (رضي الله عنه) that the Messenger of Allah (ﷺ) said:

> "Our Lord, the Blessed and the Exalted, comes down every night to the nearest Heaven when the last third of the night begins, saying: 'Is there anyone to invoke Me, so that I may respond to invocation; is there anyone to ask Me, so that I may grant him his request; is there anyone seeking My forgiveness, so that I may forgive him?'"

So a believing person should try to gain this time, if not all of it, then at least a part of it. It may be that he or she will then gain this great benefit or gift from the Lord, the Blessed and the Superior, thus Allah grants him or her their supplication.

Shaykh Muḥammad ibn 'Uthaymeen

It is allowed for a woman to pray in the market

Q. Is it allowed to offer the prayer in the market?

A. The men have to offer the *farḍ* (obligatory) prayers in the mosque. As for the women, then her house is best for her. However, if she has to pray in the market, and there is such a situation that she is hidden (from non-*maḥram* men), then there is nothing to refrain from this if Allah wills.

Shaykh Muḥammad ibn 'Uthaymeen

The ruling of the prostration (sujood) when reciting (tilaawah) the Qur'an (*sujood at-tilaawah*)

Q. If I read a verse that contains a prostration, is it obligatory upon me to prostrate?

A. *Sujood at-Tilaawah* (the prostration that comes at certain places in the Qur'an) is an emphasized Sunnah and hence should not be left. So if a person passes a verse that contains a prostration, then he should prostrate, whether he was reciting from a copy of the Qur'an or from their memory or during the prayer or when not praying.

As for it being obligatory, then that is not the case since it is not obligatory and there is no sin on a person for leaving it because it is established from the leader of the believers, 'Umar ibn al-Khaṭṭaab (رضي الله عنه), that when he read a verse of prostration in *Soorat an-Naḥl* when he was on the *minbar* (pulpit), he descended and prostrated. Then on the following Friday, he recited it again but this time he did not prostrate. He then said:

> "Verily, Allah did not make obligatory upon us this prostration except if we wish to prostrate."

He said this statement in the presence of the Companions (may Allah be pleased with them all) and no one objected.

It is also established that Zayd ibn Thaabit (رضي الله عنه) read to the Prophet (ﷺ) a verse of prostration from *Soorat an-Najm* and he did not prostrate. So if it were obligatory, the Prophet would have ordered him to prostrate. Thus we see that it is an emphasized Sunnah and it is better not to leave it, even if the time is one of the prohibited times for prayer such as after *fajr* (till sunrise) for example, or after *'aṣr* (till sunset). This is because this prostration has a reason for it and any prayer that has a reason for it, can be prayed even during the times when prayer is prohibited, such as the *sujood at-tilaawah*, the prayer for greeting the mosque and so on.

Shaykh Muḥammad ibn 'Uthaymeen

A woman is unable to stand during prayer, so is she allowed to sit?

Q. There is a woman who has a broken and dislocated back. Plaster has been put on it and now she cannot pray in a standing position like usual and thus she has been praying in a sitting position for a month now. So is her prayer valid or not?

A. Yes, her prayer is valid because she cannot stand. In an obligatory *farḍ* prayer, standing is compulsory if a person is able to and thus if this woman is not able to stand due to a broken back then she can pray in a sitting position. If she can pray in a standing position while leaning upon a stick or wall, then she should pray standing.

So based on this, her prayers performed in the past are valid and correct because she is unable to stand. The Prophet (ﷺ) said to 'Umraan ibn Ḥusayn (رضي الله عنه):

> "Pray standing up, and if you cannot, then pray while sitting and if you cannot, then pray lying down on your side."

Shaykh Muḥammad ibn 'Uthaymeen

Delaying the prayer due to sleep

Q. I am a young girl. Many times, I miss the *maghrib* prayer due to sleep. I then pray it either in the morning or at another delayed time. So what is the ruling?

A. The ruling is that it is not allowed for anyone to take the matter of prayer easy till its time ends. So if a person is sleeping, it was possible for him to appoint a person to wake him up so that he can pray. Infact, this has to be done and it is not allowed to delay the *maghrib* or *'isha'* prayer till *fajr*. It is obligatory to pray in the correct time. So this young girl should ask her family members to wake her up.

If we assume that a situation may come where there is a severe need or something unexpected happens that results in severe sleep and if she prayed *maghrib*, she fears that she may not be able to stay awake till *'isha'* due to sleep overpowering her till *fajr*, then there is no problem in such a situation to combine the *'isha'* prayer with the *maghrib* prayer such that the *'isha'* prayer is not missed past its appointed time. However, it should be noted that this is not to be done except in cases where there is a severe need or something unexpected happens that causes severe sleep. An example of this could be if she had to stay up many continuous nights without sleep or it was at the end of a sickness or similar.

Shaykh Muḥammad ibn 'Uthaymeen

Doubts during the prayer

Q. Sometimes during the prayer, I forget whether I read the *faaṭihah* (first chapter of the Qur'an) or not. So I then read it a second time. Is this action correct or should I do the prostration for forgetfulness at the end of the prayer?

A. The Satanic whisperings happen a lot to some people during the prayer. They have a doubt regarding the recitation or the *tashahhud*. The cure for this is to first have a strong desire to come to prayer and then to pray with full concentration during it such that these whisperings and imaginations reduce. Then if these still happen and the norm for you is that you read, then in this case it is disliked to repeat. However, if repetition does occur due to the person wanting to be on the safe side, then the prostration for forgetfulness is not obligatory.

Shaykh 'Abdullah ibn Jibreen

Delaying the *'isha'* prayer

Q. What is the ruling concerning delaying the *'isha'* prayer till late?

A. The best thing regarding the *'isha'* prayer is to delay it till its last appointed time. Thus whenever it is delayed, it is better. However, in the case of a man, he should not delay it because if he delays it, he will miss the congregational prayer (in the *masjid*). So it is not allowed for him to delay it and miss the congregational prayer. But for the women who stay in their houses, it is better for them to delay the *'isha'* prayer. However, the *'isha'* prayer should not be delayed past midnight (which is its end time).

Shaykh Muhammad ibn 'Uthaymeen

Repentance wipes out what happened before it

Q. I am a twenty-five year old woman. Since I was young, I did not pray or fast out of laziness till the age of twenty-one. My father and mother both used to advise me to pray and fast but I did not pay attention to their advices. So what is obligatory upon me now knowing that Allah has guided me and I pray and fast now and I repented for what already happened?

A. Repentance wipes out what happened before it. So you should regret what happened and have a firm and sincere resolve to perform acts of worship, including many voluntary prayers both in the night and day. You should also fast voluntarily, make remembrance, read the Qur'an and make supplication. Allah accepts the repentance of His slaves and forgives their sins.

Shaykh 'Abdullah ibn Jibreen

Ruling concerning the women praying behind men in the *istisqaa'* prayer (i.e. the prayer for rain)

Q. Is it allowed for women to pray behind men during the *istisqaa'* prayer and is it correct?

A. Yes, it is allowed for a woman to go out of her house for the *istisqaa'* prayer but she should be behind the men. The furtherer she is from the rows of the men, the better it is for her due to the saying of the Prophet (ﷺ):

> "The best rows for women (during prayer) are the last ones and the worst are the first ones."

It is also established from the Prophet (ﷺ) that he ordered the women to go out of their houses and attend the *'Eid* (Feast) prayer due to the good that is in it and due to the supplications that the Muslims make in it. So if a woman goes out to attend the *istisqaa'* prayer and due to the supplications that the Muslims will make, then there is no problem in that. However, it is obligatory that she should not adorn herself (such as by not wearing the *ḥijaab* or by applying make-up).

There is an important point here that must be made, which is that if the women go out of their houses to attend the prayer in congregation in the mosques, then it happens that some of them pray by themselves behind all the rows (of the other women). This is in contradiction to the Sunnah, due to the saying of the Prophet (ﷺ):

> "The best rows for women (during prayer) are the last ones..."

So this shows that women also have rows (and have to pray in them). Also, the Prophet (ﷺ) said:

> "There is no prayer for a person who prays by himself behind the rows."

Shaykh Muḥammad ibn 'Uthaymeen

Ruling on delaying the prayer

Q. What is the ruling concerning a person who prays *fajr* (dawn) before the *ẓuhr* (midday) prayer by about two hours for example, knowing that they slept all the time prior to that?

A. It is not allowed to delay the prayer from its appointed time except with an excuse. Sleep, however, may not be an excuse for every person because it is possible for him to wake up early at the time of the prayer. Similarly, it is also possible to appoint someone, such as the parents or siblings or neighbors or the like, to wake one up. Along with this, a person should pay much attention to the prayer and his heart should be busy thinking about it such that when the time of prayer comes, he will feel it, even if he is sleeping.

So a person who does not always pray *fajr* except at the time of *ḍuha* does not have in his heart even the slightest amount of concern for the prayer. In all situations, a person is ordered to perform the prayer as soon as he can. So if he was sleeping, then he should hasten to perform it when he wakes up. Similar is the case for the one who forgot to pray or the one who was absent-minded during its time.

Shaykh 'Abdullah ibn Jibreen

The upper and lower limits for saying *tasbeeh* (glorifying Allah) during the *rukoo'* and prostration positions

Q. What are the lower and upper limits for saying of *tasbeeh* during *rukoo'* and prostrations?

A. The *tasbeeh* in the *rukoo'* position is: *Subhaana rabbi al-Aẓeem* (Glory be to my Lord, the Great). And in the prostrating position, it is: *Subhaana rabbi al-A'laa* (Glory be to my Lord, the Most High). The lower perfection limit is three times and the upper limit for the Imam is ten. However, even saying it once will suffice. It is a Sunnah to praise Allah after the *tasbeeh* during the *rukoo'* and to make supplication after the *tasbeeh* during the prostration.

Shaykh 'Abdullah ibn Jibreen

Satanic whisperings during the prayer

Q. I am a woman who performs what Allah has made obligatory upon me regarding the acts of worship. The only thing is that I forget a lot during the prayer because whenever I pray, I think about some of the things that happened during that day. I only think about these things at the start of the prayer and I am unable to get rid of these thoughts except if I start to recite loudly. So what advice do you have for me?

A. This thing that you are complaining of is the same that many other people complain of, which is that the *Shayṭaan* opens for them the door of whisperings during the prayer. So it could happen that a person finishes the prayer and has no idea of what was read in it. However, the Prophet (ﷺ) guided us to the cure of this, which is to blow out on the left side three times, and then to say: *A'oodhu billahi min ash-shayṭaan ar-rajeem* (I seek refuge with Allah from the accursed *Shayṭaan*). So if a person does this, then what he finds in the prayer will be gone by the will of Allah.

A person should think that when he starts the prayer, he is in front of Allah, the Almighty, and that he is talking to Allah and is becoming closer to Him with the saying of his *takbeers*, glorifications, reciting the words of Allah, and by supplications wherever these are supposed to be done during the prayer. So if a person feels these things, then he will enter upon (get close to) his Lord, the Blessed and Glorified, with humility and glorification of Him. This will accompany love for the good He has and fear of

His punishment if he neglects something that Allah has made obligatory upon him.

Shaykh Muḥammad ibn 'Uthaymeen

Ruling concerning one who slept during the time of a prayer

Q. A person slept during the time of the *'isha'* prayer and did not remember about it except after the *fajr* prayer, so when should this *'isha'* prayer be made up? Should it be made up the next time that particular prayer comes or whenever the person remembers it?

A. It is reported in an authentic ḥadith that the Prophet (ﷺ) said:

> "Whoever sleeps during the time of a prayer or forgets it, then he should pray it whenever he remembers it. There is no expiation for it except this." He then recited the saying of Allah: "*...and establish the prayer for my remembrance.*"

Bukhari and Muslim reported this ḥadith on the authority of Anas (رضي الله عنه).

So based on this, there is no difference between the *'isha'* prayer and other prayers. Whenever a person wakes up, and the time of a particular prayer that he has not prayed has finished, then he should pray it at that time and should not delay its performance till the next time that particular prayer comes. In fact, he should pray it as soon as he becomes aware that he has missed a prayer, even if this is during one of the times wherein the prayer is forbidden, or even if it is during the time of another prayer. However, if he fears that by making up for the missed prayer, the time for the current prayer will end, then he should pray the current one and then pray the one he missed after it. And Allah knows best.

Shaykh 'Abdullah ibn Jibreen

If a barrier is placed between the men and women, then which rows are best for women?

Q. If there is a barrier between the men and women (which prevents one from seeing the other) in the mosque, then does the following saying of the Prophet (ﷺ) apply: "The best rows for men (during prayer) are the first and the worst are the last. And the best rows for women are the last and the worst are the first"? Or does this not apply anymore and thus the best rows for women would be the first ones? Please guide me and Allah will benefit you.

A. It seems that the reason for the last row of the women being the best for them is due to it being the furtherest from men. For a woman, the furtherer she is from men, the more safer it is for her and the furtherer she will be from falling into evil acts (*faaḥishah*). But if the women's place of prayer is far from men and is separated from them with a barrier, such as a wall or something else that prevents crossing, and the women rely on the microphone to follow the Imam, then the more correct would be that the first rows are better for them due to these being towards the front and closest to the *qiblah* (direction of the Ka'bah).

Shaykh 'Abdullah ibn Jibreen

The two prayers, called the prayer of need (*ṣalaat-al-ḥaajah*) and the prayer for memorization of the Qur'an, are not legislated

Q. I heard about the prayer for need and the prayer for memorizing the Qur'an. Are these prayers valid or not?

A. Both prayers are not valid. There is no special prayer for need and no prayer for memorizing the Qur'an because acts of worship, such as these, can only be considered legislated if there is some proof from the Qur'an or Ḥadith. However, in the case of these two prayers, there is no such proof from the Qur'an or Ḥadith and thus they remain unlegislated.

Shaykh Muḥammad ibn 'Uthaymeen

Breaking the prayer

Q. If I forget and pray in impure clothes and then remember it during the prayer, is it allowed for me to break my prayer and change the clothes? And what are the situations wherein a prayer can be broken?

A. Whoever prays with impurity on his clothes, which he knows about, then the prayer becomes invalid. But if he did not know until he finished the prayer, then his prayer will suffice and is valid, and there is no need for its repetition. If he knew about the impurity during the prayer and it is possible for the person to remove the impurity quickly, then it should be removed and the prayer should be completed (without breaking it). It is established from the Prophet (ﷺ) that he removed his footwear once in his prayer when Jibreel (Gabriel) (عليه السلام) (may Allah's peace be upon him) informed him that there was impurity on them. Note that the Prophet (ﷺ) just removed them and did not break his prayer. Similarly, suppose there was something on a person's headdress. In this case, he should remove it quickly (for the men only) and then continue the prayer. If however, the removal requires a lot of movements, such as removing a shirt or pants or such things, then they should be removed but afterwards, the prayer should be performed from the beginning again. Likewise, the prayer is to be broken if a person remembers that he does not have *wuḍoo'* or if he passes gas during the prayer or if the prayer becomes invalid due to him laughing or the like.

Shaykh 'Abdullah ibn Jibreen

Contractions and the prayer

Q. Is it allowed for me to pray when I feel the contractions?

A. A woman has to pray when she becomes pure after the menses or the ending of the post-natal bleeding. However, if she sees blood before delivery by a day or so, then it is considered to be post-natal bleeding and she should not pray then. But if she does not see blood, then she should pray even if she has contractions. This is similar to a sick person who prays despite feeling the pain of his sickness because the prayer is obligatory to him as long as he is sane.

Shaykh 'Abdullah ibn Jibreen

The *witr* and the night prayer

Q. I am a woman who gets very tired when I go to bed at night. So is it allowed for me to pray the *witr* prayer before I sleep because I wake up at the time of the *fajr* prayer? And is there any share for me from the night prayer?

A. If it is your habit that you do not get up except at the *adhaan* of *fajr* prayer, then it is better for you to pray what you want before you sleep because the Prophet (ﷺ) advised Abu Hurayrah (رضي الله عنه) to perform the *witr* prayer before he slept.

So you should pray whatever Allah has written for you and also the *witr* prayer before sleeping, thus you would be sleeping after praying *witr*. Then if it so happens that Allah had written for you to wake up before the *adhaan* of *fajr*, and if you want to pray *nafl* prayers, then there is no problem in you praying these voluntary prayers in sets of two *rak'ahs*, but you should not repeat the *witr*.

Shaykh Muḥammad ibn 'Uthaymeen

Completing what has been missed from the prayer as long as the time is short

Q. I prayed the *zuhr* prayer, then after that I remembered that I only prayed three *rak'ahs*. Should I then only pray the fourth *rak'ah* and perform the prostration of forgetfulness at the end or should I repeat the prayer completely?

A. Whenever a person leaves a *rak'ah* or more from a prayer and then remembers about it while still in the mosque or the place of prayer, after only a short time, such as say five minutes or the like, then he should just complete the prayer and pray only what he forgot. He should then say the *salaam*, then perform the prostration of forgetfulness and then finally say the *salaam* again. If, however, you do not remember for a long time that you missed a part of the prayer, such as say half an hour or after you leave the mosque or a long time has passed, then the prayer should be repeated completely, thus cancelling the first performance of the prayer. This is because the *rak'ahs* have to be performed continuously.

Shaykh 'Abdullah ibn Jibreen

The going out of women to attend the *'Eid al-Fitr* prayer

Q. Is it allowed for a woman to go out for the *'Eid al-Fitr* prayer?

A. Yes, it is allowed for a woman to go out for the two *'Eid* prayers and in fact, it has been stressed that they attend. Bukhari and Muslim have reported on the authority of Umm 'Atiyyah (رضي الله عنها) that she said: "We used to be ordered to come out on the Day of *'Eid* and even bring out the virgin girls from their houses and menstruating women so that they might stand behind the men and say *Takbeer* along with them and invoke Allah along with them and hope for the blessings of that day." In another narration, it says that the Messenger of Allah (ﷺ) used to order the virgins, the menstruating women and also the mature women to go out (for *'Eid*). However, the menstruating women would stay away from the place of prayer but then join in the invocations made by the Muslims. Umm 'Atiyyah (رضي الله عنها) said: "O' Messenger of Allah, what if one of us does not have a *jilbaab* to wear?" The Prophet (ﷺ) replied: "Then let her sister provide her with a *jilbaab*."

The woman, however, should not apply perfume or adornments when going out. She should also stay far away from mixing with men.

Shaykh 'Abdullah ibn Jibreen

Prostration at certain places during the recitation of the Qur'an is allowed in any situation

Q. Is it true that the *kaafir* cannot give the evil eye to a Muslim? What is the proof of this? Also, while reciting a verse that contains a prostration, should I prostrate while in the state that I am in at the time of reciting, that is, without covering the head and the body fully?

A. This is not true. The *kaafir* is just like anyone else, he can give the evil eye because the evil eye is true. Also, there is nothing wrong with prostrating in whatever condition you are in, even if the head is uncovered and other similar conditions. This is because the more correct opinion is that this prostration does not carry the rulings of the prayer.

Shaykh 'Abdullah ibn Jibreen

It is not binding upon a person who has left the prayer for many years to make them up

Q. In the past, I did not use to offer the prayer. Then Allah blessed me with guidance. Now I adhere to it strictly and perform it with eagerness. My question is regarding the prayers during the past years, is it binding upon me to make up for them?

A. Whenever a person has left the prayer for many years and then repented from that and has become strict upon its performance, then it is not binding upon him to make up for those prayers that were missed. If this were to be a condition, it would make many people run away from repenting. The person repenting should now carefully guard the prayer in the future and increase the voluntary prayers, as well as the performance of other acts of worship and good deeds so as to become closer to Allah, and the person should also fear Allah.

Shaykh 'Abdullah ibn Jibreen

Ruling concerning uncovering the head during the prayer and reciting the Qur'an

Q. What is the ruling for a Muslim woman who recites the Qur'an, prays and fasts but she does not cover her head?

A. It is not a condition to cover the head while reciting the Qur'an. As for the prayer, it is not valid until the *'awrah* is covered and as regards the free mature woman, all of her is *'awrah* during the prayer except her face. It is not obligatory upon her to cover her face during the prayer except if there are non-*maḥram* men around her which then makes the covering of the face obligatory. This is because it is not allowed for a woman to uncover her face except in front of her husband and other *maḥram* men.

Shaykh Muḥammad ibn 'Uthaymeen

Contractions expiate sins

Q. My wife used to perform her prayers until her first delivery. She then became lazy alleging that a woman who gives birth has her sins wiped off due to the pains she faces during the delivery. So what do you say to her?

A. This is not true. A woman is just like anyone else from the children of Adam, if something befalls her and she has patience and hopes for reward, then she will be rewarded for these pains and afflictions. The Prophet (ﷺ) gave an example of something much less than the pains of contractions wherein he gave an example of thorns that prick a person would expiate sins because of the pain caused.

If a person has patience and hopes to get rewarded by Allah at the time of afflictions, then he is rewarded for the patience and having hope, and the actual affliction would expiate sins. So the afflictions expiate sins in all situations, and if these are accompanied with patience, the person will be rewarded for the patience with which he bore the affliction.

So a woman no doubt has pains and hardship during her delivery, and if she then has patience and hopes for reward from Allah, she will have, along with expiation of sins, extra reward and good. And Allah knows best.

Shaykh Muḥammad ibn 'Uthaymeen

The ḥadith "The best reciter should lead the people in prayer'' is not applicable to women along with men

Q. Is it allowed for me to lead my husband in prayer considering that I know more than him and also I study in the faculty of shari'ah? He is like semi illiterate.

A. It is not allowed for a woman to lead a man during prayer whether that man is her husband, or son or father. It is not possible for her to be Imam for a man. This is because the Prophet (ﷺ) said:

> "Never will a people prosper whose affairs are managed by a woman."

This is the case even if she is the best reciter because the statement of the Prophet (ﷺ):

> "The best reciter of the book of Allah should lead the people in prayer"

— does not include a woman when she is with a man. Allah, the Almighty, says:

﴿يَٰٓأَيُّهَا ٱلَّذِينَ ءَامَنُواْ لَا يَسۡخَرۡ قَوۡمٞ مِّن قَوۡمٍ عَسَىٰٓ أَن يَكُونُواْ خَيۡرٗا مِّنۡهُمۡ وَلَا نِسَآءٞ مِّن نِّسَآءٍ عَسَىٰٓ أَن يَكُنَّ خَيۡرٗا مِّنۡهُنَّۖ ... ﴾ (الحجرات : ١١)

> *"O' you who believe, let not a group scoff at another group, it may be that the latter are better than the former. Nor let [some] women scoff at other women, it may be that the latter are better than the former..."*
> *(Qur'an 49: 11).*

Allah divided the people into two categories, the men and women. So based on this, a woman does not come under the generality of the saying of the Prophet (ﷺ): "The best reciter of the book of Allah should lead the people in prayer."

Shaykh Muḥammad ibn 'Uthaymeen

Wearing *ḥaraam* (prohibited) clothes could invalidate the prayer

Q. A woman has set aside a particular type of clothing for the prayer. These clothes are men's clothes. Is it allowed for her to perform the prayer in them? And does this come under the prohibition of imitating men?

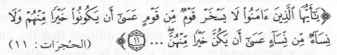

A. If the clothes that a woman wears are special for men, then it is *ḥaraam* for her to wear them, whether that is during the prayer or when she is not praying. This is because it is established from the Prophet (ﷺ) that he cursed the women who imitate men and also cursed the men who imitate women. So it is not allowed for a woman to wear clothes that are special for men and similarly, not allowed for a man to wear clothes special for women.

However, it is obligatory for us to know what makes something special for some group? It is not just with respect to color, rather with color and its type. For this reason, it is allowed for a woman to wear white colored clothes if its details are not like men's clothes. So if it is clear that for a woman to wear clothes special for men is *ḥaraam*, then her prayer performed wearing it is invalid according to those scholars who set a condition that the clothes should cover her completely and should be lawful also.

This issue has difference of opinion between the people of knowledge. Among them are who make a condition that the clothes should be covering and lawful. Others do not set this condition. The argument of the first group (i.e. those who say the prayer is invalid) is that covering the *'awrah* is a condition of the prayer (without which the prayer is invalid) and thus, this covering should be from that which Allah has allowed. So if it happens to be from what He has forbidden, the covering would then not be a shar'i (legal) covering due to the violation. The argument of the second group (i.e. those who say the prayer is valid but the person is sinful) is that the clothes have fulfilled the condition of covering and the sin is in something different and not special for the prayer. At any rate, a person praying in clothes that are not lawful is in danger of having the prayer rejected and not being accepted.

Shaykh Muḥammad ibn 'Uthaymeen

Ruling concerning a woman who prayed without the proper *ḥijaab* for a long time

Q. For a long time, I used to pray without the *ḥijaab* because I did not know about its obligation when praying. So is it necessary upon me now to repeat all those prayers knowing that it was during a period of almost six years or more, including the voluntary prayers?

A. If the situation is as has been mentioned, wherein you were ignorant regarding what has to be covered during the prayer, then you do not have to repeat the prayers you prayed during that time. What you have to do now is to make repentance to Allah of that and you should increase the performance of good deeds. This is based on the saying of Allah, the Exalted:

﴿وَإِنِّي لَغَفَّارٌ لِّمَن تَابَ وَءَامَنَ وَعَمِلَ صَٰلِحًا ثُمَّ ٱهْتَدَىٰ ﴿٨٢﴾﴾ (طه : ٨٢)

"And verily, I am indeed forgiving to him who repents, believes and does righteous good deeds, and then remains constant in doing them [till his death]."
(Qur'an 20: 82)

There are other texts with similar meaning. It should be known that the face of a woman is to be uncovered during prayer if there are no non-*maḥram* men around her (and if there are non-*maḥram* men around her, it would be obligatory to cover the face).

The Permanent Committee for Research and Verdicts

A woman forgot that there was impurity on her clothes and prayed in them

Q. If I forget that there is impurity on my clothes and pray in them, and then remember it during the prayer, is it allowed for me to break the prayer in order to change them? And what are the situations in which it is allowed to break the prayer?

A. If someone prays knowing that there is impurity on his clothes, his prayer becomes invalid. However, if the person does not know about the impurity being on the clothes until after the prayer is finished, then the prayer is correct and valid, and there is no need to repeat the prayer. If the person finds out about the impurity during the prayer and it is possible to remove it quickly, then that should be done and the prayer should be continued and not broken.

It is established that the Prophet (ﷺ) once removed his footwear during the prayer when the Angel Jibrael (Gabriel) (عليه السلام) informed him that they had impurity on them. The Prophet (ﷺ) did not break his prayer but rather continued it after quickly removing his footwear.

Similarly, if the impurity is, say for example, on the headdress and the person praying removes it quickly (then there is no need to break the prayer). However, if some effort and actions are required to remove the impure clothing, such as if it were on the shirt or the like, then in such a case the person should break the prayer, replace the clothes and then restart the prayer from the beginning. Similarly, the prayer is to be broken if one remembers that they did not perform *wuḍoo'* or if the *wuḍoo'* breaks during the prayer or if the person laughs (since that, too, breaks the prayer).

Shaykh 'Abdullah ibn Jibreen

How should a woman pray when non-*maḥram* men are around

Q. How should a woman pray if there are non-*maḥram* men around her, such as say in the *Masjid al-Ḥaram*? And similarly, during traveling if there is no special place for women to pray?

A. It is obligatory for a woman to completely cover herself during the prayer except the face and hands (up to the wrists). However, if she prays in such a situation that there are non-*maḥram* men around her who can see her, then she has to cover the complete body including the face and hands.

The Permanent Committee for Research and Verdicts

The manner in which to make up for missed prayers

Q. How are the *fajr*, *ẓuhr* and *'aṣr* prayers to be made up for, after a person remembers that these prayers have not been performed?

A. It is obligatory to make up for the missed prayers straightaway after remembering that they were missed. They also have to be made up for in the order that Allah, the Exalted, made them obligatory, such as *fajr*, then *ẓuhr*, then *'aṣr* and so on.

The Permanent Committee for Research and Verdicts

Women being Imam of other women during prayer

Q. Is it allowed for a woman to lead another woman in prayer? If so, then where should the other woman stand with respect to the woman leading the prayer?

A. It is allowed for a woman to lead other women in prayer. Shc should stand in the first row, in the middle of all other women. If a woman is leading only one other woman in prayer, then the woman should stand on the right of the woman leading the prayer.

The Permanent Committee for Research and Verdicts

Ruling concerning women appointing a female Imam during Ramaḍaan

Q. Is it permissible for women to appoint a female Imam who will lead them in the *taraaweeḥ* prayer (after 'Ishaa' prayer in Ramaḍaan) and at other times?

A. Yes, it is permissible and there is no problem in that. Some narrations have been reported from 'Aa'ishah, Umm Salamah and Ibn 'Abbaas (may Allah be pleased with them all) that show its permissibility. The female Imam of the women should stand in the middle of the first row of women and recite loudly during the prayer (as long as no non-*maḥram* men can hear her).

Shaykh 'Abdul 'Aziz ibn Baaz

Is it obligatory for women to pray in congregation?

Q. Is it obligatory for women to pray all the prayers in congregation?

A. It is not obligatory upon women to pray in congregation. It is a requirement only for men to pray in congregation and as for women, it is not necessary upon them. However, it is permissible or desirable for women to pray in congregation by appointing a woman who would stand in the middle of the first row of the women to lead them in prayer.

Shaykh Ṣaaleḥ al-Fawzaan

Is there any special intention for women when they are praying behind a man?

Q. Is it a condition for the correctness of women's prayer who pray behind a male Imam that they make a special intention? Or is it sufficient to have the intention that they are praying behind an Imam? Is there any differentiation between men and women (regarding what they are to intend)?

A. It is enough for the men and women to have the intention that they are praying behind an Imam. There is nothing to show that there is a special intention for women. During the time of the Prophet (ﷺ), the female Companions used to pray behind him and he did not order them to have any special intention.

The Permanent Committee for Research and Verdicts

Women praying in the *Masjid* (Mosque)

Q. Is it permissible for a woman to pray in the mosque in today's day and age?

A. Yes, it is permissible for a woman to pray in the mosque in today's day and age. The Prophet (ﷺ) said:

> "Do not prevent the female slaves of Allah from the mosques of Allah."

He also said:

> "The best rows for the men are the first rows and the worst are the last rows. And the best rows for the women are the last rows and the worst rows for them are the first rows."

The Permanent Committee for Research and Verdicts

Ruling concerning a woman praying all her prayers in the mosque

Q. If a religious young woman who adheres to the proper Islamic dress code and covers herself completely at all times except the face and hands wants to pray all her prayers in the mosque, is it permissible for her to do that? And is she allowed to always go to the mosque with her husband?

A. There is no problem for a woman in praying in the mosque if she wears the proper Islamic dress that covers her whole body including the face and hands, and as long as she does not apply perfume or adornments. This ruling is based on the saying of the Prophet (ﷺ):

> "Do not prevent the female slaves of Allah from the mosques of Allah."

However, it should be noted that her prayer in her house is better for her because the Prophet (ﷺ) said in the end of the above mentioned ḥadith:

> "...but their houses are better for them."

Shaykh 'Abdul 'Aziz ibn Baaz

Is the *Masjid al-Ḥarām* in Makkah better for a woman or her house?

Q. Is the prayer of a woman in her house better than in *al-Masjid al-ḥarām* in Makkah?

A. As regards the voluntary prayers, it is better to perform them in the house, both for men and women. This is based on the general saying of the Prophet (ﷺ):

> "The best prayer for a person is that which is in the house except the obligatory prayer."

For this reason, the Prophet (ﷺ) used to pray his voluntary prayers in his house despite him saying in another ḥadith:

> "The prayer in my mosque (i.e. the Prophet's mosque in Madeenah) is better than one thousand prayers performed in a normal mosque, except the *masjid al-ḥarām* (i.e. the *ḥarām* of Makkah)."

So, based on this, we say to this woman that say you are in a situation where the *adhaan* for the *Ẓuhr* prayer has been given and you are in Makkah and you want to pray in *al-Masjid al-ḥarām*. In such a case, it is better for you to pray your sunnah prayer before the *ẓuhr* prayer in your house, then go to *al-Masjid al-ḥarām* and pray the *taḥiyyatul masjid* (if there is enough time for it before the obligatory prayer).

Some scholars have taken the opinion that the multiplied reward for the prayers in the three mosques (i.e. *al-ḥaram* in Makkah, the Prophet's mosque in Madeenah and Al-Aqsa mosque in Jerusalem) is with regards to the obligatory prayers only since it is only these prayers that are prayed in them. As for the voluntary prayers, these scholars have the opinion that the reward is not multiplied.

However, the correct opinion is that multiplication of the reward is general and applies to both the obligatory and voluntary prayers. It should be noted that this does not mean that the performance of the voluntary prayers in these three mosques is better than them being performed in the house. Rather, these voluntary prayers are better in the house.

However, say if a person enters *al-ḥaram* in Makkah and prays the *taḥiyyatul masjid* in it, then this prayer is better than one hundred thousand *taḥiyyatul masjid* prayers in any other normal mosque. Similarly, *taḥiyyatul masjid* in the Prophet's mosque is better than one thousand *taḥiyyatul masjid* prayers in any other normal mosque except *al-ḥaram* (and Al-Aqsa mosque). Likewise, if you enter the *al-ḥaram* and there is still time left for the obligatory prayer after you prayed your *tahiyyatul masjid* prayer, then the voluntary prayers you pray (if you decide to) are better than one hundred thousand voluntary prayers in any other normal mosque. And so on.

The second part of this question is still left which is concerning the night prayer in Ramaḍaan, is it better to perform that in the house or in *al-Masjid al-ḥarām*?

Firstly, as regards the obligatory prayers, their performance with respect to a woman is better in the house than in *al-ḥaram* and any other mosque. Secondly, regarding the night prayer in *Ramaḍaan*, some scholars have said it is better for women to attend the mosque based on a ḥadith which reports that the Prophet (ﷺ) gathered his family and led them in the night prayer of Ramaḍaan. It is also reported that Ibn 'Umar and 'Ali (may Allah be pleased with them) ordered a man to lead the women in prayer in a mosque.

I do not have an opinion in this matter since firstly, the reports from Ibn 'Umar and 'Ali (may Allah be pleased with them) are not authentic reports and, as such, cannot be used as proofs. Secondly, the ḥadith that says that the Prophet (may the peace and blessings of Allah be upon him) gathered his family is not clear that he gathered them in the mosque and led them in prayer.

Is it better for a woman to pray the night prayer of Ramaḍaan in the *masjid al-ḥarām* or in her house? What is better is for her to pray in her house, except if there was any clear ḥadith that showed that her prayer in the *masjid al-ḥarām* was better. However, if she goes and attends the prayer, then it is hoped that she will get the reward mentioned by the Prophet (ﷺ):

> "The reward for the prayer in the *masjid al-ḥarām* is equal to one hundred thousand prayers in any other mosque."

If, however, there will be *fitnah* (trial) in a woman attending the mosque, then there is no doubt that it is better for her to pray in her house.

Shaykh Muḥammad ibn 'Uthaymeen

Concerning the passing of a woman in front of a person praying

Q. Does the passing of a woman in front of a person praying break the prayer in the *masjid al-ḥarām* of Makkah behind the Imam also or just a person praying individually?

A. It is established in a narration reported by Imam Muslim on the authority of Abu Dhar (رضى الله عنه) that the Prophet (ﷺ) said:

"A Muslim's prayer is broken, if there is nothing in front of the person praying (i.e. *sutrah*), by the passing of three things: a woman, a donkey and a black dog."

So, if a woman passes between a person and the *sutrah*, if there is one, or in front of the person till the distance of his prostration in the absence of a *sutrah*, the prayer becomes invalid and the person has to restart the prayer. This is the case even if the person was in the last *rak'ah*. There is no difference in this ruling between the *masjid al-ḥarām* in Makkah and any other mosque according to the correct opinion of the scholars because the proofs concerning this topic are general and there is nothing in them that specifies one place and not others.

For this reason, Imam Bukhari reported ḥadiths concerning this topic under a heading titled: "Chapter concerning the *sutrah* in Makkah and in other places." He deduced this from the general nature of the ḥadiths on this topic. So based on this, if a woman passes between a man and his *sutrah* (if there is one) or between him and the distance of his prostration, it becomes obligatory on the person to repeat the prayer.

This is the case except if the person is praying behind an Imam in which case the *sutrah* of the Imam is the *sutrah* for the followers and thus it is allowed in such a situation to pass in front of a person praying behind an Imam. There would not be any sin upon the one passing in front. If however a person passes in front of a person praying individually (i.e. not behind an Imam), then that is *ḥaraam*. This is based on the saying of the Prophet (ﷺ):

> "If a person passing in front of one praying knew what would be upon him, then it would be better for him or her to wait forty than to pass in front."

A narrator called Bazzaar reported that the meaning of "forty" in the ḥadith refers to years (i.e. forty years).

Shaykh Muḥammad ibn 'Uthaymeen

Requirement for straightening the rows

Q. Does the requirement for straightening the rows during prayer also apply to women's rows? And is the ruling concerning the first row and other rows the same, especially if the place of the women's prayer is completely separated from the men?

A. The rulings concerning the rows of the men also apply to the rows of women. This means that the first row should be filled before starting the second row, and they should be straightened and aligned, and the gaps between the women in the rows should be filled. If there is no separation or barrier between the men and women, then the best rows for women are the last rows as has been reported in a ḥadith. This is because of the greater distance from the men in the last rows compared to the first rows.

However, if there is a barrier or separation between the men and women, then what seems is that the best rows for women in this case would be the first rows (just like it is for the men) since the danger (of fitnah resulting from men and women being close together) is eliminated and also the first rows are the closest to the imam. And Allah knows best.

Shaykh Ṣaaleḥ al-Fawzaan

The Friday prayer takes the place of *ẓuhr* prayer

Q. If a woman prays the Friday prayer, does the *ẓuhr* prayer of that day still has to be performed?

A. If a woman prays the Friday prayer with the Imam, it suffices her the *ẓuhr* prayer, thus it is not allowed for her to pray the *ẓuhr* prayer of that day. However, if she prays by herself, then she has to pray *ẓuhr* and she cannot pray the Friday prayer in such a case (i.e. by herself).

The Permanent Committee for Research and Verdicts

Ruling concerning Friday prayer for women

Q. What is the ruling concerning the Friday prayer for women? Is it to be performed before the men pray or after them or with them?

A. The Friday prayer is not obligatory upon the women. However, if a woman prays with the Imam then her prayer is correct and valid. If she prays in her house, then she must pray four *rak'ahs* of *ẓuhr* prayer. It has to be after the start of the time, which is after the sun begins to decline after midday, and it is not allowed for her to perform the Friday prayer in such a case (since she is praying by herself in the house).

The Permanent Committee for Research and Verdicts

A menstruating woman praying due to shyness

Q. Is it allowed for a woman, who is shy, to pray while she is having her menses?

A. It is not permissible for a menstruating woman to pray. This is based on the saying of the Prophet (ﷺ):

> "Isn't it that when a woman has her menses that she does not pray nor fast?"

Both Bukhari and Muslim have reported this ḥadith. So, the menstruating woman should not pray and it is *ḥaraam* upon her to pray and even if she prayed, it would not be accepted from her. However, she does not have to make up for the prayers that she missed due to menses. This is based on the saying of 'Aa'ishah (رضي الله عنها): "We used to be ordered to make up for the missed fasts of Ramaḍaan and not for the missed prayers."

It is not permissible and *ḥaraam* for a woman to pray during menses due to shyness. Similarly, it is not permissible for her to pray after her blood flow stops (but) before taking the bath. If she does not have water with her to take a bath, she should do *tayammum* and pray until she finds water wherein she should take a bath.

Shaykh Muḥammad ibn 'Uthaymeen

A woman causing her menses

Q. A woman caused her menses by way of treatment and then she did not pray (on the days when her menses was present). So does she now have to make up for those misses prayers?

A. No, a woman is not required to make up for the prayers that she missed due to menses that she caused. This is because menses is blood and whenever it comes, its rulings apply. This is similar to if she took pills to prevent menses and then her menses did not come, then she has to pray and fast (if it's the month of Ramaḍaan) because she is not in her menses due to the blood being prevented by the pills. The rules apply whenever the reasons for it are present. Allah, the Exalted, said:

﴿وَيَسْـَٔلُونَكَ عَنِ ٱلْمَحِيضِ ۖ قُلْ هُوَ أَذًى ... ﴿٢٢٢﴾﴾ (البقرة: ٢٢٢)

"They ask you concerning the menstruation. Say it is an 'Adha' [i.e. a harmful thing]..." *(Qur'an 2: 222)*

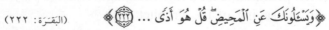

So whenever this *'Adha'* is present, its rulings apply. And whenever it is not present, its rulings no longer apply.

Shaykh Muḥammad ibn 'Uthaymeen

Ruling concerning the *'Eid* prayer

Q. Is it allowed for a Muslim not to attend the *'Eid* prayer without a valid excuse? And is it permissible to prevent a woman from performing the *'Eid* prayer with the rest of the Muslims?

A. According to many scholars, the *'Eid* prayer is *Farḍ Kifaayah*.[5] It is allowed for some people to not attend. However, its attendance is an emphasized sunnah and thus should not be left unless there is a valid shariah excuse.

Some other scholars have the opinion that the *'Eid* prayer is *Farḍ Ayn*[6] just like the ruling concerning the Friday prayer. Thus, based on this, it is not permissible for any free mature male, who is not a traveler, not to attend. This second opinion of the scholars is closer to the truth and is more in accordance with the proofs.

It is desirable for the women to attend the *'Eid* prayer after paying close attention to the proper *ḥijaab*, being covered and not applying perfume. This is based on a ḥadith narrated by Umm 'Atiyyah (رضي الله عنها) who said: "We were commanded to bring out on *'Eid al-Fitr* and *'Eid al-Aḍḥa* young women, menstruating women and *ḥijaab* observing ladies to witness the goodness and supplications of the Muslims. The menstruating women were ordered to keep back from the prayer place." Imams Bukhari and Muslim reported this ḥadith.

---

[5] *Farḍ Kifaayah* means that such an act, if performed by some people in the community, then there is no sin upon the rest for not performing it.

[6] *Farḍ Ayn* means that each and every mature Muslim must perform the particular act of worship.

In some narrations, the ḥadith ends with the following words: "I (i.e. Umm 'Atiyyah) said: 'O' Prophet, what if one of us does not have an outer garment (to cover her whole body).' He (i.e. the Prophet) said:

> 'Let her sister cover her (by providing her) with her outer garment.'"

There is no doubt that this ḥadith shows the emphasis placed on women going out to the *'Eid* prayers, both *'Eid al-Fitr* and *'Eid al-Aḍḥa*, in order to witness the goodness and the supplications of the Muslims.

Shaykh 'Abdul 'Aziz ibn Baaz

Ruling concerning women attending the *'Eid* prayers in our time

> Q. What is the ruling concerning women going out to the *'Eid* prayer especially in our times when the *fitnah* has increased. Some of the women go out adorned and perfumed. If we say that it is permissible for them to go out, then what can we say about the saying of 'Aa'ishah (رضي الله عنها) wherein she said: "If the Prophet (ﷺ) saw what the women are doing these days, he would have forbidden them."?

A. In my opinion, the women are ordered to go out for the *'Eid* prayers in order to witness the goodness and to participate with the Muslims in their prayers and supplications. However, it is obligatory upon them to go out without adorning themselves and without applying perfume. By doing what has been mentioned, they would be combining between following the Sunnah (which says for them to attend the *'Eid* prayer) and avoiding the *fitnah* (which results from them adorning and perfuming themselves).

What is witnessed from the women today, regarding adornments and perfumes, is due to their ignorance and negligence on behalf of their guardians (i.e. fathers, husbands, etc). This does not prevent the shari'ah ruling, which is for the women to go out and attend the *'Eid* prayer.

As regards the saying of 'Aa'ishah (رضي الله عنها), then it is known that if some *ḥaraam* will result from something permissible, then that permissible action becomes *ḥaraam*. So if most of the women go out in a state that goes against the shari'ah rulings, then we do not prevent everyone, but rather, we prevent only those women who are going out in such a state.

Shaykh Muḥammad ibn 'Uthaymeen

Praying three *rak'ahs* of voluntary prayer after *'Ishaa'* prayer

Q. All praise and thanks to Allah, I pray all my prayers, either in the mosque or by myself if I am unable to go to the mosque. After the *'Isha'* prayer, I pray three *rak'ahs* of voluntary prayer instead of five *rak'ahs*. I would like guidance regarding this matter. Note that I have made this a habbit and I have seen more than half of the people in all the mosques pray like this. I hope you can benefit me, may Allah guide you.

A. The least number of *rak'ahs* for *witr* prayer is one and there is no limit to the maximum number of *rak'ahs*. So it is permissible for you to pray *witr* with just one *rak'ah*, or three *rak'ahs*, or five, or seven, or nine, or eleven, or thirteen, or even more than that, there is no problem since all these are allowed. This is based on both actions and sayings of the Prophet (ﷺ). The scholar Ibn al-Qayyim has explained this matter in detail in his book titled *Zaad al-Ma'ad*. We advise you to review this book for further benefit.

The Permanent Committee for Research and Verdicts

Voluntary prayer after the *'Ishaa'* prayer

Q. I have noticed some people that they pray after *'Isha'* prayer two *rak'ahs* of voluntary prayer. Some others, like myself, pray three *rak'ahs*, while yet others pray five *rak'ahs*. So what is the correct number amongst these according to the Sunnah?

A. The Sunnah for a Muslim is to pray two *rak'ahs* of voluntary prayer after the *'Ishaa'* prayer. Its performance in the house is better than in the mosque. After that, a person can pray the *witr* prayer with either one *rak'ah*, or three, or five or more. The best is to pray eleven *rak'ahs*. After each two *rak'ahs* one should say *salam* and after ten *rak'ahs*, one should pray one *rak'ah* of *witr*. This can be performed either in the first part of the night, or the middle or the last part; whichever is easy for a person. However, the last part of the night is best for one who is able to pray then. By doing this, a person would be following what the Prophet (ﷺ) did as has been reported by 'Aa'ishah (رضي الله عنها) who said:

> "The Prophet used to perform *witr* every night, and he would (at times) complete his *witr* at the end of the night."

Imam Bukhari and Muslim reported this ḥadith.

Similarly, Imam Muslim reported on the authority of Jaabir (رضي الله عنه) that the Prophet (ﷺ) said:

> "If anyone is afraid that he may not get up in the latter part of the night, he should perform *witr* in the first part of it; and if anyone is eager to get up in the last part of it, he should observe *witr* at the end of the night, for prayer at the end of the night is witnessed (by the angels) and that is preferable."

The Permanent Committee for Research and Verdicts

Raising the hands during the *witr* prayer

Q. What is the ruling concerning raising the hands during the *Qunoot* of the *witr* prayer?

A. It is prescribed for a person to raise the hands during the *Qunoot* of the *witr* prayer. This is because the *witr* prayer is similar to the prayers performed when some calamity befalls and it is established from the Prophet (ﷺ) that he raised his hands during the *Qunoot* of these prayers. Imam Bayhaqi reported this ḥadith with an authentic chain of narrators.

Shaykh 'Abdul 'Aziz ibn Baaz

The end time for the performance of the *witr* prayer

Q. What is the end time that it is permissible to perform the *witr* prayer?

A. The end time of the *witr* prayer is the time when the night ends, which is before the *fajr* time starts (i.e. dawn). This is based on the saying of the Prophet (ﷺ):

> "Prayer during the night should be performed in pairs (i.e. two *rak'ahs*, then two *rak'ahs*, and so on). Then if one of you fears that dawn is near, he should pray one *rak'ah* which will make his prayer an odd number of *rak'ahs* for him (i.e. be his *witr* prayer)."

Shaykh 'Abdul 'Aziz ibn Baaz

Ruling concerning passing in front of a woman praying

Q. My father says that if a woman is praying an obligatory prayer, it is not allowed to pass in front of her. Please guide me in this matter, may Allah guide you.

A. The taking of a *sutrah* (i.e. something that is placed in front of a person praying) is a Sunnah for both men and women. However, it is not permissible for either a male or female to pass in front of another person who is praying or between the person and the *sutrah* (if there is one). This ruling is the same whether the person praying is a male or a female, and the one intending to pass is male or female.

However, if the person who passes in front is a woman, then the prayer of the one praying is broken. An exception to this is the *Ḥaram* in Makkah since it is not possible to avoid such a thing. Allah, the Exalted, says: "*Fear Allah as much as you can.*" He, the Exalted, also says:

﴿... وَمَا جَعَلَ عَلَيْكُمْ فِي ٱلدِّينِ مِنْ حَرَجٍ ... ﴿٧٨﴾﴾ (الحج: ٧٨)

"*...And [Allah] has not laid upon you in religion any harship...*" *(Qur'an 22: 78)*

The Permanent Committee for Research and Verdicts

Prostration when reciting the Qur'an

Q. What should a woman do when she reads a verse containing a prostration? Should she prostrate (in that state) with the head uncovered or what should she do?

A. It is better for a woman to prostrate with her head covered if she reads a verse containing a prostration. However, if she prostrates with the head uncovered, there is no problem in that. This is because the prostration performed for recitation does not take the rulings of prayer; rather it is submitting to Allah, the Exalted, and getting close to Him, and as such, it is just like other acts of remembrance and good deeds.

The Permanent Committee for Research and Verdicts

Woman reading loudly during the night prayer

Q. Is it permissible for a woman to recite in such a way that she can be heard (by those around her)? This is with respect to the prayers that are not performed loudly but rather in voluntary prayers and in prayers where the recitation is not read out loudly. The purpose for reciting loudly is to recite the Qur'an in *tarteel* (reciting according to the rules of intonation and pronunciation) form, to maintain concentration and in order not to forget. What is the ruling concerning this if there are no men or women around her?

A. As regards the night prayer, it is desirable for a woman to recite loudly in them, whether that prayer is obligatory or voluntary, as long as no non-*maḥram* man can hear her voice, thus causing *fitnah*. Infact, if she is in a place where no non-*maḥram* man can hear her and it is the night prayer, then it is preferable for her to recite loudly. If there are other people around her (i.e. such as women and *maḥram* men), then she should recite softly if that will cause disturbance to them.

With regards to the prayers performed during the day, she should recite softly since the day prayers are all recited softly. She should recite in them in such a voice that only she herself can hear. This is because reciting out loud is not desired in the day prayers since that is contradictory to the Sunnah.

Shaykh Ṣaaleḥ al-Fawzaan

A woman visiting the grave of her son

Q. Can I visit the grave of my son? I have heard from some people that if the mother goes to the grave before sunrise, does not cry and recites *Soorat al-Faatiḥah*, then it is possible for her son to see her and she would be very close to him. And if she cries over him, he cannot see her. How correct is this and what is the ruling concerning women visiting graves?

A. What has been mentioned in the question regarding if the mother goes to the grave of her son before sunrise and does not cry and recites *Soorat al-Faatiḥah*, then her son can see her as if she is very close, we say that this is incorrect and something that should not be heeded.

Regarding the ruling concerning women visiting graves, the scholars have differed on this topic. Some of them said it is disliked, others have said it is permissible if nothing prohibited is done while visiting, and some others have said it is *ḥaraam*. In my view, the correct opinion amongst what the scholars have said is that it is *ḥaraam* for women to visit graves. This is because the Prophet (ﷺ) cursed the women who visit the graves and the people who build mosques on them. It is known that a curse is not invoked upon a person for doing something permissible, nor for something that is disliked but rather it is invoked upon something *ḥaraam*.

There is a known principle among the scholars that necessitates that women visiting graves is amongst the great sins because that would bring the curse upon them. The principle among many scholars, infact most of them, is that if a sin has a curse upon its doer, then that sin is regarded as a great sin.

So based upon this, my advise to this woman (i.e. the questioner) whose son passed away, is to increase the seeking of forgiveness and supplications for him in her house. Then if Allah, the Exalted, accepts that from her, then it will benefit her son even if she is not at his grave.

Shaykh Muḥammad ibn 'Uthaymeen

Combining between the ḥadith which mentions the curse upon the women who visit graves and the ḥadith wherein it says to visit graves

Q. I have heard some scholars mention on the radio the ḥadith "Allah curses the women who visit graves". They then read the ḥadith "I used to prohibit you from visiting graves, but now visit them for they remind you of the Hereafter", or as the Prophet (ﷺ) has said. This has confused me so could you please tell me how to combine between these two ḥadiths?

A. Visiting graves for women is not permitted. As regards the ḥadith, "I used to prohibit you from visiting graves, but now visit them', it is not an abrogation of the ḥadith "Allah curses the women who visit graves".

The way to combine them is that the ḥadith, "Allah curses the women who visit graves" has specified and restricted the general nature of the ḥadith, "I used to prohibit you from visiting graves, but now visit them." So this is the way to combine between these two ḥadiths. Based on this, it is permitted for men to visit the graves and not permitted for women. This combination between the two ḥadiths is the correct opinion of the two opinions of the scholars.

The Permanent Committee for Research and Verdicts

Women visiting the grave of the Prophet

Q. What is the ruling concerning women visiting the grave of the Prophet (ﷺ)? And what is the ruling concerning women visiting graves (in general)?

A. As regards a woman visiting graves, then it is *ḥaraam*. Infact, it is amongst the great sins because the Prophet (ﷺ) cursed the women who visit graves. Also, a woman has weak reasoning, and is very emotional and becomes affected very quickly. Likewise, if a woman visits the graves, then maybe due to her emotional nature and softness, she will visit often and thus the graveyards will be filled with women. This will incite the evil men (with disease in their hearts) to gather in the graveyards for the women. The norm is that the graveyards are far away from civilian areas and separated from them, and thus enormous evil could result from this.

However, if a woman happens to pass by a graveyard without intending to visit it, there is no problem in her standing there and saying *salaam* to the people of the graves (according to what has come in the ḥadith).

As regards the women visiting the grave of the Prophet (ﷺ), then what seems to be apparent is that it too comes under the prohibition and that women are not permitted to visit that either. Some scholars have said that it is permissible because the grave of the Prophet (ﷺ) is not elevated and apparent like other graves, and also because it is surrounded by three walls. Thus, according to these scholars, if a woman visits the grave of the Prophet, it would not really be considered visiting; rather, that she just stood nearby it.

However, what seems to be apparent is that such a thing would be considered a visit to the grave according to the norms of a society (and thus would come under the prohibition). It suffices her to say: "*Assalamu 'alaikum ayyuhan Nabiyyu wa raḥmatullahi wa barakaatuhu.*"[7] Her saying this *salaam* would reach the Prophet (ﷺ) and thus she would obtain the reward for such an action.

Shaykh Muḥammad ibn 'Uthaymeen

---

[7] The meaning of this is: May the peace, mercy and blessings of Allah be upon you, O' Prophet.

Placing a woman in her grave by non-*maḥram* men

Q. Is it permissible for a non-*maḥram* man to place a woman in the grave and to untie the knots of the coffin, even if there are *maḥram* men present?

A. There is no problem in a non-*maḥram* man placing a woman in the grave and untying the knots of the coffin even if there are *maḥram* men present.

Shaykh Muḥammad ibn Ibraheem

A man placing his wife in the grave

Q. My father and I were not present when my wife passed away. However, we were present by the time she was buried. My son, one of my wife's cousins and I helped in placing her in the grave. I then heard from some people that I do not have the right to place my wife in the grave. So how true is this saying? And if it is correct, then is there any expiation I can offer or something I can do now?

A. It is permissible for you to place your wife in the grave. Whoever says that you do not have the right in doing this is incorrect. There is no requirement upon you to expiate for this and infact, you will be rewarded for this if Allah wills.

The Permanent Committee for Research and Verdicts

Placing two stones on the grave

Q. What is your view concerning the people who place two stones on the grave of a man and one stone on the grave of a woman? Is this differentiation legislated?

A. This differentiation is not legislated. The scholars have said that placing a stone or two, or brick or two such that it be known that it is a grave so that it would not be dug up a second time, they said there is no problem in doing that. As regards the differentiation between a man and woman, there is no basis for such a thing.

Shaykh Muḥammad ibn 'Uthaymeen

Burying a woman in the graveyard of men

Q. My mother says that she had a daughter who passed away in the absence of my mother and was buried in the graveyard of men. There are no women buried there at all but all men only. So is it permissible for her to be buried along with men or is it permissible to move her now? Please guide us, may Allah reward you.

A. Burying a woman in the graveyard of men and vice versa is permissible as long as each is buried in a separate grave (i.e. a man and woman should not to be buried in one grave).

The Permanent Committee for Research and Verdicts

A woman washing the body of her husband

Q. Is it permitted for a woman to see her husband after he has passed away or is it *ḥaraam*? And is it permissible for her to wash his body if there is nobody else to wash him?

A. It is permissible for a woman to see her husband after he has passed away. As regards the washing of his body, the correct opinion amongst the sayings of the scholars is that it is permissible for both a man and woman to wash the other's body, even if there is someone else who can perform the washing. This is based on the saying of 'Aa'ishah (رضي الله عنها) wherein she said: "If we had known beforehand what we have come to know afterwards, nobody would have washed the body of the Prophet (ﷺ) except his wives." Abu Dawood reported this ḥadith.

Also, Abu Bakr aṣ-Ṣiddeeq (رضي الله عنه) willed that his wife Asmaa' bint 'Umayṣ (رضي الله عنها) should wash him after he passes away. Thus she washed him as he had willed. Similarly, the wife of Abu Moosa (رضي الله عنه), whose name was Umm 'Abdullah (رضي الله عنها), washed his body.

As regards a man washing his wife's body after she passes away, then the correct saying amongst what the scholars have said is that it is permissible. The bases for this ruling, is a report by Ibn al-Mundhir that 'Ali (رضي الله عنه) washed the body of his wife Faaṭimah (رضي الله عنها) after she passed away. This incident became known among the Companions (may Allah be pleased with them all) and none of them objected, thus making it a consensus.

The Permanent Committee for Research and Verdicts

Who is the most preferable when it comes to washing a woman's body

Q. Who is the most preferable when it comes to washing a woman's body? Is it allowed for a disbeliever to wash a Muslim's body? And regarding placing a woman in her grave, is it a condition that the person doing it be some close relative of the woman or is it allowed for any person to do this job? Are the people who work in the graveyard allowed to place a woman in the grave?

A. The washing of a woman's body should be done by the closest to her, then the closest after them and so on, among her female relatives who know how to wash the body. However, it is permissible for any Muslim woman who knows how to wash a dead body to perform the duty (of washing another woman) even if she is not her close relative. Similarly, it is allowed for a husband to wash his wife's body and for a wife to wash her husband's body.

As regards a disbeliever washing a Muslim's body, then it is not allowed since the act of washing a dead body is considered as an act of worship, and acts of worship are not valid if performed by a disbeliever.

With regard to the third issue mentioned in the question: who should place a woman in her grave? The answer is that any Muslim who knows how to place the body in the grave can perform the duty, even if he is not her *maḥram*.

The Permanent Committee for Research and Verdicts

A menstruating woman washing a dead person

Q. Is it permissible for a menstruating woman to wash a dead body and to shroud it?

A. It is permissible for a menstruating woman to wash other women and to shroud them. As regards the men, a woman is only allowed to wash her husband. Menses is not considered something that prevents a woman from washing a dead person.

The Permanent Committee for Research and Verdicts

Funeral prayer by a woman

Q. Is it permissible for a woman to participate in the funeral prayer with the men?

A. The basis for acts of worship that Allah has legislated in His book (i.e. the Qur'an) or the Prophet (ﷺ) has explained in his Sunnah is that they are general and apply to both males and females. This remains the case until some proof is established that singles out the men or the women. The funeral prayer is of those acts of worship that Allah and His Prophet (ﷺ) have legislated and thus applies to both men and women. However, the rows of women are to be behind the rows of men. Also, it is established that women also performed the prayer upon the Prophet (may the peace and blessings of Allah be upon him) after he passed away just like all other men. But the women are not allowed to accompany the body to its burial because the Prophet (may the peace and blessings of Allah be upon him) forbade them from doing so.

The Permanent Committee for Research and Verdicts

Imam's position with respect to the dead body during the funeral prayer

Q. What is the position where the Imam stands when he is praying the funeral prayer on the men, women and children?

A. The position of the Imam is as follows: with respect to a man, the Imam stands near the head, and with a woman, he stands in the middle. The ruling is the same whether the man and woman are old or young. As regards a baby boy, the Imam stands near the head and with a baby girl he stands in the middle.

Sheikh Muhammad bin Uthaimeen

Announcing whether the dead person is a male or female before the funeral prayer

Q. What is the ruling concerning announcing whether the dead person is a male or female before the funeral prayer if the gathering is large?

A. There is no problem in doing that such that the gathering can use the appropriate pronoun during their supplications, the masculine pronoun for a man and the feminine pronoun for a woman. Similarly, there is no problem if this is not announced. In this case (when it is not announced), the people should intend that they are praying upon the person whose body is in front of the gathering. By doing this, their prayer would suffice and be valid. And Allah knows best.

Shaykh Muḥammad ibn 'Uthaymeen

CHAPTER: ZAKAH

Zakah (poor-due) on jewelry is obligatory

Q. Is zakah obligatory on the gold that a woman buys for beautifying herself and wearing, and not for the purpose of selling (or business)?

A. There is a difference of opinion among the scholars regarding whether zakah is obligatory on jewelry if it reaches the *niṣaab*[8] and if it is not for business. The correct opinion, however, is that zakah is obligatory on it as long as it reaches the level of *niṣaab*. This is the case even if it is for the purpose of wearing and beautification (and not business).

The *niṣaab* for gold is ninety-two grams. Hence, if the weight of gold is less than this, zakah is not obligatory on it unless it is for business in which case there is zakah on it as long as the gold and silver reach the value of the *niṣaab*. The *niṣaab* for silver is one hundred and forty *mithqaal*, i.e., (655 grams). Hence, again, if the weight of silver is less than this, zakah is not obligatory on it unless it is for business in which case there is zakah on it as long as the gold and silver reach the value of the *niṣaab*.

The proof of the obligation of zakah on gold and silver jewelry that is for the purpose of wearing, is the general statement of the Prophet (ﷺ):

[8] The *niṣaab* is the minimum amount that a person must own before it becomes obligatory to him or her to pay zakah. This value varies according to the type of item. For example, the *niṣaab* of gold is different from the *niṣaab* of silver which in turn is different from *niṣaab* on camels and so forth.

> "There is not a person who owns gold or silver and does not pay its zakah except that on the Day of Judgment they will be made into plates of fire and they will burn the sides, forehead and back of them."

Imam Muslim reported this ḥadith.

There is another ḥadith on the authority of Abdullah ibn 'Amr ibn al-'Aaṣ (ﷺ) that a woman came to the Prophet (ﷺ). Her daughter was wearing two bracelets of gold on her wrists. So he (i.e. the Prophet) asked her:

> "Do you pay zakat on those?" She replied "No". So he said to her: "Would it please you to have Allah make them into two bracelets of fire on the Day of Judgment?" The woman then removed them and said: "They are for Allah and His Messenger."

Abu Dawood and Nasaa'i reported this ḥadith with an authentic chain.

Similarly, there is another ḥadith on the authority of Umm Salamah (ﷺ) that once when she was wearing gold jewelry, she said to the Prophet (ﷺ): "O' Messenger of Allah, is this hoarded treasure?" He (i.e. the Prophet) replied:

> "Whatever out of that has reached the value of *niṣaab* and then zakah was paid on it, is not hoarded treasure."

Abu Dawood and Daaraqutni reported this ḥadith. Ḥaakim declared the ḥadith as authentic. In this ḥadith, the Prophet (ﷺ) did not tell her that there is no zakah on jewelry.

Regarding a narration wherein the Prophet (ﷺ) is reported to have said: "There is no zakah on jewelry", this ḥadith is weak and thus cannot be used (as proof) to oppose that which has been authentically established (such as the two authentic ḥadiths that have been quoted above).

Shaykh 'Abdul 'Aziz ibn Baaz

How should the zakah be given on jewelry that has gold and stones on it

Q. How should zakah be given on jewelry that is not just made out of gold but rather, it has precious stones as well? Should the weight of these stones be included (when calculating the zakah) since it is very difficult to remove the gold in order to weigh it separately?

A. Zakah must be paid on gold only even if it is for the purpose of wearing. With regard to precious stones such as pearls, diamonds and the like, there is no zakah on them. If for example a necklace contains gold and these stones, the woman herself or her husband or guardian must estimate the amount of gold or it should be given to an expert for estimation. It will suffice for a person to be reasonably sure about the amount (and is not required to be exact). Then if the amount has reached the *niṣaab*, it becomes obligatory to pay zakah on it. The *niṣaab* is ninety-two grams (for gold). Zakah is to be paid (once) every year and its amount is 2.5%. Thus, for example, on every one thousand, a person must pay twenty-five.

This is the correct opinion among what the scholars have said. If however the jewelry is for business, then zakah must be paid on all of it just like any other business item. Hence, this includes the pearls and diamonds according to their value (at the time of paying zakah). This is the opinion held by the majority of scholars.

Shaykh 'Abdul 'Aziz ibn Baaz

How should the zakah be paid on jewelry that was sold without paying its zakah

Q. I sold the jewelry that I used to wear but I did not pay zakah on it. So please tell me what I should do now regarding its zakah? I sold the gold for four thousand riyals.

A. If you did not know the obligation to pay zakah on it until after you had sold it, then you do not have to do anything. However, if you knew you had to pay zakah on gold (and still you did not pay it), then you have to now pay 2.5% for each year according to the market value of the gold. You have to give 2.5% in cash. However, if you did not know about the obligation of zakah until the last year, then in this case you have to pay zakah for only the last year.

Shaykh 'Abdul 'Aziz ibn Baaz

Ruling concerning a husband giving zakah for his wife and a person giving zakah to his nephew

Q. Is it permissible for my husband to give zakah of my wealth on behalf of me in view of the fact that he is the one who gave me the wealth (that I have)? Also, is it permissible for zakah to be given to my nephew, whose wife passed away and is a young man thinking about marriage?

A. Zakah is obligatory upon your wealth if you posses gold, silver or other items on which zakah has to be paid, if this is equal to or more than the value of the *niṣaab*. If your husband pays it for you with your permission, then there is no problem in that. Similarly, there is no problem if your father, brother or others pay it on your behalf with your permission. It is permissible for zakah to be given to your nephew in order to help him get married, if he is unable to support himself.

Shaykh 'Abdul 'Aziz ibn Baaz

A woman giving zakah to her poor or debtor husband

Q. Is it permissible for a woman to give the zakah of her jewelry to her husband who has a salary of about four thousand riyals (per month) but he has a debt of thirty thousand riyals?

A. There is no problem in a woman giving the zakah of her jewelry or of other things to her husband if he is poor or is in debt and unable to pay it off. This is according to the more correct of the two opinions of the scholars. The basis for this is the general statement of Allah, the Exalted:

﴿ إِنَّمَا ٱلصَّدَقَـٰتُ لِلْفُقَرَآءِ وَٱلْمَسَـٰكِينِ ... ﴾ (التوبة : ٦٠)

"*Zakah is only for the poor and the indigent...*"

(Qur'an 9: 60)

Shaykh 'Abdul 'Aziz ibn Baaz

It is not permissible to give zakah to one's mother

Q. Is it permissible for a person to give zakah to his or her own mother?

A. It is not permissible for a Muslim to give zakah to his or her own parents or to their children. Rather, it is obligatory upon a person to spend upon them from his own money if they (i.e. the parents or children) are in need and if the person is able to spend on them.

Shaykh 'Abdul 'Aziz ibn Baaz

Paying zakah to the *mujahideen*

Q. There is a trustworthy man who says he can collect the zakah and give it to another trustworthy person who, in turn, can give the zakah to the *mujahideen*. So should

I give the zakah of my property to him or is there some other place I can give my zakah? It is difficult for me, being a woman, to search for needy and deserving people.

A. As the scholars have mentioned, it is correct for the zakah to be given to the *mujahideen* because they are fighting the disbelievers. So, if a person has trust in another person, then it is permissible for zakah to be given to him in order to give it to the *mujahideen* himself or to get it to them through another trustworthy person. After doing this, the person has fulfilled his responsibility of giving zakah and his reward will be from Allah.

Shaykh 'Abdullah ibn Jibreen

How is zakah to be paid on jewelry?

Q. A woman possesses jewelry that has reached the value of *niṣaab*. How should she give the zakah on it in Saudi riyals? Also, how much is the amount to be given?

A. It is obligatory upon a woman every year to consult those who sell gold or others regarding the value of gold. Then when she knows its value at the time of paying the zakah, she can pay its value. There is no need for the original price to be known, rather you have to give according to the market value at the time of giving zakah.

Shaykh 'Abdullah ibn Jibreen

CHAPTER: FASTING

Intention for fasting

> Q. An Imam of a mosque mentioned to his congregation that he has a book in which it states that if the intention for the fasts of Ramaḍaan are not made before *'Isha' al-akheer* or after it or at the time of *suhoor* (the early morning meal), then there is no reward for the fast. Is this correct or not?

A. All praise is to Allah. The intention is binding upon every Muslim who believes that the fasting is obligatory upon him and wants to fast the month of Ramaḍaan. If a person knows that tomorrow is Ramaḍaan, then he must make the intention to fast. The place for the intention is the heart and everyone who knows what he wants must intend it. Uttering the intention with the tongue is not obligatory with the consensus of the Muslims. All Muslims fast with intention and there is no difference of opinion between the scholars that their fasts are correct. And Allah knows best.

Shaykh ul Islam Ibn Taymiyah

Is it required to make a new intention everyday for a person who is fasting Ramaḍaan

> Q. What does our leader have to say about fasting (the month) of Ramaḍaan, is it required to make a new intention every day?

A. Everyone who knows that tomorrow is a day of Ramaḍaan and he wants to fast it, then by that he has intended the fast. It is the same if he utters the intention with the tongue or not. This is the practice of the Muslims; all of them make the intention to fast.

Shaykh ul Islam Ibn Taymiyah

How does a person intend the fasts of Ramaḍaan?

Q. How does a person intend the fasts of Ramaḍaan? Is the mere knowledge of the beginning of Ramaḍaan sufficient (as an intention) for the remainder of the month?

A. The intention is made by having a firm will to fast. The intention for the fast in Ramaḍaan must be made at night for the following day, so this has to be done every night.

From Allah is the success. May the blessing and peace of Allah be on the Prophet Muhammad, his family and Companions.

The Permanent Committee for Research and Verdicts

Is it a condition to make the intention everyday in Ramaḍaan?

Q. At times, I fast without making an intention when starting the fast. So is it a condition to make the intention in Ramaḍaan everyday or is it enough to make one intention at the start of the month?

A. The fast and other acts of worship must be preceded by intention. The Prophet (ﷺ) said:

> "Verily all actions are by intentions and for everyone is what he intended."

Imam Bukhari reported this ḥadith. And in another report:

> "There is no act except with intention."

So to fast in Ramaḍaan, it is obligatory to make the intention during the night sometime before the *fajr* of the day being intended to fast. A Muslim's rising up from sleep in the last part of the night and eating the early morning (*suhoor*) meal is an indication of the presence of the intention. It is not required that a person utter the intention by the tongue by saying: I intend to fast. This is a *bid'ah* (reprehensible innovation in the religion) and is not allowed. The intention in Ramaḍaan is to be done every day (for the next day) because each day is a separate act of worship requiring its intention. So the intention for the fast is to be made everyday during the night in the heart. If someone makes the intention during the night, then sleeps and does not wake up until after *fajr*, then his fast is valid due to the presence of the intention from the night.

Shaykh Ṣaaleḥ al-Fawzaan

When to make the intention of fasting

Q. Is it sufficient to make the intention once in the beginning (for the whole month) or is it required every day?

A. It is known that every person wakes up in the night to eat the early morning meal because he wants to fast. There is no doubt that every sane person does an action by his choice and this is not possible except by his will.

A person's willing to do an action is his intention. One does not eat in the last part of the night except to fast that day. If he did not want to fast, then it is not of his habit to eat at that time. So this is his intention.

A question such as this is necessary to understand other situations. Suppose a person slept before sunset in Ramaḍaan and remained asleep and was not woken up by anyone till after *fajr* the next day, then he did not make his intention during that night. So do we say that his fast of that day is valid due to his previous intention (for previous days)? Or do we say that his fast is invalid because he did not make the intention during the night?

We say that his fast is valid. This is according to the more correct opinion that an intention made at the start of Ramaḍaan is sufficient and does not require renewing every day. An exception to this is a case where a person is excused from fasting and so he stops fasting during the month, then for him to restart his fasts, he must make another intention.[9]

Shaykh Muḥammad ibn 'Uthaymeen

Making the intention during the night to fast for the next day

Q. After a man slept one night, the sighting of the moon of the start of Ramaḍaan was confirmed. For this reason, he was unable to make his intention that night for the fast and woke up and did not fast that day since he did not know about the sighting of the moon. So what is obligatory upon him now?

A. This man who slept on the first night of the month of Ramaḍaan before the moon was sighted and did not make his intention to fast during the night, then woke up after *fajr* and found out that it was Ramaḍaan, it was obligatory to him to refrain from eating and drinking from the time that he found out that it was Ramaḍaan. Furthermore, it is obligatory to him to make up for that day by fasting on another day. This view is according to the majority of the scholars.

---

[9] Note that the previous question indicates that there is a difference of opinion between the scholars on whether the intention has to be made every night in Ramaḍaan or only at the start of the month.

As far as I know, only Shaykh ul Islam Ibn Taymiyah (may Allah shower His mercy upon him) holds a view contradictory to this. He said that: "Verily the intention follows the knowledge and this person (with the above mentioned scenario) did not know and, so, he is excused. It was not that the person left the intention after knowing (about the beginning of the month) but instead he was ignorant and the ignorant person is excused." Based upon this opinion, if the person refrains from eating and drinking from the point at which he knew it was Ramaḍaan, then his fast is valid and there is no need to make up for the fast of that day. But the majority of the scholars say that it is obligatory to refrain from eating and drinking, and then he should make up for that day by fasting another one. The reason for this is that: part of the day was gone without intention. In my view, as a precaution, a person should make up for the fast for that day.

Shaykh Muḥammad ibn 'Uthaymeen

Does the fast break if a person makes a firm intention to break his fast without actually eating and drinking?

Q. A person intended to definitely break his fast, so is his fast broken even if he has not actually eaten and drunk anything?

A. It is known that the fasting is a combination of intention and leaving all things that nullify the fast. A person's intention when fasting is to come closer to Allah by leaving all things that will break his fast.

So if a person has made a firm decision to break his fast, then the fast is broken but if this is in the month of Ramaḍaan, then it is obligatory upon him to refrain from eating until sunset. This is because anyone who breaks the fast in Ramaḍaan without a valid reason has to refrain from eating the rest of that day and it is also binding on him to fast another day in place of it.

However, if the decision is not made firmly and there is hesitation, then the scholars have differed in this. Some have said that the fast is nullified because hesitation is contradictory to a firm decision. And others have said that the fast is still valid because the default is the presence of intention to fast, until a firm decision is made to break and cancel it.

Shaykh Muḥammad ibn 'Uthaymeen

A person intended to keep the fasts that are upon him as an expiation, then decided to delay them till the winter

Q. I intended to fast sixty days that were upon me as an atonement. Then I put that off till the winter season. So what if I die before that?

A. It is obligatory upon a person to quickly keep the fasts that are expiations. This is because the obligatory acts have to be carried out quickly. However, if keeping the fasts of expiation in summer will be difficult upon a person due to the long daytime and the severe heat, then there is no blame upon him in delaying the fasts till the winter. If he dies before that, then there is no sin on him because he delayed it due to a valid reason. In such a case (if he dies before fasting) then someone else would have to fast on his behalf whatever is possible from the remaining.

If someone does not fast on his behalf, then a needy person has to be fed for each day missed.

Shaykh Muḥammad ibn 'Uthaymeen

A person made an intention, without vowing, to fast every Monday and Thursday. So is it obligatory to him to fast these two days of the week all his life?

Q. I intended to fast every Monday and Thursday but I did not make a vow for it. So is it obligatory to me to fast (these two days of the week) all my life? For example, if I fast on a Thursday and then break my fast (in the middle of the day), is it obligatory to me to fast another day instead?

A. An act does not become incumbent just by having an intention to do it. So if a person intended to fast every Monday and Thursday but then did not fast them, then there is no problem in it. Likewise, if someone starts to fast and then breaks it, there is no problem in it. This is because it is not binding upon a person to complete a voluntary fast. Even if a person intended to give money in charity and also decided where and how much to give, then still it is not binding upon him to donate as much as he had intended, because in matters like these, mere intention does not make the act obligatory.

Based upon this, we would say to the questioner that it is not obligatory upon you to make up for the fast that you broke on Thursday and also it is not obligatory upon you to continue to fast every Monday and Thursday. However, it is good if you do fast these two days since it is of the Sunnah to fast them.

Shaykh Muḥammad ibn 'Uthaymeen

The meaning of the ḥadith: *"There is no fast for the one who does not make his intention during the night"*

Q. What is the meaning of the ḥadith: "There is no fast for the one who does not make his intention during the night"?

A. The intention is the decision and resolution of the heart to fast. It is necessary for every Muslim who knows that Allah has made fasting in the month of Ramaḍaan obligatory. So a person's knowledge of this obligatory act and his decision to abide by it suffices his intention.

It is also enough to address oneself that he will fast the next day if there is no reason for him which may prevent him from fasting.

It is also enough if he takes the early morning meal (*suhoor*) with this intention and there it is not necessary for him to utter the intention (with the tongue) for the fast or any other act of worship. So the place for the intention is the heart and it is obligatory to a person to continue with the decision throughout the day by not intending to break or cancel the fast.

Shaykh 'Abdullah ibn Jibreen

Ruling on a conditional intention for an optional fast

Q. What is the ruling on (making) a conditional intention for an optional fast?

A. There is no problem in making a conditional intention for an optional fast. For example, by saying: "I will fast till I feel the pressure. Then if I see fatigue or hardship, I will break my fast."

Shaykh 'Abdullah ibn Jibreen

Is it necessary while making the intention to fast in Ramaḍaan to specify that it is an obligatory fast

Q. Is it necessary for a fasting person while making his intention to fast in Ramaḍaan, to specify that it is obligatory?

A. The scholars say it is obligatory to specify the intention from the night for the fast of every day, and not the intention that it is obligatory. So it is enough to intend that it is the fast of Ramaḍaan, and a person does not need to say: I intend that it is obligatory. It is known that the fast of Ramaḍaan is obligatory.

Shaykh 'Abdullah ibn Jibreen

Intending the voluntary fast after midday

Q. Is it correct for a person fasting a voluntary fast, to make the intention after midday?

A. There is freedom (for a person) in the voluntary fast. Thus it is correct to make the intention during the day. The scholars differed whether the intention is correct after midday or not? Amongst them, like the author of *Zaad al Mustaqna'*, said that it is correct after midday. And amongst them are ones who said it is not correct except before midday.

The outweighing opinion is that it is not correct except before midday. As for after midday, then most of the day has passed. The fast with its intention is the one where the intention is there for most of the day. So if only a small part of it is left, then his fast is not counted. There is a condition that has to be fulfilled, which is that he should not have eaten anything in the beginning of the day.

So if a Muslim wakes up in the morning with the intention of not fasting, but did not eat anything that breaks his fast, then during the day decides to complete the day fasting and refraining (from things that break the fast), then it is allowed.

The proof of it is the famous ḥadith of 'Aa'ishah (رضي الله عنها) who said:

> "The Prophet (ﷺ) came to me and said: 'Do you have anything (to eat)'? I said: 'No'. He said: 'Then I am fasting'."

Imam Muslim reported this ḥadith. So he (ﷺ) intended the fast during the day although he asked for food. If he had found food, he would have eaten it. So when he didn't find it, he decided to complete the day fasting.

Shaykh 'Abdullah ibn Jibreen

Is the fasting person rewarded for the time that preceded his intention in a voluntary fast?

Q. Is the fasting person rewarded for the time that preceded his intention in a voluntary fast? For example, if a person fasting a voluntary fast makes his intention after midday, then is the time that passed before he made his intention rewarded or not?

A. The correct is that the reward is from the time of the intention and what follows because the start of the day in which he didn't eat or drink is considered as though he left it due to a habit. So he is rewarded from the time he decides to fast because it is after this time, if there comes any food, he would leave it because he has already decided, even though the person fasting a voluntary fast is the boss of himself (and thus has the freedom to do what he wants). It is allowed for him to break his fast after he has decided to fast.

'Aa'ishah (رضي الله عنها) said: "The Prophet (صلى الله عليه وسلم) came to us, so we said:

> 'O' Messenger of Allah, we have been given *Hais*[10] as a gift'. So he said: 'Bring it to me, I had started the day fasting'. Then he ate (from it).'"

Imam Muslim reported this ḥadith.

Shaykh 'Abdullah ibn Jibreen

---

[10] *Hais* is a mixture made out of dates, dried milk and fat.

Ruling of uttering the intention with the tongue for the fast

Q. What is the ruling on uttering the intention (with the tongue)? Like the saying of some people when making intention to fast: "O' Allah, verily I intend to fast."

A. The place of the intention is the heart and it is not allowed to utter it (with the tongue) neither for the prayer, nor the fast, nor the purification, nor anything else.

Some of the (scholars of the) *Shafi'iyah madhhab* (school of jurisprudence) hold the opinion that it is necessary to utter the intention and have put this view in their books. In fact, they even said that uttering the intention is a Sunnah and that it is the *madhhab* of Imam Shafi'ee.

The correct opinion is that it is not the *madhhab* of Shafi'ee and it has not been narrated from him in any clear narration. Also, this is not mentioned in his books or his writings.

Shaykh 'Abdullah ibn Jibreen

The ruling of a person who hesitates in his intention to fast or to break the fast

Q. One night we heard the sound of the cannon more than once[11] and we were unsure regarding the next day, is it Ramaḍaan or is it *'Eid*? So we waited in order to hear news from the Imam before *fajr* but we did not hear anything. So what is the ruling of a person who hesitates in his intention to fast or to break the fast?

[11] The firing of the cannon is a custom used in Saudi Arabia to inform the people of the beginning of Ramaḍaan and the day of *'Eid*. It is also fired on all nights of the month. The number of firings is different for the day of *'Eid* from other days of the month.

A. It is obligatory for a person to verify and be certain. The default is to remain upon what one is sure of. In this case, if there was something, then it would have been apparent and clear to the people in order that they do not eat the early morning meal and do not fast.

In any case, this day (in question) is considered to be from the month of Ramaḍaan. If the finishing of the month were established, it would have been clear. Based upon this, it is obligatory to a person in situations such as this to fast without hesitation because the default is that Ramaḍaan is continuing. Then if it becomes clear afterwards that it is the day of *'Eid*, then he should break his fast.

Shaykh Muḥammad ibn 'Uthaymeen

It is not allowed for one who has intended to make up for a fast and has started it to break it

Q. Is it allowed for a person who has started his make-up fast (a fast being kept to make up for a missed fast) to break it? And likewise what is the ruling for a voluntary fast?

A. It is not allowed for a person to break his make-up fast after he has intended it and has started to fast the day. This is because if he has intended it and has started it, then it is obligatory to him to complete the fast. This is an obligatory act of the type *farḍ muwassa'ah*[12], which, once started, is obligatory to finish it and it is not allowed to stop it. The choice and freedom that one has in these types of obligatory acts is before starting them, for once they are started, it is not allowed to stop them.

[12] This is where the time allotted for an act is longer than it takes to perform it. An example of this is the prayer. The time allotted for it is a couple of hours whereas it takes only 10-15 minutes to perform it.

As for the voluntary fast, it is allowed for one to break it because it is not obligatory to complete them. It is better if he completes the voluntary fast, however it is allowed to break it and there is no problem in that. This is because once the Prophet (ﷺ) entered his house when he was fasting an optional fast and when he found some food in the house, which had been given as a gift to him, he ate from it and broke his fast. So this shows that it is not obligatory to complete the voluntary fasts.

Shaykh Ṣaaleḥ al-Fawzaan

The ruling of the one who fasted without intention

> Q. On the first night of Ramaḍaan, a person slept before he knew that the next day was the first fasting day. Then when he woke up for the *fajr* prayer, he asked another person in the mosque but he too did not know. The person continued not to eat and then when he went to work that day, he found the people fasting and so knew about the starting of the fasting. He continued to fast till the nighttime. So is his fast correct on that day or does he have to make up for it? Please guide us regarding this, may Allah reward you with good?

A. A person who does not know about the starting of the month of Ramaḍaan until during the day (i.e. the first day), then it is obligatory to him to fast the rest of that day and then to make up for the fast of that day later on. This is because he did not have the intention to fast from the night. It has been reported in a number of narrations that there is no fast for the one who does not make the intention during the night i.e. in the case of obligatory fasts. So this person has fasted a part of the day without any intention of fasting.

Shaykh Ṣaaleḥ al-Fawzaan

A person intended to fast on a day and then traveled during that day. So is it allowed for him to break that fast?

Q. If a resident intended to fast and traveled during that day, is it allowed for him to break that day's fast?

A. If a person intended to fast and then kept the fast, and then if he has to travel during that day, it is allowed (for such a person) to break his fast if he leaves his city as a traveler on a journey of at least a distance of 80km. If he completes the fast of the day he started, then it is better and safer since some scholars hold the opinion that it is obligatory to complete the day in which he started fasting and then traveled.

Shaykh Saaleḥ al-Fawzaan

Is it enough for a traveler who can't find food to break his fast just with the intention?

Q. The fasting person who likes to stick to the Sunnah, regardless of being a traveler or a resident at the time of sunset, wants to break his fast but cannot find anything to break his fast with. Is it enough for him (in such a case) to break his fast with mere intention?

A. Fasting while on a journey is allowed and it is better than not fasting if there is no hardship. However, if there is hardship in the journey that will prevent the fasting person from doing his duties, then it is better not to fast. This is the saying of the majority of the scholars. This is because the Prophet (ﷺ) fasted on the (day of the) battle of *Fatḥ* (conquering Makkah) until it was said to him that the people are finding the fast difficult. So the Prophet (ﷺ) broke his fast and ordered the people to also do the same to gain strength in order to meet the enemy (in battle).

It is allowed for a traveler to break his fast even without the presence of any hardship. It is enough for him to break his fast with intention only even if he does not eat anything that will break his fast. But this being his condition, there is no need for him to break his fast.

As for the one who wants to break his fast at sunset but does not find any food or drink, then it is enough for him to make the intention of breaking the fast and thus become amongst others who have broken their fasts. However, it is better to eat something as soon as the time comes to break the fast. This is because the most beloved slaves to Allah are the ones who hasten to break the fast (after the sun sets). It is reported in a narration:

> "The people will always be in good so long as they hasten to break their fast (upon its time)."

Tirmidhi reported this ḥadith.

Shaykh 'Abdullah ibn Jibreen

Fasting becoming obligatory to a young girl

Q. When does fasting become obligatory to a young girl?

A. Fasting becomes obligatory upon a young girl when she reaches the age when acts of worship become obligatory to her. As regards a girl, puberty is reached by either the completion of fifteen years of age, or the appearance of pubic hair, or by the discharge of sperm, or by the starting of menses or by pregnancy. So, whenever one of these things occur, fasting becomes obligatory to her even if she is just ten years old. Many young girls have their first menses when they are ten or eleven years old and then their parents are careless and think that they are still young and thus do not make them fast. This is wrong because with a young girl, whenever she has her first menses, she has reached puberty and has become a woman and she is accountable for all the obligatory duties.

Shaykh 'Abdullah ibn Jibreen

A twelve-year-old girl did not fast the previous year's Ramaḍaan

Q. A twelve or thirteen year old girl did not fast the month of Ramaḍaan last year. So, is there anything upon her or her family? Should she fast and if she did not fast, what is upon her?

A. A woman becomes charged with the acts of worship in Islam with the following conditions: Islam, sanity and puberty. As regards puberty, it is reached if the first menses starts or if she has a wet dream or pubic hair appears around the vagina or by reaching the age of fifteen years. So if this young girl about whom the questioner asked has satisfied the conditions by which she becomes charged with worship, then it is obligatory to her to fast. Furthermore, she has to make up for the fasts that she has missed, if any, after she fulfilled the conditions of being charged with the acts of worship. Even if one of the above conditions is not satisfied, then there is nothing upon her (i.e. no sin and no need to make up for anything).

The Permanent Committee for Research and Verdicts

A young girl who reached puberty at twelve did not fast till she was fourteen

Q. I reached puberty when I was twelve years old, just before Ramaḍaan by a month. However, I did not start fasting until I was fourteen years old. So do I have to fast, making up for the previous years or not?

A. It is obligatory to you to make up for the fasts of all the days wherein you did not fast in Ramaḍaan after you had reached puberty. You should seek forgiveness from Allah and repent to Him for the sin of not fasting in Ramaḍaan without a valid shari'ah reason. Maybe Allah will accept your repentance and forgive you for what you have neglected. Allah, the Exalted and Glorified, says:

﴿... وَتُوبُوٓا۟ إِلَى ٱللَّهِ جَمِيعًا أَيُّهَ ٱلْمُؤْمِنُونَ لَعَلَّكُمْ تُفْلِحُونَ ﴿٣١﴾﴾

(النور: ٣١)

"*...and turn to Allah in repentance, all of you, O believers, that you might succeed." (Qur'an 24: 31)*

Also, He says:

﴿وَإِنِّى لَغَفَّارٌ لِّمَن تَابَ وَءَامَنَ وَعَمِلَ صَـٰلِحًا ثُمَّ ٱهْتَدَىٰ ﴿٨٢﴾﴾ (طه: ٨٢)

"*And verily, I am indeed forgiving to him who repents, believes [in My Oneness] and does righteous good deeds, and then continues in guidance [till his death]." (Qur'an 20: 82)*

The Permanent Committee for Research and Verdicts

A fourteen-year-old girl did not fast Ramadaan even after her periods began

Q. When I was fourteen years old, my menses came for the first time. However I did not fast the month of Ramaḍaan of that year because I did not know that fasting was obligatory to me and neither did my family know. The reason for this was that we did not have any contact with the people of knowledge. I then fasted the following year when I was fifteen years old. Similarly, I have heard some people give a ruling that it is obligatory to a woman to fast when her menses begins even if she has not reached the age of puberty. I hope you can guide me.

A. This questioner who has mentioned about herself that her menses came for the first time when she was fourteen years old and she did not know that it is a sign of puberty, then there is no sin on her when she left the fasting of that year because she was ignorant and as such, there is no sin on an ignorant person.

However, since she came to know that it was obligatory to her, she must hasten to make up for the fasts that she has missed in that month of Ramaḍaan after her menses started. This is because if a woman reaches puberty, it becomes obligatory to her to fast. As regards a woman, puberty is reached by one of the following: either reaching the age of fifteen, or the appearance of pubic hair, or sexual discharge, or having menses.

So if a woman has any one of these four things, then she has reached puberty and hence, it becomes obligatory to her to perform the acts of worship just like it is obligatory to an older woman.

So I say to this questioner that it is now obligatory to her, if she has not already done so, to make up for the fast of the month of Ramaḍaan that she did not fast after her menses started for the first time. She should hasten so that the sin upon her is wiped out.

Shaykh Muḥammad ibn 'Uthaymeen

A woman becoming pure from menses after *Fajr*

Q. If a woman becomes pure straight after *Fajr*, should she refrain (from eating, drinking and other things that nullify the fast) that day, and keep a fast? Will that day be counted for her or will she have to make up for that day later by fasting on another day?

A. If a woman becomes pure after *Fajr*, the scholars have two opinions regarding whether she should refrain (from eating, drinking and other things that nullify the fast) that day. The first opinion is that she must refrain the rest of that day but it would not be counted for her as a day she has fasted. She would have to make up for that day by fasting on another day later. This is according to the opinion of Imam Aḥmad (may Allah have mercy upon him).

The second opinion is that it is not necessary for her to refrain the rest of that day because it is a day wherein her fasting is invalid since she had menses at the start of that day and thus was not among the people who fast. Furthermore, if her fast is invalid, then there is no point in her fasting (that day). She has been ordered not to fast the start of that day (since she was in menses when the day began), infact, it is *ḥaraam* upon her to fast the initial part of that day.

The definition of a shari'ah fast, as we all know, is: refraining from all things that nullify the fast and doing that as an act of worship for Allah, the Exalted, from dawn till sunset. So as we see, this second opinion of the scholars is more correct than the first opinion that necessitates refraining that day. However, according to both opinions, she has to make up for the fast of that day, later.

Shaykh Muḥammad ibn 'Uthaymeen

A woman's menses starting just before sunset

Q. A fasting woman's menses started just before the *adhaan* of *maghrib* prayer by a short time. So does this invalidate her fast of that day?

A. If her menses starts before sunset, the fast becomes invalid and she must make up for it by fasting another day. And if menses starts after sunset (even if by a short time), then her fast is valid and there is no need to make up for that day.

The Permanent Committee for Research and Verdicts

A woman feeling the beginning of menses just before sunset

Q. If a woman feels as if her menses has started but no blood came out before sunset or if she feels the pain of menses, is her fast of that day valid or is she required to make up for that day?

A. If a non-menstruating woman feels the pains of menses or feels the starting of menses while she is fasting but the blood does not come out till after sunset, then her fast of that day is valid. If that was an obligatory fast, there is no need to make up for it later and if it was a voluntary fast, her reward is not nullified.

Shaykh Muḥammad ibn 'Uthaymeen

Menstruating and post-natal bleeding women eating and drinking during Ramaḍaan

Q. Is it permissible for a menstruating and post-natal bleeding woman to eat and drink during the daytime of Ramaḍaan?

A. Yes, they are allowed to eat and drink during the daytime of Ramaḍaan. However, if there are small children in the house, then it is best that she eats and drinks secretly and not in front of them, since that may cause confusion for them (i.e. the confusion resulting from seeing the father and other people fasting, and the mother not fasting).

Shaykh Muḥammad ibn 'Uthaymeen

A small amount of blood coming out of a pregnant woman

Q. While my wife was in her second month of pregnancy, a drop of blood came out of her at the start of Ramadaan. This was after the *'Isha'* prayer time. After that by a few days, another drop came out just before sunset. This drop of blood was very light (in color). So what is upon her now knowing that she continued her fast (even after the drop came out just before sunset)?

A. If blood comes out of a pregnant woman in a pattern unlike what it used to be before pregnancy, then this blood is false blood (i.e. not to be considered menstrual blood). This is the case even if the blood that came out was a drop or two or a lot more. The blood that a pregnant woman sees is false blood unless the blood comes out with the same pattern that it used to before pregnancy, in which case it is menstrual blood. However, if the blood comes and goes, or similar to that, then the woman should pray and fast (if it is Ramadaan) and her fast would be valid and her prayers would be correct. There would be no sin or expiation upon her.

Shaykh Muḥammad ibn 'Uthaymeen

Menstruating and post-natal bleeding woman becoming pure before *fajr*

Q. If a menstruating or post-natal bleeding woman becomes pure before *fajr* but does not take a bath till after *fajr*, is the fast for that day valid?

A. Yes, the fast of a woman who becomes pure from menses before *fajr* but does not have a bath till after *fajr* is valid. Similarly, the fast of a post-natal bleeding woman whose blood stops before *fajr* is also valid. This is because as soon as the blood stops, she becomes among those people to whom fasting is obligatory. Her situation is similar to a person who is in a state of sexual defilement before *fajr*, his or her fast is also valid. The basis for this ruling is the saying of Allah, the Exalted:

﴿... فَٱلْـَٔـٰنَ بَـٰشِرُوهُنَّ وَٱبْتَغُوا۟ مَا كَتَبَ ٱللَّهُ لَكُمْ ۚ وَكُلُوا۟ وَٱشْرَبُوا۟ حَتَّىٰ يَتَبَيَّنَ لَكُمُ ٱلْخَيْطُ ٱلْأَبْيَضُ مِنَ ٱلْخَيْطِ ٱلْأَسْوَدِ مِنَ ٱلْفَجْرِ ... ﴿١٨٧﴾﴾

(البقرة: ١٨٧)

"So now have sexual relations with them (i.e. wives) and seek that which Allah has ordained for you, and eat and drink until the white thread of dawn appears to you distinct from the black thread." *(Qur'an 2: 187)*

So since Allah has made sexual intercourse permissible till *fajr*, it necessitates from that, that the bath will not be taken until after dawn (i.e. the start of *fajr*). Also, there is a ḥadith reported on the authority of 'Aa'ishah (رضي الله عنها) wherein she said that the Prophet (ﷺ) used to be in a state of major impurity resulting from sexual intercourse before *fajr*, and then fast that day.

Shaykh Muḥammad ibn 'Uthaymeen

Menstruating woman should not fast

Q. Is it permissible for a menstruating woman not to fast in Ramaḍaan and instead to fast for a number of other days equal to the number of days she missed due to menses in Ramaḍaan?

A. The fast kept by a menstruating woman are invalid, and in fact it is not permitted for her to fast. So if she has menses, she should not fast and then later on, after menses finishes, she should fast for a number of days equal to those days she missed.

The Permanent Committee for Research and Verdicts

A postnatal bleeding woman became pure within a week and then the blood flowed again before the ending of forty days

Q. If a woman with postnatal bleeding becomes pure after a week and then she fasts with the Muslims during Ramaḍaan, and then the blood returns (within the forty days), should she break her fast? And does she have to make up for the days she fasted or did not fast?

A. If a postnatal bleeding woman becomes pure before the completion of forty days and then she fasts, and then if blood starts to flow again within the forty days, then her fasts (that she kept during the days when the blood stopped) are valid. She should not pray and fast during the days when the blood returns. This is because it is postnatal blood until she becomes pure again or until the completion of forty days. Then when the forty days are finished, it becomes obligatory to her to take a bath even if the blood does not stop. This is because forty days are the limit of postnatal blood according to the more correct of the two opinions of the scholars. After that she should make a fresh *wuḍoo'* for each prayer until the blood flow stops. This ruling is based on the order of the Prophet (ﷺ) to a woman with *istiḥaaḍah* (menstrual blood).

It is permissible for the husband of a woman with such a condition to have sexual intercourse with her after the forty days finish even if the blood flow continues. This is because in such a situation, the blood that comes out is false blood and as such, does not prevent the woman from praying and fasting, and does not prevent the husband from having sexual intercourse with his wife.

However, if this blood after the forty days comes at a time when the usual menses is expected, then she should not pray or fast since she would be considered a menstruating woman (and it would not be permissible for the husband to have sexual intercourse with her in such a case).

Shaykh 'Abdul 'Aziz ibn Baaz

A woman gave birth in Ramaḍaan and did not make up for it for a year due to fear for her child

Q. A woman gave birth in Ramaḍaan but did not make up for the fasts after Ramaḍaan due to fear for her baby. She then became pregnant again and delivered in the next year's Ramaḍaan. Is it permissible for her to distribute money instead of making up for the fasts?

A. It is obligatory upon this woman to make up for the days that she did not fast even if it is after the second Ramaḍaan. This is because she has delayed the making up of the fasts till another Ramaḍaan due to a valid reason. I do not know whether it is difficult for her to make up for the fast in winter, every other day. If she is breast-feeding then Allah will give her strength and it will not have effect upon her nor upon her milk.

She should take care to try and make up for the fasts of the previous Ramaḍaan before another Ramaḍaan comes. But if she is unable to, then there is no problem in delaying it after the second Ramaḍaan (since she has a valid reason).

Shaykh Muḥammad ibn 'Uthaymeen

What is upon a breast-feeding woman who did not fast Ramaḍaan?

Q. My wife has to make up for three or four months of Ramaḍaan from previous years wherein she was unable to fast due to breast-feeding and pregnancy. She is currently breast-feeding also. She is asking you whether it is permissible for her to feed the poor (instead of making up for the fasts) since she finds making up for the fasts very difficult because they are three or four months of Ramaḍaan?

A. There is no blame on her if she delays the making up for missed fasts if her reason is due to difficulty since she is breast-feeding and pregnant. Whenever she is able to, she should hasten to make up for the missed fasts. She is now considered to be similar to an ill person and thus takes their rulings.

Allah, the Exalted and Glorified, says:

﴿...فَمَن كَانَ مِنكُم مَّرِيضًا أَوْ عَلَىٰ سَفَرٍ فَعِدَّةٌ مِّنْ أَيَّامٍ أُخَرَ...﴾ (١٨٤)
(البقرة: ١٨٤)

"*...But if any of you is ill or on a journey, [and then does not fast because of it], the same number [should be made up for] on other days...*" *(Qur'an 2: 184)*

She does not have to feed the poor.

The Permanent Committee for Research and Verdicts

What is upon a breast-feeding or pregnant woman who does not fast in Ramaḍaan

Q. If a breast-feeding or pregnant woman fears for herself or her child in Ramaḍaan and does not fast, what is upon her? Should she not fast then feed the poor and make up for it? Or should she not fast and make up for it but feed the poor? Or should she not fast and feed the poor but not make up for it? What is the correct ruling among these three?

A. If she fears that her fast will affect herself or her fetus, she should not fast. She then only has to make up for the fast later on. Her situation is similar to one who is unable to fast or fears that the fast will harm him. Allah, the Exalted, said:

﴿...فَمَن كَانَ مِنكُم مَّرِيضًا أَوْ عَلَىٰ سَفَرٍ فَعِدَّةٌ مِّنْ أَيَّامٍ أُخَرَ...﴾ (١٨٤)
(البقرة: ١٨٤)

> *"...But if any of you is ill or on a journey, [and then does not fast because of it], the same number [should be made up for] on other days..."* *(Qur'an 2: 184)*

Similarly, a breast-feeding woman who fears for herself if she feeds her baby in Ramaḍaan or fears for her child if she fasts; is permitted to miss the fast. She then has to make up for that missed fast later on (and there is nothing else upon her).

The Permanent Committee for Research and Verdicts

Forcing a wife to have sexual intercourse during the daytime in Ramaḍaan

Q. If a man forced his wife and had sexual intercourse with her during the daytime in Ramaḍaan, what is upon them? Will it suffice if they feed the poor since they are unable to free a slave and also unable to fast due to them trying to earn a living? How much and what type of food has to be fed?

A. If a man forces his wife to have sexual intercourse while both of them are fasting, then the fast of the woman is valid and correct, and there is no expiation upon her (since she was forced and did not have sexual intercourse willingly). As for the man, expiation is obligatory upon him due to the sexual intercourse that he committed if that was during the daytime in Ramaḍaan. The expiation is to free a slave. If he cannot find a slave, then he has to fast two months consecutively. If he cannot, then he has to feed sixty poor people. This is based on a ḥadith reported by Bukhari and Muslim on the authority of Abu Hurayrah (رضي الله عنه). He also has to make up for the fast of that day where he had sexual intercourse.

Shaykh Muḥammad ibn 'Uthaymeen

Leaving the fasts in Ramaḍaan due to exams

Q. I am a young girl. I was forced to leave six days of fasting in Ramaḍaan due to exams. These exams began in Ramaḍaan and the subjects were very difficult and thus if I fasted, I would not have been able to study for these subjects due to their difficult nature. So I hope you can guide me as to what I should do now so that Allah forgives me. May Allah reward you.

A. It is obligatory to you to repent of what you have done and you must make up for the missed fasts. Allah will accept the repentance from those who repent to Him. Real repentance by which Allah will wipe out sins requires you to leave the sin you are committing as a sign of glorification of Allah, the Exalted, and fearing His punishment. You should feel regret for what happened and make a firm and honeṣt resolution never to return to such a sin again. If a sin is related to a person and involves, say for example, oppressing him, then for the repentance to be complete, you must free yourself from their rights (i.e. if something was taken, it should be returned and if some harm was caused, forgiveness should be sought from the person etc).

Allah, the Exalted, says:

﴿...وَتُوبُوٓا۟ إِلَى ٱللَّهِ جَمِيعًا أَيُّهَ ٱلْمُؤْمِنُونَ لَعَلَّكُمْ تُفْلِحُونَ ﴿٣١﴾﴾

(النور : ٣١)

"*...and turn to Allah in repentance, all of you, O believers, that you might succeed.*" *(Qur'an 24: 31)*

He, the Exalted, also says:

﴿يَٰٓأَيُّهَا ٱلَّذِينَ ءَامَنُوا۟ تُوبُوٓا۟ إِلَى ٱللَّهِ تَوْبَةً نَّصُوحًا... ﴿٨﴾﴾ (التحريم : ٨)

"*O' you who believe, turn to Allah with sincere repentance...*" *(Qur'an 66: 8)*

The Prophet (ﷺ) said:

> "Repentance wipes out what was before it."

He (ﷺ) also said:

> "Whoever has oppressed another person concerning his reputation or anything else, he should beg him to forgive him, before the Day of Resurrection when there will be no money (to compensate for wrong deeds), but if he (i.e. the person who wronged another) has good deeds, those good deeds will be taken from him according to his oppression which he has done, and if he has no good deeds, the sins of the oppressed person will be loaded on him (i.e. he will have to bear the punishment for those sins)."

Imam Bukhari reported this ḥadith.

Shaykh 'Abdullah ibn Baaz

Bleeding and its effect on the fast

Q. In the noble month of Ramaḍaan, I was pregnant. While I was fasting, blood flowed from me on the twentieth day of the month. As a result of that, I did not fast for four days whilst I was in the hospital. After Ramaḍaan, I made up for the fasts of those four days. So now do I have to fast a second time? My baby is still in my stomach. Please guide me, may Allah guide you.

A. The bleeding you had while you were pregnant does not have any effect on your fast just like the extra blood flow does not affect a woman with *istaḥaaḍah*. Your fasts are valid and those four fasts that you missed whilst in the hospital and then you made up for them later will suffice you and you do not have to fast them a second time.

The Permanent Committee for Research and Verdicts

Kissing one's wife whilst fasting

Q. If a man kisses his wife in the daytime of Ramaḍaan or flirts with her, does that invalidate the fast or not? Please benefit me, may Allah guide you.

A. It is permissible for a man to kiss his wife or flirt with her or enjoy her without having sexual intercourse whilst he is fasting. There is no problem in that. The Prophet (ﷺ) used to kiss and enjoy his wives while he was fasting.

However, if there is fear that doing this will lead to what Allah has forbidden (i.e. sexual intercourse during the daytime of Ramaḍaan) because the man becomes aroused very quickly and easily, then kissing and enjoying the wife is disliked. If whilst doing that sperm comes out, he has to refrain the rest of that day (from things that nullify the fast) and make up for that day's fast. There is no expiation upon him according to the opinion of the majority of the scholars.

If, however, only the prosthetic fluid comes out (as a result of kissing or enjoying), then it does not invalidate the fast according to the most correct opinion of the scholars. This is because the basis for such things is that they do not break the fast (unless if some proof says otherwise) and that the fast is valid since it is very difficult to protect oneself from the discharge of the prosthetic fluid.

Shaykh 'Abdul 'Aziz ibn Baaz

A man had sexual intercourse with his wife during the daytime in Ramaḍaan

Q. A man had sexual intercourse with his wife three days consecutively during the daytime in Ramaḍaan. So what is obligatory upon him now?

A. If a fasting person has sexual intercourse during the daytime, then he has committed a great sin. He must now repent to Allah of that sin and must fast another day in place of the day he had sexual intercourse. As regards the expiation, he has to free a slave. If he cannot find a slave to free, then he must fast two consecutive months. If he cannot, he must feed sixty poor people with two handfuls of food each. He should make a separate expiation for each time he had committed sexual intercourse. And Allah knows best.

Shaykh Ṣaaleḥ al-Fawzaan

Applying henna while fasting

Q. Is it permissible to apply henna on the hair when fasting and praying? I have heard that applying henna nullifies the fast?

A. This saying has no basis because applying henna when fasting has no effect on the fast and does not nullify it. It is similar to applying *kohl* or a drop in the ear or drop in the eye. All of these actions do not nullify the fast.

As regards applying henna when praying, I do not know how this would be since when a woman is praying, it is not possible for her to apply henna. Maybe the questioner's intention is whether the henna is something that affects the correctness of the *wuḍoo'* if a woman has applied it?

The answer is that it does not affect the correctness of the *wuḍoo'*, since henna does have a solid status that prevents the water reaching (the skin). It is only a color. What does affect the *wuḍoo'* is anything that has a solid nature that prevents water from reaching the skin, in which case that thing must be removed so that the *wuḍoo'* be correct.

Shaykh Muḥammad ibn 'Uthaymeen

Does the discharge of the water before delivery invalidate the fast

Q. There is a woman who was pregnant in her ninth month when the month of Ramadaan came. At the start of the month, water started discharging from her but there was no blood flow with it. She kept on fasting even with the water flowing. This incident happened ten years ago. My question is whether there is any expiation upon this woman, knowing that she fasted those days when the water was still coming out of her?

A. If the situation is as described in the question, then her fasts are correct and valid, and there is no need for any expiation.

The Permanent Committee for Research and Verdicts

A woman did not fast in Ramaḍaan and was unable to make up for the missed fasts

Q. I am a woman with an illness. In the previous Ramaḍaan, I did not fast some days and was unable to make up for those fasts due to my continued illness. So what is the expiation upon me? Similarly, due to the illness, I will not be able to fast this coming Ramaḍaan either. So what is the expiation upon me? May Allah reward you.

A. It is permitted for a person not to fast if an illness will make the fast more difficult. Then whenever Allah cures the person, he must make up for the missed fasts. The basis for this ruling is the saying of Allah, the Exalted:

﴿...فَمَن كَانَ مِنكُم مَّرِيضًا أَوْ عَلَىٰ سَفَرٍ فَعِدَّةٌ مِّنْ أَيَّامٍ أُخَرَ...﴾ (١٨٤)

(البقـرة: ١٨٤)

> *"...So whoever among you is ill or on a journey [during them] - then an equal number of days [are to be made up]..."* *(Qur'an 2: 184)*

There is no blame upon you (i.e. the questioner) if you do not fast in this coming month of Ramaḍaan as long as the illness is present. This is because the permission for a sick person or a traveler not to fast is a concession from Allah and He likes to give concessions and does not like to be disobeyed. You have to make up for the missed fasts (whenever you recover from your illness). May Allah cure you from all the evil, and expiate for all of us our sins.

Shaykh 'Abdul 'Aziz ibn Baaz

A woman did not fast some days in Ramaḍaan and then passed away soon afterwards before making up the missed fasts

> Q. My wife became ill in the month of Ramaḍaan. She was able to fast twenty-two days, and when only eight days were remaining, her illness became more severe and she was unable to fast the rest of the month. She then passed away after the end of Ramadaan by a few days. So please advise us what we should do about the days she missed? I thank you very much.

A. This woman who was ill during the month of Ramaḍaan and could not fast because of her illness which continued with her till she passed away, there is nothing upon her for the days she did not fast. This is because she did not fast for a valid reason and was not negligent in making up for the missed fasts. Her illness prevented her from fasting and from making up for the missed fasts, and thus there is no need for any expiation. Allah, the Exalted, says:

﴿لَا يُكَلِّفُ ٱللَّهُ نَفْسًا إِلَّا وُسْعَهَا ... ﴿٢٨٦﴾﴾ (البقرة: ٢٨٦)

"Allah does not burden a soul more than it can bear..."
(Qur'an 2: 286)

The Permanent Committee for Research and Verdicts

One who died without making up for all the missed fasts

Q. If a man or a woman died and there are fasts that have not been made up for from Ramaḍaan, should these days be fasted on behalf of them, or is it required to feed the poor? And what is the ruling concerning a person who vowed to fast (i.e. not connected with Ramaḍaan) but did not fast?

A. As regards the fasts of Ramaḍaan, a person who died and there are days remaining to be made up for due to illness, then the answer is as follows:

Firstly, if the illness continued and the person was unable to make up for the days missed till he died, then there is no expiation upon him, and no need to fast on his behalf, and no need to feed the poor since such a person is excused (i.e. had a valid reason of illness for not fasting and not making up for those days).

Secondly, if the person became well after the illness that prevented the fasts, and then another Ramaḍaan came without the person making up for the fasts, then died; it is obligatory to feed one poor person for each day missed on behalf of this person. This is because such a person was negligent and delayed the making up for the fasts until another Ramaḍaan came when he or she passed away. There is however a difference of opinion between the scholars regarding whether this will suffice the fasts or not.

As regards the fasts that the person vowed to fast but did not before death, then these have to be fasted on behalf of the person. This is based on the saying of the Prophet (ﷺ):

"If anyone dies in a state that he had to complete some fasts, his heir must fast on his behalf."

In another narration, the wordings are:

"...had to complete some fasts that he vowed..."

The Permanent Committee for Research and Verdicts

A woman did not fast during her menses and did not make up for the fasts

Q. I did not fast during Ramaḍaan when my menses came. Till now, which is many years after the incident, I have not made up for those fasts. I would now like to make up for them, so what is upon me now? I do not know the exact number of days I missed, so what should I do?

A. There are three things upon you:

Firstly: You should repent to Allah for delaying the making up for the fasts. You should also regret your negligence and make a firm resolve never to commit such a thing again. This is because Allah, the Exalted, says:

﴿...وَتُوبُوٓاْ إِلَى ٱللَّهِ جَمِيعًا أَيُّهَ ٱلْمُؤْمِنُونَ لَعَلَّكُمْ تُفْلِحُونَ ﴿٣١﴾﴾

(النور: ٣١)

"*...and turn to Allah in repentance, all of you, O believers, that you might succeed.*" *(Qur'an 24: 31)*

Your delay in making up for the fasts is a sin and thus repenting of it is obligatory.

Secondly: You should now hasten to make up for the fasts based upon what you think is the most likely number of days missed. Allah does not burden a soul more than it can bear. So whatever you think you have missed, you should now make up for. So, for example, if you think it is ten days, then fast ten days. Or if you think it is more or less then make up for them according to what you think it most likely is. Allah, the Exalted, says:

﴿لَا يُكَلِّفُ ٱللَّهُ نَفْسًا إِلَّا وُسْعَهَا ... ﴿٢٨٦﴾﴾ (البقرة : ٢٨٦)

"*Allah does not burden a soul more than it can bear.*"

(Qur'an 2: 286)

Also, Allah, the Glorified, says:

﴿فَٱتَّقُوا۟ ٱللَّهَ مَا ٱسْتَطَعْتُمْ ... ﴿١٦﴾﴾ (التغابن : ١٦)

"*...And fear Allah as much as you can...*"

(Qur'an 64: 16)

Thirdly: If you are able to, you should feed a poor person for each day missed. It is permissible for you to feed all this to one person. If however you are yourself poor and unable to feed others, then there is nothing upon you except to make up for the fasts and to repent of the sin. The amount that is obligatory to feed (if you are able to) is two handfuls from the normal food of the country. In terms of weight, it is one and a half kilograms (for each day you missed to a poor person).

Shaykh 'Abdul 'Aziz ibn Baaz

A woman has two hundred days to make up for

Q. A woman who is in her fifties is ill with diabetics. She finds it very difficult to fast but still she fasts the month of Ramaḍaan. She did not know until recently that the fasts missed due to menses have to be made up for. Now she has a total of about two hundred days wherein she did not fast. So what is the ruling concerning these days especially in view of her present status where she is ill? Will Allah forgive what passed or does she have to fast them or can she feed a fasting person? And is it obligatory to feed a fasting person or can it be any poor person?

A. If this woman is as described, wherein fasting will harm her due to old age and illness, then a poor person should be fed on behalf of her for each day she missed. An estimate should be made of how many days have been missed and for each day, a poor person should be fed on behalf of her. Similarly, if it is difficult for her to fast the present Ramaḍaan[13], and her illness is not expected to finish, then she should feed a poor person for each day she will miss as we have just mentioned.

Shaykh Muḥammad ibn 'Uthaymeen

A woman ate medicine just after *fajr* started

> Q. My mother took her medicine after the *adhaan* of *fajr* by a short time during Ramaḍaan. I told her that if she takes her medicine at that time, she will have to make up for the fast of that day. So what is upon her now?

A. If an ill person takes medicine during Ramaḍaan after *fajr* starts, then his fast is invalid because he has intentionally eaten something. It then becomes obligatory upon him to refrain from what nullifies the fast for the rest of that day except if the fast will be difficult upon him due to the illness, in which case it is permissible to eat and drink. However, the person has to make up for that day since he ate something intentionally. It is not permissible for an ill person to take medicine while he is fasting during Ramaḍaan, except if there is a real necessity such as if we fear death (or something like that), in which case it is permissible to take medicine to reduce the illness. In such a case, the person would not be fasting (since he has taken the medicine) and there is no blame upon him for breaking the fast due to illness.

Shaykh Muḥammad ibn 'Uthaymeen

---

[13] It seems that this question was answered by the shaykh during the month of Ramaḍaan.

Fasting in front of people but eating in seclusion

Q. When I first reached puberty, I used to fast in front of my family but when I was by myself, I used to eat and drink. I did this for three months of Ramaḍaan. However, after I got married, I repented to Allah of that and when I want to make up for those months, my husband says that repentance wipes out what was before it. He also says that by me fasting, I am neglecting him and our children. So is it obligatory upon me to fast or to feed one hundred and eighty poor people?

A. If you were such that you did not actually start to fast in all those days, then making for them up will not benefit because there is a principle that says: if a person delays the acts of worship that have a specific time to perform them until after the end of that time without a valid reason, then that act will not be accepted from him (even if performed later on). So based on this, if this woman did not actually fast on those days, then she does not have to make up for them, and repentance will wipe out what was before it.

However, if she was fasting but then she broke the fast during the daytime, she has to make up for the fasts. It is not permitted for her husband to prevent her from this because it is obligatory upon her to make up for the fasts. It is not permissible for a husband to prevent his wife from making up for a missed obligatory fast (such as Ramaḍaan).

Shaykh Muḥammad ibn 'Uthaymeen

Not making up for fasts of Ramaḍaan till after the next Ramaḍaan

Q. Some women do not make up their fasts missed from one Ramaḍaan till after the second Ramaḍaan passes. So what is obligatory upon them?

A. It is obligatory upon them to repent to Allah of this sin because it is not permissible for someone who has to make up for missed fasts to delay them past the next Ramaḍaan without a valid reason. This is based on the saying of 'Aa'ishah (رضي الله عنها) wherein she said: "I had to make up for some of the fasts of Ramaḍaan that I missed, but I could not do it except during the month of Sha'baan."

So this shows that it is not permissible to delay it past the next Ramaḍaan. These women should repent to Allah, the Exalted and Glorified, for what they have done, and make up for the fasts that have been missed after the second Ramaḍaan.

Shaykh Muḥammad ibn 'Uthaymeen

A woman did not make up for fasts she missed due to menses from the time fasting became obligatory upon her

Q. Ever since fasting became obligatory upon me, I have been fasting the month of Ramaḍaan. However, I have never made up for the days I missed due to menses. I do not know how many days I have missed. I would like to know what is obligatory upon me now?

A. It saddens me that such a thing should occur among the believing women. Not making up for the missed fasts during Ramaḍaan is either due to ignorance or due to laziness, both of which are a problem. As regards ignorance, its cure is to gain knowledge and ask those who know. And as regards laziness, its cure is to have *taqwa* (fear) of Allah, the Exalted and Glorified, to fear his punishment and to hasten to perform whatever makes Him happy.

This woman should repent to Allah of what she had committed and seek His forgiveness. She should estimate, as best as possible, the number of days she missed and make up for them. If she does these things, she would have fulfilled her obligation and I hope that Allah will accept her repentance.

Shaykh Muḥammad ibn 'Uthaymeen

Wisdom behind a menstruating woman making up for fasts but not for prayers

Q. What is the wisdom behind a menstruating woman making up for the fasts she misses but not the prayers?

A. Firstly, there is no doubt that what is obligatory upon a Muslim is to perform whatever Allah has made obligatory. This includes both what He has ordered to perform and what He has ordered to refrain from. A Muslim is required to do this whether he understands and knows the wisdom behind these orders and prohibitions or not. It is also obligatory upon a Muslim to believe that Allah does not order the servants to perform something except that there is a benefit for them in performing it, and does not forbid them from something except that it contains harm for them. Similarly, all of Allah's shari'ah is based on the wisdom that He knows. Some of it He makes known to His servants in order that a believer increases in his belief, while with other things, He does not reveal the wisdom behind them such that a believer increases in his belief by submitting to the orders of Allah.

Secondly: It is known that the prayers are performed five times everyday during the daytime and nighttime. So making up for these for only one day or two would be difficult for a menstruating woman. Allah, the Great, said the truth wherein He said:

﴿يُرِيدُ ٱللَّهُ أَن يُخَفِّفَ عَنكُمْ ۚ وَخُلِقَ ٱلْإِنسَٰنُ ضَعِيفًا ﴿٢٨﴾﴾

(النساء : ٢٨)

"Allah wishes to lighten [the burden] for you, and man was created weak." *(Qur'an 4: 28)*

The Permanent Committee for Research and Verdicts

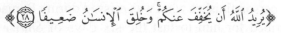

Making up for six days of Ramaḍaan in *Shawwal*, will that suffice for *Shawwal* also?

Q. If a woman fasts six days that she missed from Ramaḍaan in the month of *Shawwal*, will that suffice her the six-day-fast of *Shawwal*, and will she have the reward written for her?

A. It is reported from the Prophet (ﷺ) that he said:

> "Whosoever fasts the month of Ramaḍaan, then follows it up with six days of *Shawwal*, it will be as if he has fasted the whole year."

In this ḥadith there is a proof that a person must complete the fasts of Ramaḍaan, which are obligatory, and then add to them six days of *Shawwal*, which are voluntary, so that it be like fasting the whole year.

In another ḥadith, the words are:

> "The fast of Ramaḍaan is equal to ten months and the six days of *Shawwal* are equal to two months."

This means that the reward of these deeds is ten fold.

So based on this, whoever fasted some days from the month of Ramaḍaan and missed some days, either due to illness or traveling or menses or post-natal bleeding, then that person should first complete what has been missed in *Shawwal* or at any other time, before fasting the six days of *Shawwal* or other voluntary fasts. So if the person finishes what was missed during Ramaḍaan, it is then prescribed for him to fast the six days of *Shawwal* in order to obtain the reward mentioned in the ḥadith. Thus, this woman's making up for the missed fasts will not suffice her the voluntary fasts of *Shawwal* as is evident.

Shaykh 'Abdullah ibn Jibreen

Is it permissible for a husband to prevent his wife from voluntary fasts

Q. Do I have the right to prevent my wife from keeping voluntary fasts such as the six days of *Shawwal*? Will there be any sin upon me for that?

A. It has been reported that it is not permissible for a woman to keep a voluntary fast while her husband is present and wants to enjoy her, except after gaining his permission. So if a woman kept her voluntary fast, it is permissible for the husband to make her break it if he is in need of sexual intercourse. If however he does not have the need, it is disliked for him to prevent her from fasting as long as the voluntary fast does not harm her or does not interfere with her duties towards her kids or breast-feeding. This ruling is the same for the six days of *Shawwal* and any other voluntary fasts.

Shaykh 'Abdullah ibn Jibreen

Ruling concerning tasting food by a woman who is fasting

Q. What is the ruling concerning tasting the food during the daytime in Ramaḍaan by a woman who is fasting?

A. The ruling of such a thing is that there is no problem in doing it since there is a need for it. However, she should not swallow what she tastes (but should spit it out).

Shaykh Muḥammad ibn 'Uthaymeen

Women spending time during Ramaḍaan shopping, sleeping and watching television

Q. There are women who spend Ramaḍaan by staying up at night watching television or serials or films via satellite dish, or by going to shopping centers and by sleeping. So what do you advise these women?

A. It is obligatory upon a Muslim, whether male or female, to respect the month of Ramaḍaan and to spend it in acts of worship and avoid sins and evil deeds. This should be done at all time and it is even more emphasized in Ramaḍaan due to its sacredness. Staying up late at night to watch films or serials on television or satellite dish or to listen to music, all of these actions are *ḥaraam* (forbidden) and are sins both in Ramaḍaan and at other times. However, they are much more severe during the month of Ramaḍaan.

And if all these forbidden things are accompanied with neglecting obligatory acts of worship or sleeping during the times of prayer, then these are more sins upon sins. It should be known that sins attract a person and lead him to other sins. We ask Allah for safety.

It is *ḥaraam* for the women to go out to shopping centers except if there is a necessity. In such a case, she should only go out as much as needed, and upon condition that she is covered properly and decently, and avoiding mixing with men or talking to them, except as much as is necessary, without causing *fitnah* (temptation). Also women should not go out for too long during the night which will lead her to sleep during the times of prayer and to neglect the rights of her children and husband.

Shaykh 'Abdul 'Aziz ibn Baaz

Means that will help a woman to perform good acts during Ramaḍaan

Q. What are the means that will help a woman to perform good acts during the month of Ramaḍaan?

A. The means that will help a man and woman to perform good acts during Ramaḍaan are:

Firstly: Fearing Allah, the Exalted and Glorified, and having a firm belief that He is watching and aware of all actions, sayings and intentions, and that He will take a person to account for these. If a Muslim realizes this, he will spend the time performing good deeds, will leave sins and hasten to repent of them.

Secondly: Increasing the remembrance of Allah and the recitation of the Qur'an. This is because such deeds soften the heart. Allah, the Exalted, says:

﴿ٱلَّذِينَ ءَامَنُوا۟ وَتَطۡمَئِنُّ قُلُوبُهُم بِذِكۡرِ ٱللَّهِۗ أَلَا بِذِكۡرِ ٱللَّهِ تَطۡمَئِنُّ ٱلۡقُلُوبُ ﴿٢٨﴾﴾

(الرّعد : ٢٨)

"*Those who believed [in the Oneness of Allah] and whose hearts find rest in the remembrance of Allah. Verily, in the remembrance of Allah do hearts find rest.*"

(Qur'an 13: 28)

He, the Exalted, also says:

﴿إِنَّمَا ٱلۡمُؤۡمِنُونَ ٱلَّذِينَ إِذَا ذُكِرَ ٱللَّهُ وَجِلَتۡ قُلُوبُهُمۡ... ﴿٢﴾﴾

(الأنفال : ٢)

"*The believers are only those who, when Allah is mentioned, feel fear in their hearts...*"

(Qur'an 8: 2)

Thirdly: Avoiding actions that harden the heart and distance it from Allah. These actions are sins, spending time with evil-doers, eating from *ḥaraam* sources, being neglectful of the remembrance of Allah, the Exalted and Glorified, watching evil films and so on.

Fourthly: A woman should stay in her house and not go out except for necessity; and when she goes out, she should hasten to return quickly to the house when the necessity is fulfilled.

Fifthly: Sleeping early at night because it helps a person to wake up early at the end of the night (for *tahajjud*). It will also reduce the need for sleep during the day, thus helping a person to perform all the prayers at their proper times and allowing him to make use of his time in performing good deeds.

Sixthly: Controlling the tongue from engaging in backbiting, slandering, lying and other prohibited speech, and, instead, using the tongue for Allah's remembrances.

Shaykh Ṣaaleḥ al-Fawzaan

CHAPTER: ḤAJJ AND 'UMRAH

Ruling concerning a woman who wears her *iḥraam* (Islamic dress during 'Umrah or Hajj), then before performing 'umrah, her menses starts

Q. This is a question regarding a woman who wore her *iḥraam* and made the intention for 'Umrah. But before she reached the Ka'bah, her menses started. So what should she do? Should she do the Ḥajj before 'Umrah (i.e. in the situation where she came to do the 'Umrah and follow that with Ḥajj)?

A. She should remain in her *iḥraam* of 'umrah, and if she becomes pure before the ninth of *dhul-hijjah*, and she is able to complete her 'umrah at that time, she should complete it. She should then put the *iḥraam* on for Ḥajj and go to *'Arafah* to complete the rest of the rites of Ḥajj. However, if she does not become pure before the day of *'Arafah*, she should then include the Ḥajj in her 'Umrah with her saying "*Allahumma inni ahramtu bi Ḥajj ma' 'umrati*" (which means "O' Allah, I am making *iḥraam* for Ḥajj with my 'Umrah"). She would then be performing the *Qiraan Ḥajj*. She should stay with the people and complete her rites of Ḥajj. Her *iḥraam* and *ṭawaaf* on the day of *'eid* or after it will suffice her the *ṭawaaf* of *ziyaarah*, and her *sa'ee* will suffice for the *sa'ee* of Ḥajj and 'Umrah. She has to make a sacrifice of *Qiraan Ḥajj* just like a person making the *Mutamatti'* type of Ḥajj does.

Shaykh 'Abdullah ibn Jibreen

There is nothing upon a woman who happens to trim her hair before making the intention of *iḥraam*

Q. My wife made her *iḥraam* and before she came out of the bathroom and put on her clothes, she cut a bit of her hair. What is obligatory upon her to do now?

A. There is no problem in this for her and no sacrifice necessary since the prohibition is in cutting hair after the intention of *iḥraam* is made. This woman did not make her intention before cutting her hair nor did she wear her clothes, so there is no problem in that for her. Even if she had done that after entering in *iḥraam* due to ignorance or forgetfulness, she would not have to sacrifice due to the reason of ignorance.

Shaykh ‘Abdullah ibn Jibreen

I want to perform Ḥajj but my husband is preventing me from doing so

Q. I am an old and rich woman. I said to my husband more than once that I would like to perform Ḥajj, but he refuses to give me permission without any reason. I have an elder brother who also wants to perform Ḥajj, so can I perform it with him even if my husband does not allow me? or should I leave the Ḥajj and stay in my country in obedience to my husband? Please provide me with a ruling, may Allah reward you with good.

A. In view of the fact that it is obligatory to perform the Ḥajj as quickly as possible, once its conditions are fulfilled, and as the woman asking the question has fulfilled these conditions of maturity, ability and *maḥram* (unmarriageable) to accompany her, it is obligatory to her to hasten to perform Ḥajj and it is *ḥaraam* for her husband to prevent her from doing so.

In the situation mentioned in the question, it is allowed for the woman to perform the Ḥajj with her brother, even if her husband does not give her permission, since the obligation is upon her. This is similar to when the prayer or the fast becomes obligatory. So the right of Allah is more deserving of being put forward, and this husband who is preventing her without any reason does not have the right to stop his wife from fulfilling the obligation of Ḥajj. However, Allah is the One Who gives success and guides to the right path.

Shaykh 'Abdullah ibn Jibreen

Face-cover is among the things that are disallowed in the state of *iḥraam* (ritual consecration) as long as no non-*maḥram* men are around

Q. I wore a face-cover when performing 'Umrah since I did not know that it was disallowed. So what is the atonement for this?

A. Since the face-cover is among the disallowed things during *iḥraam* (when there are no non-*maḥram* men around), the obligation upon a woman who wears it is to either sacrifice or feed six needy people or to fast three days. However, this is on the condition that she knew the rule and she remembered it. So whoever wears it out of ignorance regarding its ruling, or out of forgetfulness that she is in *iḥraam*, or that it is disallowed, then in such cases there is no sacrifice to be given. The sacrifice is to be given only by the one who wears it intentionally (even after knowing the ruling).

Shaykh 'Abdullah ibn Jibreen

Ruling concerning using menses-preventing pills to perform Ḥajj

Q. Is it allowed for a woman to use pills that will prevent the menses or delay it at the time of Ḥajj?

A. It is allowed for a woman to use these pills to prevent the menses from coming at the time of Ḥajj. However, a specialist doctor should be consulted before taking these pills in order to protect her health. Similarly, she can do this during the month of Ramaḍaan if she would like to fast with the rest of the people.

The Permanent Committee for Research and Verdicts

Ruling concerning a woman performing Ḥajj without a *maḥram*

Q. A woman performed Ḥajj with other people strange to her (i.e. not related to her and not her *maḥrams*). She first asked her close relatives to accompany her but they refused. So she then went with a man who had two women with him. So is her Ḥajj correct or not?

A. Her Ḥajj is correct but she committed a sin since she traveled without a *maḥram*. This is because of evidences that show that it is prohibited for a woman to travel by herself. She should repent to Allah, the Glorified, of this sin.

Shaykh 'Abdul 'Aziz ibn Baaz

A woman can wear any clothes in her *iḥraam*

Q. Is it allowed for a woman to wear any clothes she desires in her *iḥraam?*

A. Yes, she can wear whatever she likes for her *iḥraam* since it is not required for a woman to wear any special clothes as some people think. But her clothes should not be beautiful or eye-catching since she will be with other people in Ḥajj. So her clothes should be normal, without any possibility of causing *fitnah*, and not attractive or eye-catching.

Shaykh 'Abdul 'Aziz ibn Baaz

Ruling concerning changing the clothes while in *iḥraam*

Q. Is it allowed for a person to change the clothes while in *iḥraam* in order to wash them?

A. There is no problem in washing the clothes while in *iḥraam*, or changing them and wearing other clean or new clothes.

Shaykh 'Abdul 'Aziz ibn Baaz

Performing Ḥajj for one's father

Q. My father, may Allah have mercy upon him, passed away ten years ago. He used to perform all his obligatory duties but he was unable to perform Ḥajj due to lack of money. Then, due to the Will of Allah, I came to Saudi Arabia for a teaching position and performed my Ḥajj. I would like to perform Ḥajj on behalf of my father. Is this allowed and will there be a reward for me?

A. It is prescribed for you to perform Ḥajj for your father, and you will have a great reward for this. May Allah accept from you and make it easy for you. And Allah is the source of success.

Shaykh 'Abdul 'Aziz ibn Baaz

Ḥajj is not obligatory to a woman who does not have a *maḥram*

Q. A righteous woman, who is between middle and old age, would like to perform Ḥajj but she does not have a *maḥram*. There is a man in the same city who is well known for his righteousness and who also wants to perform Ḥajj with a group of women who will accompany him to Ḥajj. So is it correct for this woman to travel to Ḥajj with this man and his group of women, the man being an observer? Or is Ḥajj not obligatory to her anymore due to her not having a *maḥram*? She has enough money to go for Ḥajj. Please give us a ruling, may Allah bless you.

A. Ḥajj is not obligatory upon a woman who does not have a *maḥram*, because having a *maḥram* for her is among the conditions that need to be fulfilled for Ḥajj to be obligatory. Allah, the Exalted, said:

﴿...وَلِلَّهِ عَلَى ٱلنَّاسِ حِجُّ ٱلْبَيْتِ مَنِ ٱسْتَطَاعَ إِلَيْهِ سَبِيلًا...﴾ (٩٧)

(آل عمران: ٩٧)

"*...And Ḥajj to the House [i.e. Ka'bah] is a duty that mankind owes to Allah, for those who have the ability...*"

(Qur'an 3: 97)

And it is not allowed for a woman to travel to perform Ḥajj or (to travel) anywhere except with her husband or a *maḥram* because of a ḥadith recorded by Bukhari in which the Prophet (ﷺ) is reported to have said:

> "It is not allowed for a woman to travel the distance of one day and night except with a *maḥram*."

In another ḥadith recorded by Bukhari and Muslim on the authority of Ibn 'Abbaas (رضي الله عنه) who said he heard the Prophet (ﷺ) say:

> "No person should be alone with a woman except when there is a *maḥram* with her, and the woman should not undertake journey except with a *maḥram*." A person stood up and said: "O' Allah's Messenger, my wife has set out for pilgrimage, whereas I am enlisted to fight in

such and such battle." So the Prophet said: "You go and perform Ḥajj with your wife."

Among the scholars who hold this opinion are Al-Ḥasan, An-Nakh'ee, Aḥmed, Isḥaaq, Ibn al-Mundhir and others. It is a correct opinion because of its conformity with the ḥadiths stating the prohibition for a woman traveling without her husband or *maḥram*. Among the scholars who hold a different opinion on this issue are Maalik, Shafi'ee and Al-Aouzaa'ee. Each of them has stated a condition for which there is no proof (from the Qur'an or ḥadith). Ibn al-Mundhir said about the conditions laid down by this second group of scholars: "They left what is apparent from the ḥadith and each of them has put forward a condition for which there is no proof." And with Allah is success.

The Permanent Committee for Research and Verdicts

Ruling on a woman wearing socks and gloves when in *iḥraam*

Q. What is the ruling concerning a woman wearing socks and gloves while she is in her *iḥraam*? And is it allowed for her to remove what she has initially made *iḥraam* with?

A. The best for her is to wear *iḥraam* with socks or shoes and sandals on. This is better because it covers her more than anything else. However, if her clothes are long (such that they pass the feet and touch the ground), then it will suffice. If she makes her *iḥraam* in socks and then removes them later on (making sure that her feet are still covered), there is no problem in that, because it would be just like a man who made his *iḥraam* with sandals and then removed them, it would not affect his *iḥraam*.

But it is not allowed for a woman to wear gloves during *iḥraam*, because a woman in the state of *iḥraam* is prohibited from that. Similarly, she should not wear something that covers the face, because the Messenger (ﷺ) forbade that. But if non-*maḥram* men came close to her such that they can see her, she should drop her *khimaar* or *jilbaab* (Islamic dress) or anything else like that, over her head and cover the face. This is to be done during *ṭawaaf* (circumambulation) or *sa'ee* or anywhere else when non-*mahram* men come close to her. This is based on a hadith reported by Abu Dawood and Ibn Maajah on the authority of 'Aa'ishah (رضي الله عنها) who said: "The riders used to pass by us when we were in a state of *iḥraam* with the Messenger of Allah (ﷺ). So when they came close to us, we would drop our *jilbaab* over the head and on the face. Then when they passed by, we would uncover the face."

It is allowed for a man to wear socks even if they are not cut. This is according to the correct opinion of the scholars. Most of the them have said that they should be cut, but the correct opinion is that cutting them is not necessary when one has lost the sandals or shoes and is replacing them with socks. This is the case because on the day of *'Arafah* (a Mountain in Makkah), the Prophet (ﷺ) delivered an address and said:

> "So far, as the trousers are concerned, one who does not find lower garment, he may wear them; as regards socks, one may wear them when he does not find shoes."

Bukhari and Muslim reported this ḥadith. So we see in this ḥadith that the Prophet (ﷺ) did not order to cut the socks. This shows abrogation of the (previous) ruling to cut them. And Allah is the source of success.

Shaykh 'Abdul 'Aziz ibn Baaz

A woman should wait till she becomes pure after menses and then performs *ṭawaaf al-ifaaḍah* (circumbulation of Ka'bah immediately after 'Arafah)

> Q. There is no doubt that *ṭawaaf al-ifaaḍah* is a basic element of the Ḥajj that must be done. But how about if a menstruating woman leaves it due to insufficient time wherein there was no time to wait for her to become pure again. So what is the ruling?

A. It is obligatory to her and her guardian to wait for her to become pure and then to perform *ṭawaaf al-ifaaḍah*. This is based on the saying of the Prophet (ﷺ) when he was informed that Safiyyah bint Huyay cntered her menses after performing *Ṭawaf al-Ifaaḍah*, he said:

> "Well, then she will detain us." Then he was informed she has already performed *ṭawaaf al-ifaaḍah*, and it was after this that she entered the menses. Thereupon Allah's Messenger said: "(If it is so), then proceed forth."

However, if she is unable to wait but can come back to perform the *ṭawaaf* after becoming pure, it is then allowed for her to travel and then come back for the *ṭawaaf al-ifaaḍah*. But if she is unable to come back or fears that she may not be able to return, such as for people who live in countries far away from Makkah, such as Indonesia or Morocco or like that, then according to the correct opinion of the scholars, she can put something on the spot to reduce or stop the blood and then perform the *ṭawaaf* with the intention of Ḥajj. Some of the scholars have said that this will be sufficient for her. Among these scholars are Shaykh ul-Islam Ibn Taymiyah, his student Ibn al-Qayyim (may Allah have mercy upon them) and others.

Allah is the source of success, may peace be upon our Prophet Muhammad, his family and Companions.

Shaykh 'Abdul 'Aziz ibn Baaz

Ruling concerning a woman who did not trim her hair out of ignorance

Q. A woman completed all the rites when she performed Ḥajj except she did not cut her hair out of ignorance or forgetfulness. After she reached her country, she did everything that should not be done in the state of *iḥraam* (thinking she was out of *iḥraam*). So what is obligatory upon her now?

A. If the situation is as mentioned in the question, wherein she did all the rites except the cutting of the hair and that it was out of forgetfulness or ignorance, then she should now cut her hair in her country whenever she remembers. She does not have to do anything else in view of the fact that she delayed the hair cut due to forgetfulness or ignorance, that she has not actually finished the Ḥajj. We ask Allah success and acceptance for all.

However, if her husband had sexual intercourse with her before she cut her hair (but whilst still in Makkah), she then has to offer a sacrifice. This can be either a sheep or one seventh of a camel or one seventh of a cow (of the animals that are suitable for sacrifice), and should be sacrificed in Makkah and the meat distributed to the poor people of the *ḥaram* (holy place). If, however, her husband had sexual intercourse with her after she left the *ḥaram* and went to her country or wherever, she can then offer the sacrifice anywhere she wishes and distribute the meat to the poor. May the peace and blessings of Allah be upon our Prophet Muhammad, his family and his Companions.

The Permanent Committee for Research and Verdicts

Does a woman have to uncover her face and hands during Ḥajj

Q. It is known that all of a woman is considered *'awrah* during the prayer except the face and hands. But what if she is on Ḥajj or a trip with strange non-*maḥram* men and she is praying in a group, is she allowed to uncover her face and hands during the prayer or should she cover them fearing that the non-*maḥram* might see her? Similarly, in the *ḥaram*, should she drop her *jilbaab* over her head on the face and cover her hands or is it allowed for her to uncover them? Please give us a ruling.

A. A free woman is *'awrah* and thus it is *ḥaram* for her to uncover her face and hands when non-*maḥram* men are around her, whether that is in prayer or during the state of *iḥraam* or other normal situations according to the more correct of the two opinions of the scholars. This is based on a ḥadith on the authority of 'Aa'ishah (رضي الله عنها) who said:

> "The riders used to pass by us when we were in a state of *iḥraam* with the Messenger of Allah (ﷺ). So when they came close to us, we would drop our *jilbaab* over the head and on the face. Then when they passed by, we would uncover the face."

Aḥmed, Abu Dawood and Ibn Maajah reported this ḥadith.

So if this is the situation in the state of *iḥraam* wherein she is required to uncover the face but if non-*maḥram* men are around she is required to cover it, then in other situations it is more so that she should cover the face. This is based on (a number of evidences including) the general saying of Allah, the Glorified and Exalted:

﴿...وَإِذَا سَأَلْتُمُوهُنَّ مَتَاعًا فَسْئَلُوهُنَّ مِن وَرَآءِ حِجَابٍ ذَٰلِكُمْ أَطْهَرُ لِقُلُوبِكُمْ وَقُلُوبِهِنَّ... ﴿٥٣﴾﴾

(الأحزاب: ٥٣)

> *"...And when you ask [women] for anything you want, ask them from behind a screen. That is purer for your hearts and for their hearts..."* *(Qur'an 33: 53)*

The Permanent Committee for Research and Verdicts

Ruling concerning *ṭawaaf al-wadaa'* (farewell circumambulation) for a person performing 'umrah and buying something after the *ṭawaaf*

Q. Is *ṭawaaf al-wadaa'* obligatory in 'Umrah? And is it allowed to purchase anything from Makkah after performing it, whether that is in Ḥajj or 'Umrah?

A. *Ṭawaaf al-wadaa'* is not obligatory in 'Umrah but performing it is better. Thus if a person leaves Makkah and does not perform it after 'Umrah, there is no problem. However, it is obligatory in Ḥajj because of the saying of the Prophet (ﷺ):

> "None of you should leave until you make the *ṭawaaf* as the last action of the Ka'bah." He said this to the people doing Ḥajj.

It is allowed for a person to purchase whatever he needs, even for business, after *ṭawaaf al-wadaa'* as long as the duration is not long according to what is seen as long in society. If the duration is long, *ṭawaaf al-wadaa'* should be performed again. However, if it is not long, according to the customs and traditions of the people, there is no need to re-perform the *ṭawaaf*.

Shaykh 'Abdul 'Aziz ibn Baaz

Ruling concerning a menstruating woman's Ḥajj

Q. What is the ruling concerning a woman who menstruated during the days of Ḥajj? Will that Ḥajj suffice her?

A. If a woman has her menses during the days of Ḥajj, she should do all the rites of Ḥajj except that she should not do the *ṭawaaf* nor do the *sa'ee* between *safa* and *marwa* until she becomes pure again. Then when she becomes pure, she should have a bath and then do *ṭawaaf* and *sa'ee*.

However, if her menses came at a time when she only had *ṭawaaf al-wadaa'* left, she can then travel and there will not be anything upon her since she does not have to do it in such a situation. Her Ḥajj would be correct. The basis for this is a hadith reported by Tirmidhi and Abu Dawood on the authority of 'Abdullah ibn 'Abbaas (رضي الله عنه) that the Prophet (ﷺ) said:

> "If the post-natal bleeding and menstruating women come to the *meeqaat* (the starting place of iḥraam), they should take a shower, wear the *iḥraam* and do all the rites of Ḥajj except the *ṭawaaf*."

Another hadith reported in *Ṣaḥeeḥ* on the authority of 'Aa'ishah (رضي الله عنها) that her menses came before she could do the rites of 'Umrah. So the Prophet (ﷺ) ordered her to make the *iḥraam* for Ḥajj and not to do *ṭawaaf* until she becomes pure again. She can do whatever a person performing Ḥajj does and should enter the Ḥajj in her 'Umrah (i.e. combine the Ḥajj after the 'Umrah).

Also, Bukhari reported from 'Aa'ishah (رضي الله عنها) that Safiyyah bint Huyay, one of the wives of the Prophet (ﷺ) entered her menses after performing *ṭawaf al-ifaaḍah*. So 'Aa'ishah informed the Prophet about this and he said:

> "Well, then she will detain us." Then he was informed she has already performed *ṭawaaf al-ifaaḍah*, and it was after this that she entered the menses. Thereupon Allah's Messenger said: "(If it is so), then proceed forth."
> Another hadith has been reported with similar wording.

May the peace and blessings of Allah be upon our Prophet Muhammad, his family and his Companions.

The Permanent Committee for Research and Verdicts

Concerning a woman whose *mahram* dies during Ḥajj

Q. What should a woman do if her *maḥram* dies during Ḥajj?

A. If she has another *maḥram* in Makkah, who can take care of her and bring her back, that is better. Otherwise, she can travel even without a *maḥram* in this case. However, she should not travel through an area that will have danger for her.

Shaykh Muḥammad ibn Ibraheem

Ruling concerning performing Ḥajj without the husband's permission

Q. What is the ruling concerning a woman who leaves for Ḥajj without the permission of her husband?

A. The Ḥajj is to be performed once in a lifetime, so it is obligatory if all its conditions are fulfilled. And gaining the permission of the husband is not among these conditions. It is not allowed for him to prevent her from going for Ḥajj (as long as all the conditions are fulfilled and it is her obligatory Ḥajj). In fact, it is prescribed for him to cooperate with her in fulfilling this obligation.

The Permanent Committee for Research and Verdicts

Is it allowed for a woman to perform Ḥajj with her husband's money?

Q. Is it allowed for my wife, who is poor, to perform Ḥajj with my money? Will this suffice her for her obligatory Ḥajj or is it not allowed?

A. Yes, it is allowed for her to do that and it will suffice her the obligatory Ḥajj. May Allah reward you well due to your kindness towards her (by giving her the money for her Ḥajj).

The Permanent Committee for Research and Verdicts

Making *iḥraam* from Jeddah

Q. I spent the month of Ramaḍaan in Jeddah and fasted there. Then I stayed there and on the eighth of the month of *Dhul Hijjah*, I put on the *iḥraam* from Jeddah and performed all the rites of Ḥajj. So is there any sacrifice upon me for this action?

A. No, there is no sacrifice upon you or anyone who was with you and did what you did.

Shaykh Muḥammad ibn Ibraheem

Ruling concerning a woman who passed by the *meeqaat* in a state of menses and did not put *iḥraam* on till she reached Makkah

Q. I was going to 'Umrah and when I was passing by the *meeqaat*, my menses came, so I did not put on the *iḥraam*. I stayed in Makkah until I became pure and then put on the *iḥraam* from Makkah. So is this allowed or what should I have done? And what is upon me now?

A. What you have done is not allowed. It is not allowed for a woman who wants to perform 'Umrah to pass the *meeqaat* without *iḥraam*, even if she is menstruating. In such a case, she should wear her *iḥraam* and it would be correct. The proof of this is that Asmaa' bint Umays, the wife of Abu Bakr (رضي الله عنه) gave birth when the Prophet (ﷺ) descended *dhul hulayfah* (the *meeqaat* of

Madeenah) wanting to perform the farewell pilgrimage. So she sent a person to the Prophet asking him what she should do. The Prophet (ﷺ) told her:

> "Take a shower and tie a cloth to the area where the blood is coming out and then wear *iḥraam.*"

The blood of menses is the same in ruling as the post-natal bleeding mentioned in this ḥadith.

So we say to a menstruating woman who passes by the *meeqaat* wanting to perform either Ḥajj or 'Umrah to take a shower and tie a cloth to the spot where the blood is coming from, and wear *iḥraam*. Then when she reaches Makkah, she should not go to the Ka'bah nor perform the *ṭawaaf* until she becomes pure. This is based on the saying of the Prophet (ﷺ) to 'Aa'ishah (رضي الله عنها) when her menses came during the 'Umrah:

> "Perform everything that others are doing except do not do *ṭawaaf* of the house (i.e. Ka'bah) until you become pure." Bukhari and Muslim reported this ḥadith.

Another ḥadith by Bukhari mentions on the authority of 'Aa'ishah (رضي الله عنها) that when she became pure from menses, she performed the *ṭawaaf* and did *sa'ee* between *safa* and *marwa*. So this ḥadith shows us that if a woman makes her *ihraam* for either Ḥajj or 'Umrah when she is menstruating or her menses comes after her intention but before the *ṭawaaf*, she should not perform the *ṭawaaf* nor the *sa'ee* until she becomes pure and takes a shower.

However, if she does the *ṭawaaf* when she is pure and after she finishes it, her menses starts, she can continue with the *sa'ee* even if she is in menses. She can then cut her hair and finish her 'Umrah. This is because being pure (from menses or having *wuḍoo'*) is not a requirement when performing the *sa'ee* between *safa* and *marwah*.

Shaykh Muḥammad ibn 'Uthaymeen

Kissing the black stone at the start of the *ṭawaaf*

Q. What is the ruling concerning kissing the black stone at the start of the *ṭawaaf*?

A. The Sunnah is that you should not crowd around to kiss the stone. It is not something that is prescribed for women just like *ramal* (i.e. the hastening performed by men during the first three rounds of *ṭawaaf*) is not prescribed for them. They should, however, try to stay at a distance from the Ka'bah and not be too close. This is because a woman is *'awrah* and if she kisses the stone, there will be desires there with all the men around. Making sure that the woman is covered is more important than these things that are desirable but not compulsory.

Shaykh Muḥammad ibn Ibraheem

Hastening between the two green marks when doing *sa'ee* between *safa* and *marwah*

Q. Is it prescribed for women to hasten between the two green marks when doing *sa'ee*? Similarly, what about a man who is accompanying women?

A. The women should not hasten between these two green marks. Likewise, a man who is with a woman or other women should also not hasten such that he can take care and guard them.

Shaykh Muḥammad ibn 'Uthaymeen

Shaving the head with respect to women during Ḥajj and 'Umrah

Q. Is a woman allowed to shave her head in 'Umrah and Ḥajj?

A. A woman has to cut her hair in 'Umrah and Ḥajj equal to one third of the length of a finger and it is not allowed for her to shave.

It is stated in the book *Mughni*: “Cutting the hair and not shaving is prescribed for a woman. There is no difference of opinion on this among the scholars.”

Ibn al-Mundhir said: “The scholars have a consensus upon this (i.e. that cutting the hair is prescribed for women) and that shaving the hair is considered repulsive for women.” Ibn ‘Abbaas (رضي الله عنه) reported that the Prophet (ﷺ) said:

“Women should not shave, but they have to trim.”

Abu Dawood reported this ḥadith. It is also reported on the authority of ‘Ali (رضي الله عنه) that the Prophet (ﷺ) prohibited a woman from having a haircut.

Imam Aḥmed used to say that a woman should cut the hair equal to one third of the finger from all over her head. Ibn ‘Umar (رضي الله عنه), Imam Shafi‘ee, Isḥaaq and Abu Thour have all said the same. Abu Dawood said: “I heard Aḥmed say ‘yes’ when asked whether a woman should trim her hair from all over her head. He further said that she should gather her hair all at the front and then cut from its end equal to one third of the length of the finger.” Imam an-Nawawi said in his book *Majmoo‘*: “The scholars have a consensus that a woman is not ordered to shave, but rather, she is required is to trim her hair because shaving is an innovation (*bid‘aa*) and repulsive for a woman.”

Shaykh Ṣaaleḥ al-Fawzaan

Are there any specified clothes for a woman to wear when performing Ḥajj?

Q. Is it necessary for a woman to wear clothes with specific colors when performing the rites of Ḥajj?

A. There are no specific clothes that a woman should wear during Ḥajj. Rather, she should just wear whatever is her habit of wearing as long, as it fully covers her body and is not attractive. It should not resemble men's clothes. However, what a woman has been prohibited from doing is wearing the *burqu'*[14] which is especially sewn to cover the face and from wearing gloves that is especially sewn to cover the hands. At the same time, however, she is required to cover her face and hands (as well as the whole body) with something else that is not made especially for that purpose because these parts are from her *'awrah* and thus must be covered. A woman has not been prohibited from covering the face and hands during *iḥraam*; rather she has been prohibited from covering them with *burqu'* and gloves only (and not with something else).

Shaykh Ṣaaleḥ al-Fawzaan

A woman did everything during Ḥajj except the throwing of the stones because she had a baby with her

Q. A woman performed all the rites of Ḥajj except the throwing of the stones for which she appointed someone to do it on her behalf because she had a baby with her. This Ḥajj is her first one. So what is the ruling?

A. If she did not have anyone with her who could take care of the baby, then there is no problem in appointing someone else to throw the stones on her behalf. However, if there is someone who can stay with the baby and take care of him or her, then it is not allowed for her to appoint someone to throw stones on her behalf, whether that is her first Ḥajj or subsequent ones.

Shaykh Muḥammad ibn 'Uthaymeen

---

[14] The prohibition here is not in reference to covering the clothes of a woman with the outer garment. Rather, a woman is required to cover her whole body except the face and hands during the *iḥraam*. She should use something other than the *burqu'* to cover her whole body and clothes.

Appointing someone for throwing stones

Q. A man performing Ḥajj has many young girls with him who fear a large crowd and it is known that the crowd of Ḥajj is extreme. There was also the fear of them possibly falling on the ground or even dying. So should they try to throw the stones themselves or appoint somebody close to them to throw for them when there is extreme congestion? Furthermore, if they only stone *jamrat al-'aqabah* before the sunrise on *'Eid* day, and then somebody else stones for them the rest after midday, what is the ruling?

A. It is allowed for a person to appoint someone else to throw stones (on their behalf) if they are unable to throw (by themselves). It is the same for *jamrat al-'aqabah* and the rest of the *jamrahs*. The person being appointed should be reliable and be one who is also performing Ḥajj in that very year. There is no problem if the young girls mentioned in the question appoint somebody because they fear the congestion.

Likewise, there is no problem if stoning *jamrat al-'aqabah* on the night of *'Eid* (i.e. the night before *'Eid* day) and before sunrise on *'Eid* day morning, because the Prophet (ﷺ) made a concession for weak people to do that.

The Permanent Committee for Research and Verdicts

Performing Ḥajj with the proper *iḥraam* clothes

Q. My father performed Ḥajj last year and because he was suffering a severe illness, he was unable to wear the proper *iḥraam* clothes. So what is obligatory upon him now?

A. If a person performing Ḥajj wears his normal clothes due to a reason such as severe cold or illness or something like that, then he is permitted to do that according to the shari'ah. However, now he must either fast three days or feed six poor people, each of whom is to be given two handfuls of the country's normal food, or he may sacrifice a sheep which fulfils the conditions of sacrifice. He must do this since he wore sewn clothes.

Likewise, the ruling is the same for a person who covers his head (i.e. with respect to a man). The fasting, if chosen, can be done anywhere, whereas the feeding of poor and sacrifice must be done in the *ḥaram* of Makkah.

The Permanent Committee for Research and Verdicts

If hair falls out without one's will

Q. What should a woman do if some of her hair falls off without her doing when she is in a state of *iḥraam*?

A. If hair falls off a person, whether male or female, who is in *iḥraam*, either due to touching it during *wuḍoo'* or when washing it for example, it will not affect the *iḥraam*. Similarly, if some hair falls off a man's moustache or beard, or his fingernail breaks, it will not affect his *iḥraam* since he did not do that intentionally. What is considered disallowed in *iḥraam* is cutting hair or nails intentionally. It is the same for a woman. But if something (like hair or nails) falls out unintentionally, they are in fact dead hairs that fall off due to movement, and thus it will not affect a person's *iḥraam*.

Shaykh 'Abdul 'Aziz ibn Baaz

Ruling concerning socks and gloves for a woman

Q. Is a woman allowed to wear gloves and socks during Ḥajj (when in *iḥraam*)?

A. As for the socks, she is allowed to wear them during Ḥajj (when in *iḥraam*) because the Prophet (ﷺ) did not forbid a woman from that. As for gloves, she cannot wear them because the Prophet (ﷺ) forbade a woman from wearing gloves during *iḥraam* (however, she is required to cover her hands with the rest of her clothes).

Shaykh Muḥammad ibn 'Uthaymeen

A menstruating woman praying the two *rak'ahs* of *iḥraam*

Q. How should a menstruating woman pray the two *rak'ahs* of *iḥraam*? Also, is it permissible for a menstruating woman to read verses from the Qur'an?

A. Firstly, it should be known that there is no prayer for *iḥraam*. This is because it was not reported from the Prophet (ﷺ) that he legislated praying two *rak'ahs* for *iḥraam*. He did not pray himself, or order anyone to pray and did not approve anyone else who may have prayed it.

Secondly, it was possible for this woman (i.e. the questioner) who had her menses before *iḥraam* to make her *iḥraam* even though she was menstruating. The basis for this is a ḥadith wherein the Prophet (ﷺ) ordered Asmaa' bint Umays, the wife of Abu Bakr (رضي الله عنها), when her postnatal bleeding started at the *meeqaat* of *dhul hulayfah* (in Madeenah) to take a bath and then to enter the state of *iḥraam*. The ruling is the same for a menstruating woman. She should remain in her *iḥraam* till she becomes pure and then perform the *ṭawaaf* of the Ka'bah and *sa'ee* between *safa* and *marwah*.

With regard to her question concerning whether it is permissible for her to recite the Qur'an or not? The answer is yes; it is permissible for a menstruating woman to recite the Qur'an if there is a necessity or benefit. As for a situation wherein there is no necessity or benefit, and she wants to recite as an act of getting closer to Allah, then it is better for her not to recite (until she becomes pure from menses).

Shaykh Muḥammad ibn 'Uthaymeen

It is not permissible for a menstruating woman to enter the *ḥaram*

Q. Is it permissible for a menstruating woman to enter the *ḥaram* of Makkah?

A. No, it is not permissible for her to enter the *ḥaram* of Makkah except if she is passing through it. As regards staying inside for *ṭawaaf* or for remembrances and *dhikr*, then it is not allowed.

There arises a question, what should a woman do if she feels that her menses has started while she is performing the *ṭawaaf*? The answer is that she should continue with her *ṭawaaf* as long as she is not sure that the blood has come out. Then whenever she becomes sure that blood has come out, it becomes obligatory upon her to leave. She should wait till she becomes pure from menses and then re-starts the *ṭawaaf* from the beginning (i.e. she should not continue from where she left off).

Shaykh Muḥammad ibn 'Uthaymeen

Menses starting on the day of *'Arafah*

Q. What should a woman do if her menses starts on the day of *'Arafah*?

A. If a woman's menses starts on the day of *'Arafah*, she should continue with her Ḥajj and perform all the rites of Ḥajj that other people perform, except that she should not perform the *ṭawaaf* until she becomes pure.

Shaykh Muḥammad ibn 'Uthaymeen

A woman's aunty was rich but passed away without performing Ḥajj

Q. My aunty was very rich during her life. However, she passed away without performing her Ḥajj. So is it obligatory to perform Ḥajj on her behalf from her money? Or is it permissible for someone else to perform Ḥajj for her from their own money?

A. It is obligatory to perform Ḥajj on her behalf from her money. However, it is permissible for you to perform from your money.

Shaykh Muhammad ibn Ibraheem

Wife performing Ḥajj on behalf of her husband

Q. Is it permissible for my mother to perform Ḥajj on behalf of my father knowing that my mother has already performed her own obligatory Ḥajj?

A. In view of the fact that your mother has performed her own obligatory Ḥajj, there is no problem in her performing Ḥajj on behalf of your father.

Shaykh Muḥammad ibn Ibraheem

A woman performing the eighth Ḥajj on behalf of her mother

Q. My mother has performed Ḥajj seven times. Is it permissible for me to perform for her the eighth Ḥajj?

A. Yes it is permissible for you to perform on her behalf her eighth Ḥajj or more. This will be kindness towards her and you will have a great reward for this as long as you have performed your own obligatory Ḥajj. We ask Allah, the Exalted and Glorified, to grant us the understanding of His religion and to remain firm upon it.

The Permanent Committee for Research and Verdicts

A woman performing Ḥajj on behalf of her dead parents

Q. Is it permissible for me to perform Ḥajj on behalf of my parents who died without performing Ḥajj because they were poor?

A. Yes, it is permissible for you to perform Ḥajj on behalf of your parents or even to appoint someone else to perform it on their behalf. However, the person performing Ḥajj on their behalf (whether that is you or someone else) must have already performed their own obligatory Ḥajj. This is based on a ḥadith reported by Abu Dawood on the authority of 'Abdullah ibn 'Abbaas (رضي الله عنه) that the Prophet (ﷺ) once heard a person saying that he is going to do Ḥajj on behalf of someone named Shubrumah. So the Prophet asked who is Shubrumah? The man replied that Shubrumah is his brother or close relative. Then the Prophet asked him whether he had performed his own Ḥajj? So when the man replied that he had not performed, the Prophet said to him:

> "Perform your own Ḥajj first and then perform on behalf of Shubrumah."

Ibn Majah also reported this ḥadith and Bayhaqi said: there is no ḥadith more authentic regarding this topic.

The Permanent Committee for Research and Verdicts

The permissibility of a woman sacrificing an animal by herself

Q. Is it permissible for a woman to sacrifice (with her own hands)? Also, is it permissible to eat from the sacrificed animal?

A. Yes, it is permissible for a woman to sacrifice just like it is permissible for a man. The basis for this ruling is what has been established from the Prophet (ﷺ) regarding this issue. Similarly, it is permissible to eat from the animal sacrificed as long as the woman who performed the sacrifice was a Muslim or from the People of the Book (i.e. either a Jew or Christian), and also as long as she sacrificed according to the proper shari'ah guidelines. The ruling is the same even if there is a man who can perform the sacrifice instead of her, since there is no condition of sacrificing, that states that a man should not be available.

Shaykh 'Abdul 'Aziz ibn Baaz

CHAPTER: MISCELLANEOUS

A *du'aa'* (supplication) that is not acceptable

Q. I fast voluntarily such that Allah should wipe out my errors and slips that might have happened from me without me knowing, and I adhere very much to my religion, all praise is to Allah. But my parents make *du'aa'* that my fasts should not be accepted and I do not know why they do this. My fasts do not affect the duties in the houses and my mother does not need me either. I am confused and also worried that Allah may not accept my deeds and fasts because the supplications of the parents are accepted. So what is your view, O' Noble Shaykh?

A. We thank you for your attention towards acts of worship and optional deeds as well. You should stay firm on these as much as you can. Try to explain to your mother that this is a good and virtuous deed (i.e. fasting) and that the right of the mother is being fulfilled, as fasting does not hinder the person from fulfilling the rights of the mother and serving her. Also explain to her that it is obligatory to her to urge you to do these good deeds and she should try to follow you as well. She is more in need of such optional prayers, fasts and other deeds because of her seniority and for the expiation of sins.

As for her supplication against you, it will not be accepted if Allah wills, especially since the deed is virtuous and good, and since she did not intend except mercy and compassion.

Shaykh 'Abdullah ibn Jibreen

My mother likes me a lot and thus treats me like a baby

Q. My mother likes me a great deal and has a lot of affection for me. Maybe this is due to my weakness and illness, but at any rate, her love has crossed the limit. I am currently twenty-one years old and still my mother treats me as if I am only ten years old. In fact, if it occurred to her, she would even feed me with her hands. I am soft-spoken and obedient towards her. So what should I do?

A. This usually happens from the father wherein he loves his children and inclines towards them. However, the effect of this varies a lot in the hearts of the parents or one of them, with or without a reason. Maybe one of the reasons could be that they want total obedience or maybe because of weakness or illness that makes them do this.

Because such a thing can lead to harm, as has been mentioned in the question, it is upto the son or daughter to talk to the parents and explain to them that there is no need for such observation or concern. Similarly, it is upon the parents to be just and have equality in their treatment of children regarding love, compassion and affections. It is reported that some of the pious predecessors used to even be equal in their kissing of their children and other similar things. It is reported from the Messenger of Allah (ﷺ) that he said:

"Fear Allah and be just with your children."

Sheikh Abdullah bin Jibreen

My mother died when she was angry with me

Q. My mother passed away six years ago in the month of Ramaḍaan. When I was little, I used to be very bold with her and always reply back. She died when she was angry with me. When I got older, I became mature and now I regret all that happened but I can't do anything except seek forgiveness, regret and seek repentance from Allah and to make supplication for her for mercy and forgiveness. So is this enough such that Allah forgives my sins and has mercy upon me on the Day when I meet Him? Secondly, we have not kept the fasts on her behalf. So is this a sin upon us and is it allowed for us now to fast on her behalf, knowing that we did not know about this except sometime ago?

A. Perhaps, when your mother was alive, you were young with ignorance and silliness. Thus you are excused for what occurred in that situation. In general, since you have regretted after becoming mature and gaining senses, and have repented to Allah and sought His forgiveness for that, then whatever happened will be wiped out if Allah wills. This is because repentance wipes out what happened before it. Similarly, you said that you also make supplication for her and seek forgiveness and mercy for her, and give charity on her behalf. Allah forgives sins because of all these deeds and similar actions. As for the fasting that your mother has left and did not observe while she was ill, she is excused for that due to her illness which disabled her to make up for it.

Shaykh 'Abdullah ibn Jibreen

I made *du'aa'* to Allah and it was not answered

Q. I spent more than ten years, on and off, making *du'aa'* to Allah to bless me with a pious husband and children. But nothing of my *du'aa'* has been accepted, and this is the will of Allah, the Almighty, and there is nothing that can go against His decree. My question is: since a short period of time, I have stopped making *du'aa'*. This is not due to giving up hope in Allah's response, but because I began to think that maybe this matter is not good for me, since Allah has not responded to my *du'aa'*. So, I decided not to make *du'aa'* because Allah, the Almighty, is more knowledgeable than me in what is beneficial for me even though I still have a strong desire for what I made *du'aa'* for, and would like it to be answered. So what is obligatory upon me to do in this situation? Should I continue with this *du'aa'* or be satisfied that maybe this *du'aa'* is not beneficial for me and thus stop making *du'aa'*?

A. It is established in a ḥadith that the supplication of a slave (of Allah) is answered as long as he does not hasten. This hastening has been explained to mean that the slave does not see the response quickly for his *du'aa'*, and thus becomes sad and disheartened, and leaves making the *du'aa'*, and says that I made *du'aa'* repeatedly but it was not answered for me. This is because Allah, the Almighty, sometimes delays the response to the *du'aa'*, either due to general or specific reasons. It has come in a ḥadith that Allah gives one of three things to a person who makes *du'aa'*: either He answers the *du'aa'* and gives the person what he asked, or keeps it for the person for the day of Judgment, or evil is warded off this person according to how sincerely the *du'aa'* was. So you, O' sister, should not hasten, but should continue in your *du'aa'* always, even if that means many years. Similarly, you should not reject a proposal that comes from good people of your standard, even if they are old and even if they are married. Maybe Allah will put great benefit in this for you.

Shaykh 'Abdullah ibn Jibreen

Du'aa' against the children

Q. Many fathers and mothers make *du'aa'* against their children when the latter make errors or slips. I hope you can give some advice to them regarding this matter.

A. We advise the parents to pardon and overlook the shortcomings of their children as long as they are young. They should also have patience and bear what they face regarding bad speech or behavior. Children's senses have not yet matured and this causes errors in both speech and actions. So whenever the father is fore-bearing and patient, he will forgive that and teach the children with gentleness, kindness and advices. This will have the greatest impact on their acceptance and future behavior.

However, some parents fall into a greater error than this, which is to make *du'aa'* against the children, for them to either die, or fall ill, or be afflicted with trials. Some of them persist in this *du'aa'*. Then when they have calmed down, they realize that it was wrong of them to do that, and they admit that they do not want to see that *du'aa'* being accepted. This is due to the sympathy and compassion they have been created with. It is only a case of severe anger that drove them to make these *du'aa's*. Allah will forgive them, as He said:

﴿ وَلَوْ يُعَجِّلُ ٱللَّهُ لِلنَّاسِ ٱلشَّرَّ ٱسْتِعْجَالَهُم بِٱلْخَيْرِ لَقُضِىَ إِلَيْهِمْ أَجَلُهُمْ... ﴾ (١١)

(يونس : ١١)

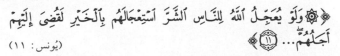

"*And were Allah to hasten for mankind the evil [of what they invoke for themselves and for their children, while*

in a state of anger] as He hastens for them the good [they invoke] then they would have been ruined..."

(Qur'an 10: 11)

It is obligatory on the parents to have patience and bear this, and to discipline their children by hitting them in a manner that will deter them. This is because hitting has a greater effect on a child than just teaching what is right and disciplining. As for making du'aa' against them, it will not benefit. A person does not know what will be written about him regarding what he said. So it maybe that this du'aa' by the parents is written against them but will not have any beneficial effect on the child. And Allah knows best.

Shaykh 'Abdullah ibn Jibreen

It is not allowed to cheat in exams

Q. I write the answers for my friends in the class during the exams after I obtain the answers myself by all means possible. So what does the religion have to say in this matter?

A. It is not allowed to cheat in exams or to help someone who is cheating, whether by looking at the answers from the person next to you or by speaking softly to someone or by other such tricks. This has a harmful effect on the society, because the person who cheats will hold a qualification that he does not deserve, and might be given a position that is not for him, based on that false qualification. This is harmful and dangerous. And Allah knows best.

Shaykh 'Abdullah ibn Jibreen

There is nothing wrong with humor if it is the truth

Q. What is the ruling regarding humor? Is it considered to be wasteful speech? Please note that it is not mocking the religion. Please give us a *fatwa*, may Allah reward you.

A. Jokes and amusement with speech, if it is the truth, there is nothing wrong with it, especially if it is not done often. The Messenger of Allah (ﷺ) used to joke, but, even then, he used to say the truth. As for jokes that are lies and false, it is not allowed due to the saying of the Messenger of Allah (ﷺ):

> "Woe to the one who speaks and tells a lie to make people laugh, woe to him, then woe to him."

Abu Dawood, Tirmidhi and Nasaa'i reported this ḥadith with a good chain of narrators. And Allah is the source of success.

Shaykh 'Abdul 'Aziz ibn Baaz

The ḥadith regarding the seven who will have the shade on the Day of Judgment is not specific to men

Q. The ḥadith wherein is mentioned the seven who Allah will shade in His shade when there will be no shade except His, is it specific to men or is it that anyone who does those good deeds from amongst the women will also get the reward mentioned in the ḥadith?

A. The virtue mentioned in the ḥadith is not specific to men but rather it encompasses both men and women. So, firstly, a young girl who grows up in the worship of Allah comes under the ḥadith. Secondly, two women who love each other for the sake of Allah only, also come under the ḥadith. Thirdly, any woman who is called to have illegal sexual intercourse by a beautiful and high status man, but she refuses and says to him: I fear Allah, then she would also come under the ḥadith. Fourthly, whoever gave in charity from their pure wealth, while concealing it to such an extent that their left hand would not know what the right hand has given in charity, would come under the ḥadith. Fifthly, whoever among the women remembered Allah in seclusion and then cried out of fear of Him would also come under the ḥadith.

As for the sixth aspect, which is the leadership, it is specific to men. So also the last category concerning the congregational prayer in the mosques is specific to men. A woman's prayer in her house is better for her as has been reported in authentic ḥadiths from the Messenger of Allah (ﷺ). And Allah is the source of success.

Shaykh 'Abdul 'Aziz ibn Baaz

A woman working along with men

Q. What is the view of Islam regarding a woman working with men?

A. It is a known fact that when a woman enters the fields of men, it causes mixing between the two and also seclusion of men with women. These things are very dangerous for them due to what they could lead to, and more importantly, it is contradictory to the texts of the shari'ah that order the woman to stay in her house and to perform the duties which are specific to her and which require the characteristics that Allah has created her with. These duties keep her far away from mixing with men.

There are clear and authentic proofs showing the prohibition of seclusion with strange women (for whom a man is not a *maḥram*) and from looking at them. In fact, Islam has also prohibited any means that can lead one to falling into what Allah has prohibited, and the outcome of these would not be praiseworthy.

Among these proofs is the saying of Allah, the Almighty, the All-Glorious, to women:

﴿وَقَرْنَ فِى بُيُوتِكُنَّ وَلَا تَبَرَّجْنَ تَبَرُّجَ ٱلْجَٰهِلِيَّةِ ٱلْأُولَىٰ ۖ وَأَقِمْنَ ٱلصَّلَوٰةَ وَءَاتِينَ ٱلزَّكَوٰةَ وَأَطِعْنَ ٱللَّهَ وَرَسُولَهُۥٓ ۚ إِنَّمَا يُرِيدُ ٱللَّهُ لِيُذْهِبَ عَنكُمُ ٱلرِّجْسَ أَهْلَ ٱلْبَيْتِ وَيُطَهِّرَكُمْ تَطْهِيرًا ﴿٣٣﴾ وَٱذْكُرْنَ مَا يُتْلَىٰ فِى بُيُوتِكُنَّ مِنْ ءَايَٰتِ ٱللَّهِ وَٱلْحِكْمَةِ ۚ إِنَّ ٱللَّهَ كَانَ لَطِيفًا خَبِيرًا ﴿٣٤﴾﴾

(الأحزاب : ٣٣-٣٤)

"*And stay in your houses and do not display yourselves like that of the times of ignorance, and perform the prayer and give the zakah, and obey Allah and His Messenger. Allah wishes only to remove evil deeds and sins from you, O' members of the family [of the Messenger of Allah] and to purify you with a thorough purification. And remember [the Graces of your Lord] that which is recited in your houses of the Verses of Allah and the Messenger of Allah's ways. Verily, Allah is Ever Most Courteous, Well-Acquainted with all things.*"

(Qur'an 33: 33-34)

Also, Allah says:

﴿يَٰٓأَيُّهَا ٱلنَّبِىُّ قُل لِّأَزْوَٰجِكَ وَبَنَاتِكَ وَنِسَآءِ ٱلْمُؤْمِنِينَ يُدْنِينَ عَلَيْهِنَّ مِن جَلَٰبِيبِهِنَّ ۚ ذَٰلِكَ أَدْنَىٰٓ أَن يُعْرَفْنَ فَلَا يُؤْذَيْنَ ۗ وَكَانَ ٱللَّهُ غَفُورًا رَّحِيمًا ﴿٥٩﴾﴾

(الأحزاب : ٥٩)

"*O' Prophet, tell your wives and your daughters and the women of the believers to draw their cloaks [i.e. veils] all over their bodies. That will be better that they should be known [as free respectable women] so as not to be annoyed. And Allah is Ever Oft-Forgiving, Most Merciful.*" *(Qur'an 33: 59)*

He, the Almighty, also says:

﴿قُل لِّلْمُؤْمِنِينَ يَغُضُّوا۟ مِنْ أَبْصَٰرِهِمْ وَيَحْفَظُوا۟ فُرُوجَهُمْ ۚ ذَٰلِكَ أَزْكَىٰ لَهُمْ ۗ
إِنَّ ٱللَّهَ خَبِيرٌۢ بِمَا يَصْنَعُونَ ﴿٣٠﴾ وَقُل لِّلْمُؤْمِنَٰتِ يَغْضُضْنَ مِنْ أَبْصَٰرِهِنَّ
وَيَحْفَظْنَ فُرُوجَهُنَّ وَلَا يُبْدِينَ زِينَتَهُنَّ إِلَّا مَا ظَهَرَ مِنْهَا ۖ وَلْيَضْرِبْنَ
بِخُمُرِهِنَّ عَلَىٰ جُيُوبِهِنَّ ۖ وَلَا يُبْدِينَ زِينَتَهُنَّ إِلَّا لِبُعُولَتِهِنَّ أَوْ ءَابَآئِهِنَّ
أَوْ ءَابَآءِ بُعُولَتِهِنَّ أَوْ أَبْنَآئِهِنَّ أَوْ أَبْنَآءِ بُعُولَتِهِنَّ أَوْ إِخْوَٰنِهِنَّ أَوْ
بَنِىٓ إِخْوَٰنِهِنَّ أَوْ بَنِىٓ أَخَوَٰتِهِنَّ أَوْ نِسَآئِهِنَّ أَوْ مَا مَلَكَتْ أَيْمَٰنُهُنَّ أَوِ
ٱلتَّٰبِعِينَ غَيْرِ أُو۟لِى ٱلْإِرْبَةِ مِنَ ٱلرِّجَالِ أَوِ ٱلطِّفْلِ ٱلَّذِينَ لَمْ يَظْهَرُوا۟
عَلَىٰ عَوْرَٰتِ ٱلنِّسَآءِ ۖ وَلَا يَضْرِبْنَ بِأَرْجُلِهِنَّ لِيُعْلَمَ مَا يُخْفِينَ مِن زِينَتِهِنَّ ۚ
وَتُوبُوٓا۟ إِلَى ٱللَّهِ جَمِيعًا أَيُّهَ ٱلْمُؤْمِنُونَ لَعَلَّكُمْ تُفْلِحُونَ ﴿٣١﴾﴾

(النور: ٣٠-٣١)

"*Tell the believing men to lower their gaze [from looking at haraam things] and protect their private parts [from illegal sexual acts]. That is purer for them. Verily, Allah is All-Aware of what they do. And tell the believing women to lower their gaze [from looking at haraam things] and protect their private parts [from illegal sexual acts] and not to show off their adornments except only that which is apparent and to draw their veils all over their bodies, faces, necks and bosoms, and not to reveal their adornments except to their husbands, or their fathers, or their husbands' fathers, or their sons, or their husbands' sons, or their brothers or their brothers' sons, or their sisters' sons, or their [Muslim] women or the [female] slaves whom their right hands possess, or old male servants who lack vigor or small children who have no sense of feminine sex. And let them not stamp their feet so as to reveal what they hide of their adornment. And turn to Allah in repentance, all of you, O believers, that you might succeed."* *(Qur'an 24: 30-31)*

And Allah says to the companions:

﴿...وَإِذَا سَأَلْتُمُوهُنَّ مَتَٰعًا فَسْـَٔلُوهُنَّ مِن وَرَآءِ حِجَابٍۚ ذَٰلِكُمْ أَطْهَرُ لِقُلُوبِكُمْ وَقُلُوبِهِنَّۚ ...﴿٥٣﴾﴾ (الأحزاب : ٥٣)

"*And when you ask [the Messenger of Allahs' wives] for anything [such as Islamic rulings etc.], ask them from behind a screen, that is purer for your hearts and for their hearts."* *(Qur'an 33: 53)*

The Messenger of Allah (ﷺ) said:

> "Beware of meeting women (i.e. the strange women for whom you are not a *maḥram*)." It was said to him: "O' Messenger of Allah, what about the *Hamu* (the husband's brother)?" The Messenger of Allah said: "He is death."

The Messenger of Allah (ﷺ) forbade a man from being in seclusion with a strange woman at any cost when he said about a man and a woman being alone:

> "... the third of them is the *Shayṭaan* (Satan)."

Also, the Messenger of Allah (ﷺ) forbade a woman from traveling except with a *maḥram* man in order to cut the means that lead to evil acts, to close the door on sins and to guard both the man and woman from the traps and plans of the *Shayṭaan*.

It is authentically established that the Messenger of Allah (ﷺ) said:

> "Beware of the world and beware of the women, for verily the first *fitnah* of the children of Israel was with women."

He (ﷺ) also said:

> "I have not left after me a more harmful *fitnah* upon men than women."

All these verses and ḥadiths are clear cut regarding the obligation to stay far away from mixing, which will lead to evil, the destruction of the family and the ruining of society.

When we look at the status of the woman in some of the Islamic countries, we find that she has become disgraced and vulgar due to her being taken out of her house and being made to take up roles outside of her areas. Some of the people of senses there and in some Arab countries have made a call that it is obligatory for the woman to return to her natural place that Allah has made her suitable for, both in terms of intellect and physique. However, this call has come too late.

It suffices women that they have to work in their houses and in the field of teaching (only to women) from them having to work in the field of men. We ask Allah to protect our country and all the Muslim countries from the tricks of the enemies and their destructive plans. May Allah guide the Muslims and the journalists in writing things that will amend their matters, both in this world and in the Hereafter. This would be in accordance with the order from their Lord and Creator. May Allah also guide the Muslims in the Muslim lands to all that will amend the slaves of Allah and the countries, and regarding their homes here and abodes in the Hereafter. May Allah protect all Muslims from all trials and tribulations, and the causes of Allah's wrath. Verily, Allah has the ability to do this.

Shaykh 'Abdul 'Aziz ibn Baaz

Ruling concerning a woman remaining with her alcoholic husband

Q. I have three boys and one daughter and my husband is an alcoholic, may Allah protect us from it. Previously, he was imprisoned for it. He is addicted to it and has punished my children and me before as a result of it. I am divorced from him now and I live with my family along with my children. He does not spend any money on us and I do not have any desire of going back to him. He threatens me that he will take the children from me, which I cannot bear. I am a mother before all else. I hope you can advise.

A. This is a matter specific for the shari'ah court without a doubt. A person addicted to drinking should not be stayed with because he will harm his wife and children. You should distance yourself from him except if Allah guides him and he returns to the correct way. If the judge breaks up between husband and wife, then most often he will give custody of the children to the mother because she is more suited for that and he is not.

But since the problem is his addiction to drinking, then he is definitely not suited for his children because he will lose them and also make them corrupt. Thus the mother is more suitable for the children than the father, even if the children were daughters. This is what is apparent from the judges and this is what is correct, that the children should be with this mother because she is better than this father, since he is an evildoer (i.e. drinks alcohol).

She has done well in refusing to go back to him because it is dangerous for her. And if it is such that he does not pray, then it is obligatory not to go back to him. This is because whoever leaves the prayer has disbelieved, may Allah protect us from this, as the Messenger of Allah (ﷺ) said:

"The covenant between us and them is the prayer. Whoever leaves it has disbelieved."

So it is not obligatory upon you to stay with a person who does not pray. Allah (ﷻ) says:

﴿...لَا هُنَّ حِلٌّ لَّهُمْ وَلَا هُمْ يَحِلُّونَ لَهُنَّ ... ﴿١٠﴾﴾ (المُمتحنة : ١٠)

"...They are not lawful [wives] for the disbelievers nor are the disbelievers lawful [husbands] for them..."
(Qur'an 60: 10)

This is the case until Allah guides them and they repent, in which case, for example, this woman can go back to her husband. Otherwise, she and her children stay with her family and away from him until Allah forgives him and until he returns to what is correct.

If he is such that he prays but drinks alcohol, then this is a great sin and disobedience, yet, he is not a *kaafir* but an evildoer. She has the choice of staying away from him or leaving him. She will be excused if she stays away from him and if she has patience with him and can bear him, then there is no problem.

Shaykh 'Abdul 'Aziz ibn Baaz

Ruling concerning the publishing, distributing, purchasing and working with deviant magazines

Q. What is the ruling regarding publishing magazines which contain pictures of uncovered women and in seductive ways? They concentrate on the news concerning actors and actresses. And what is the ruling regarding a person who works for such magazines and helps in their distribution and also regarding one who purchases them?

A. It is not allowed to publish magazines that contain pictures of women and that contain calls to illegal sexual intercourse, evil acts, homosexuality, taking drugs or the like, all of which call to falsehood and help it. Similarly, it is not allowed to work for such magazines with articles or circulation, because that comes under the scenario of helping one another upon sin and transgression. It would also be considered spreading evil on earth and calling for the corruption and disgracing of the society. Allah, the Almighty, said in His clear Book:

﴿... وَتَعَاوَنُوا۟ عَلَى ٱلْبِرِّ وَٱلتَّقْوَىٰ ۖ وَلَا تَعَاوَنُوا۟ عَلَى ٱلْإِثْمِ وَٱلْعُدْوَٰنِ ۚ وَٱتَّقُوا۟ ٱللَّهَ ۖ إِنَّ ٱللَّهَ شَدِيدُ ٱلْعِقَابِ ﴿٢﴾﴾ (المائدة : ٢)

"... *and help one another in virtue and righteousness and do not help one another in sin and transgression. And fear Allah, verily, Allah is severe in punishment.*"

(Qur'an 5: 2)

The Messenger of Allah (ﷺ) said:

"Whoever calls to good will have the reward similar to those who act upon it and it will not decrease from their reward a bit. And whoever calls to evil, will have the sin similar to those who act upon it and it will not decrease from their sins at all."

Muslim reported this ḥadith in his *Ṣaheeh*.

The ḥadith of Abu Hurayrah (رضي الله عنه) who said that the Messenger of Allah (ﷺ) said:

"Two are the types of the people of Hell whom I did not see: people having flogs like the tails of the ox with them and they would be beating people, and the women who would be dressed but appear to be naked, who would be inclined (to evil) and make their husbands incline towards it. Their heads would be like the humps of long-necked camels inclined to one side. They will not enter Paradise and they would not smell its odor whereas its odor would be smelt from such and such a distance."

Reported by Muslim in his *Ṣaḥeeḥ*.

There are many verses and ḥadiths that carry this meaning. We ask Allah to guide the Muslims to what is good for them and for their success. May He guide the people responsible for media and advertising to all the beneficial things that lead to the success of the society. May Allah protect them from the evil of their own actions and from the plans of *Shayṭaan*. Verily, He is Generous and Bountiful.

Shaykh 'Abdul 'Aziz ibn Baaz

Ruling concerning reading deviant magazines

Q. What is the ruling concerning women who read deviant magazines?

A. It is *haraam* for any male or female to read books that contain innovations and deviations, as well as magazines that spread evil and call to falsehood. They also call to the changing of noble characteristics. The only exception is if a person is reading such things in order to rebut the deviances and heresies in them, and if such a person is going to advise the people involved in such magazines to come to the right path. Also, such a person is allowed if they will condemn the people involved and warn the public against their evil.

The Permanent Committee for Research and Verdicts

The Qur'an is the alternative

Q. What is the advice of the Shaykh for people who let a month or many months go by without touching the

Noble Book of Allah without an excuse? You find that such people follow closely magazines that are of no benefit.

A. It is desirable for both male and female believers to increase the recitation of the Book of Allah with reflection and pondering. This is the same whether they are reciting from a copy of the Qur'an or from their memory. Allah, the Almighty, says:

﴿كِتَٰبٌ أَنزَلْنَٰهُ إِلَيْكَ مُبَٰرَكٌ لِّيَدَّبَّرُوٓا۟ ءَايَٰتِهِۦ وَلِيَتَذَكَّرَ أُو۟لُوا۟ ٱلْأَلْبَٰبِ ﴿٢٩﴾﴾

(ص : ٢٩)

"*A Book We have sent down to you, full of blessings, that they may ponder over its verses and that men of understanding may remember.*" *(Qur'an 38: 29)*

Also, Allah, the Almighty, says:

﴿إِنَّ ٱلَّذِينَ يَتْلُونَ كِتَٰبَ ٱللَّهِ وَأَقَامُوا۟ ٱلصَّلَوٰةَ وَأَنفَقُوا۟ مِمَّا رَزَقْنَٰهُمْ سِرًّا وَعَلَانِيَةً يَرْجُونَ تِجَٰرَةً لَّن تَبُورَ ﴿٢٩﴾ لِيُوَفِّيَهُمْ أُجُورَهُمْ وَيَزِيدَهُم مِّن فَضْلِهِۦٓ ۚ إِنَّهُۥ غَفُورٌ شَكُورٌ ﴿٣٠﴾﴾

(فاطر : ٢٩-٣٠)

"*Verily, those who recite the Book of Allah and perform the prayer and spend out of what We have provided for them, they hope for a trade-gain that will never perish. That He may pay them their wages in full, and give them more out of His Grace. Verily, He is Oft-Forgiving, Most Ready to appreciate.*" *(Qur'an 35: 29-30)*

The reciting mentioned in this verse includes both reading and following. Reading with reflection and pondering, and also sincerely for Allah are all means that aide a person in following the Qur'an and has a lot of rewards. The Messenger of Allah (ﷺ) said:

"Read the Qur'an for verily it will come on the Day of Judgment as an intercessor for the person."

Imam Muslim reported this ḥadith in his *Ṣaḥeeḥ*.

The Messenger of Allah (ﷺ) also said:

"The best of you is the one who learns the Qur'an and then teaches it."

Imam Bukhari reported this ḥadith in his *Ṣaḥeeḥ*. Also, there is another Hadith with the wording:

"Whoever reads a letter from the Qur'an will have a reward and each reward is ten-fold. I do not mean that *alif laam meem* is a letter, but rather, *alif* is a letter, *laam* is a letter and *meem* is a letter."

It is also established that the Messenger of Allah (ﷺ) said to 'Abdullah ibn 'Amr ibn 'Aaṣ:

"Read the Qur'an (completely, at least) once every month." So the Companion said: "I can recite more than that." So he said: "Read it every week (i.e. finish it every week)."

The Companions of the Messenger of Allah (ﷺ) used to finish the recitation of the Qur'an completely every week.

My advice to all the reciters of the Qur'an is to increase its recitation and to recite it with reflection and pondering, and to recite it for the sake of Allah only. They should have the intention of gaining knowledge and benefiting (both themselves and others). If possible, they should try to finish it each month and better still, for those who can, should finish it in less time than that, because it is a great benefit. It is allowed to finish in less than a week, but the better approach is to not finish it in less than three days because that is what the Messenger of Allah (may the peace and blessings of Allah be upon him) guided his Companion 'Abdullah ibn 'Amr ibn 'Aaṣ (in another ḥadith).

Another reason for not finishing it in less than three days is that it may lead to hastening and thus a person will not be able to ponder and reflect upon it. It is not allowed for a person to recite the Qur'an from the copy (i.e. *muṣḥaf*) except in a state of purity (i.e. with *wuḍoo'*). However, if he is reading it from memory, then there is no problem if he does not have *wuḍoo'*.

As for a person in the state of *janaabah* (ritual impurity) after having sexual intercourse and before taking a bath, it is not allowed for him to read from the *muṣhaf* nor from his memory until a bath is taken. This is based on a ḥadith reported by Imam Aḥmed and the other Imams who collected the books of *Sunan* with a good chain of narrators, on the authority of 'Ali (رضي الله عنه) who said: "There was nothing that used to prevent the Messenger of Allah (ﷺ) from the Qur'an except the state of *janaabah*." And with Allah is success.

Shaykh 'Abdul 'Aziz ibn Baaz

Ruling concerning listening to (radio) programs that have music in between them

Q. What is the ruling concerning listening to radio programs, such as news or the like, that have music being played in them during intervals?

A. There is no problem in listening to these programs and benefiting from them as long as it is turned off when the music starts until it is finished. Music is one of the tools of entertainment (that are prohibited). May Allah make it easy for us to leave it and protect us from its evil.

Shaykh 'Abdul 'Aziz ibn Baaz

Rulings concerning songs and watching destructive serials

Q. What is the ruling concerning listening to music and songs? And the ruling regarding watching TV serials in which women are adorned and beautified?

A. The ruling of these things is that they are forbidden (*ḥaraam*) because they drive away from the path of Allah, cause diseases of the heart, and contain the danger of falling into what Allah, the Almighty, has forbidden such as illegal sexual intercourse. Allah, the Almighty, says:

﴿وَمِنَ ٱلنَّاسِ مَن يَشۡتَرِي لَهۡوَ ٱلۡحَدِيثِ لِيُضِلَّ عَن سَبِيلِ ٱللَّهِ بِغَيۡرِ عِلۡمٖ وَيَتَّخِذَهَا هُزُوًاۚ أُوْلَٰٓئِكَ لَهُمۡ عَذَابٞ مُّهِينٞ ۝٦ وَإِذَا تُتۡلَىٰ عَلَيۡهِ ءَايَٰتُنَا وَلَّىٰ مُسۡتَكۡبِرٗا كَأَن لَّمۡ يَسۡمَعۡهَا كَأَنَّ فِيٓ أُذُنَيۡهِ وَقۡرٗاۖ فَبَشِّرۡهُ بِعَذَابٍ أَلِيمٍ ۝٧﴾

(لقمان : ٦-٧)

"*And of mankind is he who purchases idle talks to mislead [people] from the path of Allah without knowledge, and takes it [i.e. the path of Allah] by way of mockery. For such there will be a humiliating torment. And when Our verses are recited to such a person, he turns away in pride as if he did not hear them, as if there were some deafness in his ear. So announce to him a painful torment.*" *(Qur'an 31: 6-7)*

So in these two noble verses there is proof that listening to the tools of idle talks and songs are means of one going astray and leading others astray as well. They are also a means that will lead a person to take the verses of Allah as mockery and make him turn away in pride from listening to them.

Shaykh 'Abdul 'Aziz ibn Baaz

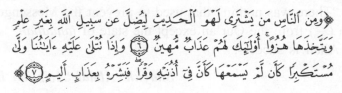

People say about me that I am complicated and difficult

Q. I am a young girl who lives in a dormitory with other female students. Allah has guided me to the truth and I have thus become firm upon it, all praises are to Allah. However, I become very depressed when I see the sins and evil actions performed around me by my colleagues such as listening to songs, backbiting and slandering. I have advised them many times but some of them make fun of me and mock at me also. They say I am complicated and difficult. Noble Shaykh, I hope you can guide me on this issue as to what I should do. May Allah reward you with good.

A. It is obligatory to you to speak out against evil according to your ability. You should be soft-spoken and have good manners along with mentioning the verses and ḥadiths that you know are related to the topic. You should not participate with them in the songs or in other acts that are forbidden. Try to stay away from them as much as you can until they change the topic. Allah, the Almighty, says:

﴿وَإِذَا رَأَيْتَ ٱلَّذِينَ يَخُوضُونَ فِيٓ ءَايَٰتِنَا فَأَعْرِضْ عَنْهُمْ حَتَّىٰ يَخُوضُوا۟ فِى حَدِيثٍ غَيْرِهِۦ ...﴿٦٨﴾﴾ (الأنعام: ٦٨)

"*And when you see those who engage in false conversation about Our verses by mocking at them, stay away from them till they turn to another topic...*"

(Qur'an 6: 68)

As long as you forbid them with your tongue and stay away from their actions, it will not harm you and the blame of their actions will not come upon you. Allah, the Almighty, says:

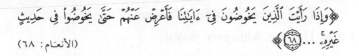

﴿ يَٰٓأَيُّهَا ٱلَّذِينَ ءَامَنُوا۟ عَلَيْكُمْ أَنفُسَكُمْ ۖ لَا يَضُرُّكُم مَّن ضَلَّ إِذَا ٱهْتَدَيْتُمْ ۚ إِلَى ٱللَّهِ مَرْجِعُكُمْ جَمِيعًا فَيُنَبِّئُكُم بِمَا كُنتُمْ تَعْمَلُونَ ١٠٥ ﴾

(المائدة: ١٠٥)

"*O' you who believe, take care of yourselves. If you follow the right guidance and forbid what is wrong, no harm can come to you from those who are in error. The return of you all is to Allah, then He will inform you about all that which you used to do.*"

(Qur'an 5: 105)

So Allah made it clear that, as long as a believer sticks to the truth and stays firm upon it, the wrongdoers will not be able to harm him. A person is to do this by forbidding the wrong actions, as well as being firm upon the truth and calling to it in a wise manner. If you do this, Allah will then make a way out for you and make them benefit from your advices if you have patience and hope for reward, if Allah wills. Rejoice at the great reward and the happy end as long as you are firm upon the truth and prohibit what opposes it. As Allah, the Almighty says:

﴿ ... وَٱلْعَٰقِبَةُ لِلْمُتَّقِينَ ٨٣ ﴾ (القصص: ٨٣)

"*And the good end is for the pious...*" *(Qur'an 28: 83)*

And also He, the Almighty, says:

﴿ وَٱلَّذِينَ جَٰهَدُوا۟ فِينَا لَنَهْدِيَنَّهُمْ سُبُلَنَا ۚ وَإِنَّ ٱللَّهَ لَمَعَ ٱلْمُحْسِنِينَ ٦٩ ﴾

(العنكبوت: ٦٩)

"*As for those who strive hard in Our cause, We will surely guide them to Our paths. And verily Allah is with the good doers.*" *(Qur'an 29: 69)*

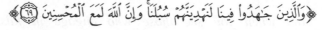

May Allah guide you to what pleases Him, give you patience and firmness, and guide your friends and family to what He loves and is pleased with. Verily, He is the Hearer, the Near, and He guides to the straight path.

Shaykh 'Abdul 'Aziz ibn Baaz

Being shy in condemning the people from backbiting and slandering

Q. I am a young girl who dislikes backbiting and slandering. Sometimes I find myself in the middle of a group of people who are talking about the affairs of people and then they start to backbite and slander. I dislike this within myself, but I am very shy and cannot prohibit them from this. Similarly, there is no other place where I can distance myself from them. Allah knows that I want them to change the topic. So is it a sin upon me to sit with them? What is obligatory upon me to do in such a situation? May Allah guide you to what will benefit Islam and Muslims.

A. There is a sin upon you unless you condemn the wrong. If they accept from you, then all praise is to Allah. But if they do not, it becomes obligatory upon you to distance yourself from them and not to sit with them. This is based on the saying of Allah, the Almighty:

﴿وَإِذَا رَأَيْتَ ٱلَّذِينَ يَخُوضُونَ فِىٓ ءَايَٰتِنَا فَأَعْرِضْ عَنْهُمْ حَتَّىٰ يَخُوضُوا۟ فِى حَدِيثٍ غَيْرِهِۦ ... ﴿٦٨﴾﴾ (الأنعام : ٦٨)

"*And when you see those who engage in false conversation about Our verses by mocking at them, stay away from them till they turn to another topic...*"

(Qur'an 6: 68)

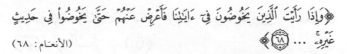

The Messenger of Allah (ﷺ) said:

> "Whoever sees an evil deed being performed should change it with his hand. If he is not able to change it with his hand, then (he should change it) with his tongue. And if he is not able to change it with his tongue, then (he should change it) with his heart, and that is the weakest form of *Eemaan*."

Imam Muslim reported this ḥadith in his *Ṣaḥeeḥ*. The verses and ḥadiths on this topic are numerous. And Allah is the source of success.

Shaykh 'Abdul 'Aziz ibn Baaz

You should enjoin good and forbid evil even if it means that the people who you are forbidding from evil will become angry with you

Q. If we enjoin the people with what is good and forbid what is evil, then what happens is that these people, who we speak to, start to abuse and insult us, and also become angry with us. So is there a sin upon us due to their anger, even if these people include our parents? Should we forbid them or leave them in affairs that do not concern us? Please guide us, may Allah guide you.

A. One of the most important obligatory actions is to enjoin good and forbid evil. Allah, the Almighty, says:

﴿وَٱلْمُؤْمِنُونَ وَٱلْمُؤْمِنَٰتُ بَعْضُهُمْ أَوْلِيَآءُ بَعْضٍ يَأْمُرُونَ بِٱلْمَعْرُوفِ وَيَنْهَوْنَ عَنِ ٱلْمُنكَرِ ... ﴿٧١﴾﴾ (التوبة : ٧١)

"*The believers, men and women, are auliyaa' [helpers, supporters, friends and protectors] of one another. They enjoin what is good and forbid what is evil...*"

(Qur'an 9: 71)

So Allah made it clear in this verse that among the obligatory traits of the believing men and women is the enjoining of good and forbidding from evil.

Allah, the Almighty, says:

﴿كُنتُمْ خَيْرَ أُمَّةٍ أُخْرِجَتْ لِلنَّاسِ تَأْمُرُونَ بِالْمَعْرُوفِ وَتَنْهَوْنَ عَنِ الْمُنكَرِ وَتُؤْمِنُونَ بِاللَّهِ ... ﴿١١٠﴾﴾ (آل عمران: ١١٠)

"*You are the best of people ever raised up for mankind; you enjoin good and forbid evil and you believe in Allah...*" *(Qur'an 3: 110)*

The Messenger of Allah (ﷺ) said:

> "Whoever sees an evil deed being performed should change it with his hand. If he is unable to change it with his hand, then (he should change it) with his tongue. And if he is not able to change it with his tongue, then (he should change it) with his heart, and that is the weakest form of *Eemaan*."

Imam Muslim reported this ḥadith in his *Saheeh*. The verses and ḥadiths are numerous that state the obligatory nature of enjoining good and forbidding evil, and condemning those who abandon such an act.

So, it is obligatory upon you and upon all male and female believers, to enjoin good and forbid evil, even if that means that the people whom you forbid will become angry with you. If they insult you, then you must have patience just like the Messenger of Allah (ﷺ) and those who followed him in goodness had patience. As Allah says, speaking to His Messenger (ﷺ):

﴿فَاصْبِرْ كَمَا صَبَرَ أُولُوا الْعَزْمِ مِنَ الرُّسُلِ ... ﴿٣٥﴾﴾ (الأحقاف: ٣٥)

"*Therefore be patient as did the Messengers of strong will [had patience before you]...*" *(Qur'an 46: 35)*

Also He, the Almighty, says:

﴿... وَٱصْبِرُوٓا۟ إِنَّ ٱللَّهَ مَعَ ٱلصَّـٰبِرِينَ ﴿٤٦﴾﴾ (الأنفال: ٤٦)

"*And be patient, surely Allah is with those who are patient.*" *(Qur'an 8: 46)*

Allah, the Almighty, said regarding the advice of the wise Luqmaan:

﴿يَـٰبُنَىَّ أَقِمِ ٱلصَّلَوٰةَ وَأْمُرْ بِٱلْمَعْرُوفِ وَٱنْهَ عَنِ ٱلْمُنكَرِ وَٱصْبِرْ عَلَىٰ مَآ أَصَابَكَ ۖ إِنَّ ذَٰلِكَ مِنْ عَزْمِ ٱلْأُمُورِ ﴿١٧﴾﴾ (لقمان: ١٧)

"*O' my son, perform the prayer and enjoin good and forbid evil, and bear with patience whatever befalls you. Verily, these are some of the important commandments.*" *(Qur'an 31: 17)*

There is no doubt that the amending of the community and their uprightness is due to Allah, the Almighty, and then due to enjoining good and forbidding evil. Similarly, its opposite, the corruption and destruction of the community, among the greatest causes that lead to it is the leaving of this act. This is based on an established ḥadith from the Messenger of Allah (ﷺ) who said:

"If the people see evil and wrongdoing and do not change it, then it maybe that Allah's punishment will come upon all of them."

Allah, the Almighty, cautioned His servants by mentioning how the disbelievers from the children of Israel were, with His saying:

﴿لُعِنَ ٱلَّذِينَ كَفَرُوا۟ مِنۢ بَنِىٓ إِسْرَٰٓءِيلَ عَلَىٰ لِسَانِ دَاوُۥدَ وَعِيسَى ٱبْنِ مَرْيَمَ ۚ ذَٰلِكَ بِمَا عَصَوا۟ وَّكَانُوا۟ يَعْتَدُونَ ﴿٧٨﴾ كَانُوا۟ لَا يَتَنَاهَوْنَ عَن مُّنكَرٍ فَعَلُوهُ ۚ لَبِئْسَ مَا كَانُوا۟ يَفْعَلُونَ ﴿٧٩﴾﴾

(المائدة: ٧٨-٧٩)

> *"Those among the children of Israel who disbelieved were cursed by the tongue of Dawood and 'Eesa, the son of Maryam. That was because they disobeyed and were transgressing beyond bounds. They did not use to forbid one another from evil and wrongdoing that they committed. Vile indeed was what they used to do."*
>
> *(Qur'an 5: 78-79)*

We ask Allah to guide all the Muslims, both leaders and general public, to hold up this obligation, and to amend their affairs. May He also protect everyone from the means that lead to His anger and punishment. Verily, He is the Hearer and the One who answers.

Shaykh 'Abdul 'Aziz ibn Baaz

Rulings concerning removal of bodily hair of a woman

Q. What is the ruling regarding the following for women:

1. Removing the hair from the armpits and the private parts
2. Removing the hair from the legs and arms
3. Removing the hair from the eyebrows when the husband requests it?

A. The following are the answers:

1. Removing the hair from the armpits and private parts is Sunnah. As for the armpits, it is better to pluck them, while for the private parts, it is better to shave them. However, if these hairs are removed in some other way, there is no problem.

2. As for removing the hair from the legs and arms of women, there is no blame in that on them. I do not know a problem in this.

3. Removing the hair from the eyebrows on request from the husband (or without it) is not allowed because the Messenger of

Allah (ﷺ) said:

> "Cursed is a woman who removes (or cuts) the eyebrows of other women and a woman who has it removed (or trimmed) from her."

Shaykh 'Abdul 'Aziz ibn Baaz

Ruling concerning giving preference to one of the children over others with wealth or other things

Q. Is it allowed for me to give one of my children what I do not give to others due to the others being rich?

A. No, it is not allowed for you to single out one of your children, whether male or female, with something. Instead, it is obligatory upon you to be just with all of them according to the rules of inheritance, or you can leave them all out. This is because the Messenger of Allah (ﷺ) said:

> "Fear Allah and be just with your children."

The two Imams, Bukhari and Muslim, reported this ḥadith.

However, if all your children agree to your singling out a child with something, then there is no problem if they are all mature and pious. Similarly, if one of your children is unable to work and earn, say due to an illness preventing work, and that child does not have a father or brother to spend on him, and does not have a monthly stipend from the government, then you should in this case spend on him according to the need until Allah makes him self sufficient.

Shaykh 'Abdul 'Aziz ibn Baaz

Dumping the food-remains along with the rest of the garbage and using newspapers as tablecloth

Q. Firstly, is it allowed to use newspapers (or other such things that contain the Names of Allah or verses of Qur'an) as tablecloths? And if it is not allowed, then what should be done after reading them? Secondly, with respect to the food-remains, some people put them in a carton or something like that and place it on the street for the animals to eat. But the cleaners come and put that with the rest of the garbage. My question is: is it allowed to put the food-remains with the rest of the garbage?

A. Firstly, it is not allowed to use the newspapers as tablecloths if they contain verses of the Qur'an or the Names of Allah, in which case they cannot be mistreated like other things. They should be kept in an appropriate safe place or burnt or buried in clean ground. (But if the newspapers do not contain verses from the Qur'an or the Names of Allah, then it is permissible to use them as one desires.)

Secondly, the food-remains should be handed over to the needy, if any. If there are no poor people, they should be placed far away from being misused, such that the animals can eat them. And even if that is not possible, they should be kept in cartons or bags or similar things and handed over to the council. They should make sure their workers put them in clean places such that the animals can eat from them, or people can take them for their animals, thus protecting the food from wastage and mistreatment.

Shaykh 'Abdul 'Aziz ibn Baaz

Relation of sins and the depriving of blessings

Q. I read that among the results of sins is punishment from Allah and depriving of blessings. The fear of this makes me cry. Please guide me, may Allah reward you with good.

A. It is obligatory to every male and female Muslim to avoid sins and to repent of whatever has happened along with having a good opinion of Allah, hope in His mercy and fearing His punishment. Allah, the Blessed and Almighty, said in His Noble Book about His pious slaves:

﴿...إِنَّهُمْ كَانُوا۟ يُسَٰرِعُونَ فِى ٱلْخَيْرَٰتِ وَيَدْعُونَنَا رَغَبًا وَرَهَبًا ۖ وَكَانُوا۟ لَنَا خَٰشِعِينَ ﴿٩٠﴾﴾ (الأنبياء: ٩٠)

"*...Verily, they used to hasten to do good deeds, and they used to call on Us with hope and fear and used to humble themselves before Us.*" *(Qur'an 21: 90)*

He, the Almighty, the All-Glorious, also said:

﴿أُو۟لَٰٓئِكَ ٱلَّذِينَ يَدْعُونَ يَبْتَغُونَ إِلَىٰ رَبِّهِمُ ٱلْوَسِيلَةَ أَيُّهُمْ أَقْرَبُ وَيَرْجُونَ رَحْمَتَهُۥ وَيَخَافُونَ عَذَابَهُۥٓ ۚ إِنَّ عَذَابَ رَبِّكَ كَانَ مَحْذُورًا ﴿٥٧﴾﴾

(الإسراء: ٥٧)

"*Those whom they invoke seek means of access to their Lord, as to which of them should be the nearest; and they hope for His mercy and fear His torment. Verily, the torment of your Lord is ever feared.*" *(Qur'an 17: 57)*

He, the Blessed and Almighty, also said:

﴿وَٱلْمُؤْمِنُونَ وَٱلْمُؤْمِنَٰتُ بَعْضُهُمْ أَوْلِيَآءُ بَعْضٍ ۚ يَأْمُرُونَ بِٱلْمَعْرُوفِ وَيَنْهَوْنَ عَنِ ٱلْمُنكَرِ وَيُقِيمُونَ ٱلصَّلَوٰةَ وَيُؤْتُونَ ٱلزَّكَوٰةَ وَيُطِيعُونَ ٱللَّهَ وَرَسُولَهُۥٓ ۚ أُو۟لَٰٓئِكَ سَيَرْحَمُهُمُ ٱللَّهُ ۗ إِنَّ ٱللَّهَ عَزِيزٌ حَكِيمٌ ﴿٧١﴾﴾

(التوبة: ٧١)

"The believers, men and women, are allies [helpers, supporters, friends and protectors] of one another. They enjoin what is good and forbid what is evil. They perform the prayer and give the zakah and obey Allah and His Messenger. Allah will have His mercy upon them. Surely, Allah is All-Mighty, All-Wise."

(Qur'an 9: 71)

It is also prescribed for a believer, both male and female, to strive to perform good deeds using means that have been allowed by Allah. By doing this, you will be combining both fear and hope, together with the performance of good deeds and reliance upon Allah. Verily, He is Generous and Bountiful.

He, the Almighty, also said:

﴿...وَمَن يَتَّقِ ٱللَّهَ يَجْعَل لَّهُۥ مَخْرَجًا ۝٢ وَيَرْزُقْهُ مِنْ حَيْثُ لَا يَحْتَسِبُ... ۝٣﴾ (الطّلاق : ٢-٣)

"...And whosoever fears Allah - He will make for him a way out [of every difficulty]. And He will provide for him from where he does not expect..."

(Qur'an 65: 2-3)

He, the Almighty, also said:

﴿...وَمَن يَتَّقِ ٱللَّهَ يَجْعَل لَّهُۥ مِنْ أَمْرِهِۦ يُسْرًا ۝٤﴾ (الطّلاق : ٤)

"And whosoever fears Allah - He will make his matter easy for him." (Qur'an 65: 4)

And finally, He, the Almighty, also said:

﴿... وَتُوبُوٓا۟ إِلَى ٱللَّهِ جَمِيعًا أَيُّهَ ٱلْمُؤْمِنُونَ لَعَلَّكُمْ تُفْلِحُونَ ۝٣١﴾ (النّور : ٣١)

"...And turn to Allah in repentance, all of you, O believers, that you might succeed." (Qur'an 24: 31)

So, it is obligatory upon you, O' sister, to repent to Allah, the Almighty, of what has happened of sins and then become upright in His obedience. Along with this, you should have a good opinion of Him and be cautious of deeds that lead to His anger. Have glad tidings of great reward and a praiseworthy end. And with Allah is success.

Shaykh 'Abdul 'Aziz ibn Baaz

Keeping photos for remembrance

Q. Is it permissible or not to keep photos with the intention of remembering?

A. It is not permissible for a male or female Muslim to keep photos for the purpose of remembering. That is, photos of living things among children of Adam and others. It is obligatory to destroy them due to what has been established from the Messenger of Allah (ﷺ) that he said to 'Ali (رضي الله عنه):

> "Do not leave a photo except that you efface and destroy it, and do not leave a raised grave except that you flatten it."

It is also established from the Messenger of Allah (ﷺ) that he prohibited photos being hung in the Ka'bah. So on the day of the conquer of Makkah when he entered the Ka'bah, he saw photos on its walls. He then requested water and a piece of cloth and wiped them off. As for photos of non-living things, such as mountains, trees and the like, there is no problem in keeping them.

Shaykh 'Abdul 'Aziz ibn Baaz

The voice of a woman

Q. It is said that a woman's voice is *'awrah*. Is this correct?

A. A woman is where man fulfils his desires, and thus men lean towards women due to the sexual desire. So if a woman makes her voice soft or flirts, the *fitnah* increases. For this reason, Allah ordered the believers to ask women what they need from behind a curtain. He, the Almighty, said:

﴿... وَإِذَا سَأَلْتُمُوهُنَّ مَتَٰعًا فَسْـَٔلُوهُنَّ مِن وَرَآءِ حِجَابٍ ۚ ذَٰلِكُمْ أَطْهَرُ لِقُلُوبِكُمْ وَقُلُوبِهِنَّ ... ﴿٥٣﴾﴾

(الأحزاب: ٥٣)

"...And when you ask [women] for anything you want, ask them from behind a screen. That is purer for your hearts and for their hearts..." *(Qur'an 33: 53)*

Women are prohibited from softening their speech when talking to men, such that one in whose heart is a disease should not be moved. As Allah, the Almighty, says:

﴿ يَٰنِسَآءَ ٱلنَّبِىِّ لَسْتُنَّ كَأَحَدٍ مِّنَ ٱلنِّسَآءِ ۚ إِنِ ٱتَّقَيْتُنَّ فَلَا تَخْضَعْنَ بِٱلْقَوْلِ فَيَطْمَعَ ٱلَّذِى فِى قَلْبِهِۦ مَرَضٌ وَقُلْنَ قَوْلًا مَّعْرُوفًا ﴿٣٢﴾﴾

(الأحزاب: ٣٢)

"O' wives of the Prophet, you are not like any other women. If you keep your duty [to Allah] then be not soft in speech lest in whose heart is a disease should be moved with desire, but speak in an honorable manner." *(Qur'an 33: 32)*

If this was the case when the believers were strong in their belief (at the time of the Companions), then how about our time, where the belief is really weak and the people who are adhering to the religion are few? So you should decrease your speaking to strange non-*maḥram* men. You should only speak when there is a necessity and even then, you should not soften your speech due to the order mentioned in the verse quoted above.

From this, you will know that normal voice and speech which does not have any softening in it is not considered to be *'awrah*. This is because the women at the time of the Messenger of Allah (ﷺ) used to speak to him and ask him questions concerning matters of the religion. Similarly, they used to speak to the Companions regarding any need that arose, and nobody ever forbade them from doing so. And with Allah is success.

The Permanent Committee for Research and Verdicts

Ruling concerning a woman leaving her house without permission from the husband

Q. What is the ruling concerning a woman going out to the market without her husband's permission?

A. If a woman wants to go out of her husband's house, she must inform him where she intends to go. Then if the husband allows her, she can then go out as long as there is no evil resulting from this. This is better and more safer for her due to the general saying of Allah, the Almighty:

﴿... وَبُعُولَتُهُنَّ أَحَقُّ بِرَدِّهِنَّ فِي ذَٰلِكَ إِنْ أَرَادُوٓا۟ إِصْلَٰحًا ۚ وَلَهُنَّ مِثْلُ ٱلَّذِى عَلَيْهِنَّ بِٱلْمَعْرُوفِ ۚ وَلِلرِّجَالِ عَلَيْهِنَّ دَرَجَةٌ ... ﴿٢٢٨﴾﴾ (البقـرة: ٢٢٨)

"...And their husbands have more right to take them back in this ('iddah period) if they want reconciliation. And due to them (wives) is similar to what is expected of them, according to what is reasonable. But men have a degree over them..." *(Qur'an 2: 228)*

Also, He, the Almighty, said:

﴿ٱلرِّجَالُ قَوَّٰمُونَ عَلَى ٱلنِّسَآءِ بِمَا فَضَّلَ ٱللَّهُ بَعْضَهُمْ عَلَىٰ بَعْضٍ...﴿٣٤﴾﴾ (النساء : ٣٤)

"*Men are in charge of women by (right of) what Allah has given one over the other...*" *(Qur'an 4: 34)*

The Permanent Committee for Research and Verdicts

Prohibited gifts

Q. I used to live in a society wherein men and women used to mix. A man gave me a bracelet as a gift due to something satanic he interpreted. And now, all praise is to Allah, I have managed to get out of such a society and know the true path. I regretted what happened in the past. So is this gift something that I have a right to keep and adorn myself with or should I give it away in charity or what should I do? I cannot return it to the person who gave it to me since I detest that society.

A. Praise and thank Allah for your well-being. What was given to you as a gift, do not return it but rather, give it away in charity.

The Permanent Committee for Research and Verdicts

Ruling regarding a woman boarding a taxi with a strange (i.e. non-*maḥram*) driver

Q. What is the ruling concerning a woman getting in a taxi with a strange (i.e. non-*maḥram*) driver?

A. It is not allowed for a man to seclude with a woman in a car except if he is a *maḥram* to her, because the Messenger of Allah (ﷺ) said:

"A man should not be alone with a woman except in the presence of a *maḥram* to the woman."

But, if there were to be two or more women in the car with the driver, that is not a problem, since it would not be considered seclusion. However, this should be on the condition of safety i.e. it should be safe for them to get in the car, and it should also not be a journey (wherein she is obliged to have a *maḥram* with her). And Allah is the One who gives success.

Shaykh Muḥammad ibn 'Uthaymeen

Shaking hands with a non-*maḥram*

> Q. We live in a town that has evil and disgusting customs. Among these, for example, is a practice that when a guest comes to the house, then all those present, both men and women, shake the guest's hands. If I abstain from this, they say to me I am abnormal and weird. So what is the ruling?

A. It is obligatory upon a Muslim to obey Allah, the Glorified and Almighty, by following His orders and staying far away from His prohibitions. Adhering to this is not abnormal or weird, but rather the abnormal is the one who goes against the orders of Allah. This custom, mentioned in the question, is an evil and a disgusting custom. It is prohibited for a woman to shake hands with a non-*maḥram* man, whether that is from behind a barrier or directly. This touching of a man and woman, when shaking hands, leads to *fitnah*. There are numerous ḥadiths reported on this topic that mention punishment for a person who does that. Some of them are authenticated as regards their chain of narrators, but the meaning put forward in each is correct. And Allah knows best.

I ask the questioner not to listen to the comments of her family. It is obligatory to her to advise them that they should stop this disgusting custom and do what would please Allah and His Messenger.

Shaykh Muḥammad ibn 'Uthaymeen

Purchasing magazines

Q. I take a lot of care in reading only magazines that are useful and ones that I can benefit from during my life. But I am faced with a problem, which is that there are photos in these magazines. So is there a problem in buying these magazines? And what should I do after that, should I keep them since I need them, or should I burn them?

A. You are allowed to read beneficial newspapers and magazines, and thus benefit from them, in terms of religion or language skills or manners. As for the photos contained therein, wipe them out with ink or something else that will get rid of them or of the faces shown therein. You can also cover them or leave the magazine in a closed place such, as inside a drawer or a box. When you no longer need these magazines, burn them.

Shaykh Muḥammad ibn 'Uthaymeen

Keeping a dog in the house

Q. We have a female dog in our house. We purchased it at a time when we did not know the ruling concerning keeping dogs without a reason. After we knew about this, we threw it out of the house but it did not go. It knows our house due to it being there for sometime. I do not want to kill it, so what is the solution?

A. There is no doubt that it is *ḥaraam* for a person to keep a dog except in things which the shari'ah has specified and has allowed its keeping. Whoever keeps a dog, except for the purpose of guarding, or hunting or farming, will have the equivalent of a *qiraaṭ* reduced from his reward everyday. If this is the case, then he is actually sinning because losing reward is like committing sin since both show that it is *ḥaraam*.

Let me take this opportunity to advise all those ignorant people who have been deluded by the disbelievers in keeping dogs. It is malicious and its impurity is the greatest of all animal impurities since it is required to wash its impurity (i.e. what it has licked with its tongue) seven times to clean it, once with soil. Even the pig, which Allah has mentioned in the Qur'an as being *ḥaraam* and filthy, its impurity is not to such a degree.

A dog is repugnant and impure. So it is with regret that we see some people being deluded by the disbelievers who tame these foul animals and keep them without any reason or necessity. They keep them, raise them and clean them, even though it can never ever become clean, even if you cleaned it with all the water of the sea. This is because it itself is impure. Furthermore, they spend a lot of money on them that leads to wastage of money, something that the Messenger of Allah (ﷺ) forbade.

So I advise these deluded people to repent to Allah, the Glorified and Almighty, and to remove the dogs from their houses. As for the one who needs a dog for hunting or guarding or on the farm, then there is no problem in that because the Messenger of Allah (ﷺ) allowed the keeping of dogs for these purposes.

What remains is the answer to the question: if you removed the dog from your house and threw it out, you are not responsible for it. Do not keep it in the house and do not give it shelter. Maybe if it remains outside the door for sometime (due to you not letting it in), it may go and leave your area, and eat from the provision of Allah, the Almighty, as all the other dogs eat.

Shaykh Muḥammad ibn 'Uthaymeen

Lying is prohibited, both as a joke and when being serious

Q. When some people speak with their friends, they lie a bit when joking with one another just to make the others laugh. So is this prohibited in Islam?

A. Yes it is prohibited in Islam because all forms of lying is prohibited and one should be wary of it. The Messenger of Allah (ﷺ) said:

"Telling the truth is a virtue and virtue leads to Paradise and a servant who endeavors to tell the truth is recorded as truthful with Allah. And be careful of lying for it leads one to obscenity and obscenity leads to Hell-Fire, and the servant who endeavors to tell a lie is recorded as a liar with Allah."

It is also reported that the Messenger of Allah (ﷺ) said:

"Woe to the one who lies to make people laugh...woe to him and woe to him."

So based on this, one should be careful not to lie at all, whether it is as a joke or when serious. If a person accustoms himself to speaking the truth and endeavors upon it, he will become truthful both inwards and outwards. For this reason, the Messenger of Allah (ﷺ) said:

"...and a servant who endeavors to tell the truth is recorded as truthful with Allah."

It is not hidden from us the results of speaking the truth (which are always good) and the results of lying (which are always evil).

Shaykh Muḥammad ibn 'Uthaymeen

Interpretation of seeing a dead person in a dream

Q. What is the interpretation of every time seeing a dead person in a dream?

A. If this dream in which the dead person was seen was good, then good can be expected for the dead person. However, if it was not as such, then it is from the actions of the *Shayṭaan* because the *Shayṭaan* does this sort of a thing to make the person alive feel sad. This is because the *Shayṭaan* is keen to employ any means that will instill sadness or grief or depression in a believer, as Allah, the Almighty, said:

﴿إِنَّمَا ٱلنَّجْوَىٰ مِنَ ٱلشَّيْطَٰنِ لِيَحْزُنَ ٱلَّذِينَ ءَامَنُوا۟ وَلَيْسَ بِضَآرِّهِمْ شَيْـًٔا إِلَّا بِإِذْنِ ٱللَّهِ ... ﴿١٠﴾﴾ (المجادلة : ١٠)

"*Secret counsels are only from Shayṭaan in order that he may cause grief to the believers. But he cannot harm them in the least except as Allah permits...*" *(Qur'an 58: 10)*

So based upon this, if a person sees in a dream what he dislikes concerning the dead, then he should seek refuge with Allah from the evil of the *Shayṭaan* and from the evil of what he saw. He should also not speak to anybody about the dream or what he saw regarding the dead. If this is done, the dead person will not be harmed at all. Furthermore, if anyone sees in his dream something he dislikes, it is prescribed for him to seek refuge with Allah from the evil of the *Shayṭaan* and from the evil of what he saw. He should also blow on his left side three times and then go back to sleep lying on the opposite side to which he was lying when he saw the dream. However, if he makes *wuḍoo'* and prays (after waking up from the dream), then it is good and better for him. He should not speak to anybody regarding what he saw in the dream and then it will not harm him.

Shaykh Muḥammad ibn 'Uthaymeen

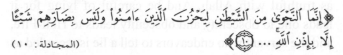

It is not permissible for a woman to kiss a non-*maḥram* man

Q. A woman kisses her sister's husband when giving *salaam* when he comes back from a journey. However, she does not shake his hands. So is this permissible, keeping in mind that one man she kisses is her cousin and the other is her sister's husband? I hope you can benefit, may Allah reward you with good.

A. It is not permissible for a woman to kiss a non-*maḥram* man, such as her sister's husband or her cousin, just like she is not permitted to display her adornments in front of them. This is because they are not *maḥrams* for her. It is permissible for her to give *salaam* to them while being covered and hidden, and without shaking hands. Similarly, this should not be done in seclusion with the man. If anyone sees such wrong acts, it is obligatory to him to forbid them and explain that such practices are similar to pre-Islamic practices that Islam nullified.

Shaykh 'Abdullah ibn Jibreen

This deed is not permissible

Q. Is it permissible for a woman to trim her eyebrows if they are broad and resemble that of men, and in order to beautify herself for her husband?

A. This is not permissible under any circumstances. Trimming of the eyebrows is not permissible and the Messenger of Allah (ﷺ) cursed both the woman who trims it for other women and the woman who has her eyebrows trimmed. This curse shows that the act is *ḥaraam*. There is no doubt that her beauty is in the way Allah has created her. The hairs of the eyebrows in a person's body have been created for beauty of the face. They protect the eyes from particles and other such things from the head. Hence removing or trimming them is changing the creation of Allah which is not permissible.

Shaykh 'Abdullah ibn Jibreen

The women will have husbands in Paradise

Q. We know that the men will have wives, *Ḥoor al-'een*, in Paradise. But what about the women in Paradise, will they have husbands or not?

A. Allah, the Glorified and Almighty, says regarding the pleasures of Paradise:

﴿...وَلَكُمْ فِيهَا مَا تَشْتَهِيٓ أَنفُسُكُمْ وَلَكُمْ فِيهَا مَا تَدَّعُونَ ﴿٣١﴾ نُزُلًا مِّنْ غَفُورٍ رَّحِيمٍ ﴿٣٢﴾﴾ (فُصِّلَت : ٣١-٣٢)

"*...Therein you shall have all that your inner-selves desire, and therein you shall have all for which you ask. An entertainment from [Allah] the Oft-Forgiving, Most Merciful.*" *(Qur'an 41: 31-32)*

Also, He, the Almighty, says:

﴿...وَفِيهَا مَا تَشْتَهِيهِ ٱلْأَنفُسُ وَتَلَذُّ ٱلْأَعْيُنُ وَأَنتُمْ فِيهَا خَٰلِدُونَ ﴿٧١﴾﴾ (الزخرف : ٧١)

"*...There will be in it all that the inner-selves could desire and all that eyes could delight in and you will abide therein forever.*" *(Qur'an 43: 71)*

It is known that marriage is one of the most desired things for the inner-selves and thus it will also happen in Paradise for its inhabitants, both male and female. As for the woman, Allah, the Glorified and Almighty, will get her married in Paradise to whoever she was married to in this world, as He, the Almighty, says:

﴿رَبَّنَا وَأَدْخِلْهُمْ جَنَّٰتِ عَدْنٍ ٱلَّتِى وَعَدتَّهُمْ وَمَن صَلَحَ مِنْ ءَابَآئِهِمْ وَأَزْوَٰجِهِمْ وَذُرِّيَّٰتِهِمْ... ﴿٨﴾﴾ (غافر: ٨)

"*Our Lord, and make them enter the Paradise which you have promised them and to the righteous among their fathers, their wives and their offspring...*"

(Qur'an 40: 8)

If it so happens that a woman had two husbands in this world (say for example, the first died and then she remarried), then she will be given the choice to choose between them in Paradise. And if a woman never got married in this world, then Allah, the Exalted, will get her married to someone who will be the delight of her eyes (i.e. she will be pleased with him) in Paradise.

Thus the pleasures in Paradise are not restricted to men but rather for men and women. And among these pleasures is marriage. However, one might say that Allah, the Exalted, mentioned *Ḥoor al-'een* who are the wives and did not mention husbands for women. So on this, we say that He mentioned wives for the husbands because it is the husband who seeks and desires.

Shaykh Muḥammad ibn 'Uthaymeen

The worst of people is one with two faces

Q. I see some people with "two faces", they speak to me in a way and to others in another way. Should I be quiet about it or inform others?

A. It is not allowed to be two-faced because the Messenger of Allah (ﷺ) said:

"You will find the worst of people a two-faced person, he comes to some people with a face and to others with another face."

The meaning of this is that he praises a person on his face, and does a good job of it for some worldly purpose, and then in his absence, he speaks ill of him in front of others and tries to find faults with him. This behavior of his will be the same with those whom he does not like.

So it is obligatory upon one who knows this to advise and warn him about this action that is a characteristic of the hypocrites. Also, that the people will soon know about him and his two-faced characteristic, thus resulting in the people disliking him, be cautious of him and stay away from him. This will ensure that this person's evil intentions will not be realized.

But if he does not take the advice and benefit from it, then it becomes obligatory to warn others of him and his actions, even if that is done in his absence. This is based on a ḥadith wherein the Messenger of Allah (ﷺ) said:

> "Mention to the people the evildoer so that they be careful of him."

Shaykh 'Abdullah ibn Jibreen

The voice of a woman is *'awrah*

Q. What is the ruling regarding a non-*maḥram* man hearing the voice of a woman over the phone or other communication channels?

A. The voice of a woman is *'awrah* for a non-*maḥram* man according to the correct opinion of the scholars. For this reason, she is not allowed to raise her voice during prayer when the Imam makes a mistake, the men are required to do so, but rather she may only clap or tap her hands. Similarly, she is not permitted to give the *adhaan* for prayer that is given in mosques since that requires the raising of the voice. Moreover, she is to lower her voice when saying the *talbiya* during the state of *iḥraam* (for Ḥajj or 'Umrah) such that only her companion (another woman or a *maḥram* man near her) can hear.

Some scholars have allowed her to speak to men only as much as is necessary such as answering a question. However, even this is to be done on the condition that it does not lead to anything harmful and on the condition of safety from arising desires. This is based on the saying of Allah, the Exalted:

﴿... فَلَا تَخْضَعْنَ بِٱلْقَوْلِ فَيَطْمَعَ ٱلَّذِى فِى قَلْبِهِۦ مَرَضٌ ... ﴿٣٢﴾﴾

(الأحزاب : ٣٢)

"*...Be not soft in speech, lest in whose heart is a disease should be moved with desire...*" *(Qur'an 33: 32)*

The disease of desiring illegal sexual intercourse may come in the heart if the woman softens her speech or if she discusses or enters into what happens between the husband and wife or the like. So based on this, a woman should speak on the phone only as much as is necessary whether she is the one who started the phone conversation or answered the phone, in which case she would have no choice but to speak (only as much as is necessary) since she did not initiate the call.

Shaykh 'Abdullah ibn Jibreen

Ruling concerning preferring some children over others

Q. Is it permissible for a woman to single out a child over others regarding greetings and welcoming. Note that all children behave the same towards the mother. Similarly, what about the case of the grandchildren who are equal in their behavior and greetings towards the grandmother but the grandmother is not equal in return. Please guide us, may Allah reward you with good.

A. A father should be just between all his children and should not prefer some to the others with gifts or other such things. This is because the Messenger of Allah (ﷺ) said:

"Fear Allah and be just with your children."

He (ﷺ) also said:

> "Do you want the children to be the same in the obedience to you? Then be equal with them all."

Some of the greatest scholars liked to be equal among their children, even when it came to kissing, smiling and greeting them. This is because of the order contained in the words of the Messenger of Allah (ﷺ) to be just with the children.

However, there may be times and situations when not being equal may be pardonable sometimes, such as when a father may prefer the youngest one or the ill child or similar due to affection and compassion. Otherwise, the required behavior is to be equal in all types of behavior especially if all the children are equal in the piety, obedience and faithfulness.

Shaykh 'Abdullah ibn Jibreen

Applying henna during menses is permissible

> Q. What is the ruling concerning applying henna during menses? And is it considered impure as long as its color remains on the hand?

A. It is permissible for a woman to apply henna on her hands (and hair etc.) during menses because her body is pure which is why it is permissible to shake hands with her (for a *maḥram*). It is established from the Messenger of Allah (ﷺ) that, when 'Aa'ishah (رضي الله عنها) was in her menses, he drank after her from the same glass and by putting his mouth on the same place where her mouth had touched the glass. He (ﷺ) said to her:

"Your menses is not in your hands (i.e. not in your control)."

So henna is pure and is applied to pure parts of the body and thus there is no objection in that.

Shaykh Muḥammad ibn 'Uthaymeen

Ruling concerning beating female students for discipline

Q. What is the ruling concerning beating the female students who require discipline and guidance regarding knowledge?

A. Being soft and kind is preferable on behalf of the teacher who teaches both small children and elder kids. However, if the situation calls for disciplining and beating, it is allowed as long as it is not severe. It is from the habit of the silly children to misbehave and disrespect, thus arising the need for serious action or sternness or more than just softness and kindness.

Shaykh 'Abdullah ibn Jibreen

Is it desirable to bury the nails and hair after cutting them

Q. I have seen some people when they cut their nails or hair, especially amongst the women, that they bury these nails and hair in the belief that throwing them outside and leaving them like that is a sin. So to what extent is this correct?

A. The people of knowledge have mentioned that it is better and more preferable to bury the hair and nails. Some reports to this effect have been narrated from the Companions (may Allah be pleased with them all). However, the belief that it is a sin to throw them outside and leave them like that in the open, is not at all true.

Shaykh Muḥammad ibn 'Uthaymeen

Follow the best course of action when advising a sinner

Q. Is it permissible to inform others about a close relative or friend who is doing *ḥaraam*, such as drinking, after I have advised him many times? Or would it be like a scandal for him, knowing that one who keeps quiet from portraying the truth is like a dumb *Shayṭaan*?

A. It is obligatory to a Muslim to advise his fellow Muslim brother whom he has seen committing a sin and to warn him against persisting in his disobedience to Allah, the Exalted. He should also be told of the punishment of sins and their ill effects upon the heart, soul and the body. Similarly, the sins have an ill effect on a person and the community as well. It maybe that due to continuous advices, he may desist from committing the sin and come to the right path.

But if that does not benefit him, then the person advising should choose the best course of action to stop this person from committing the sin. It maybe that he can inform people responsible for such things or someone who is higher in the eyes of the sinner than the person who has already tried to advise him.

At any rate, it is important that the best course of action is taken that will achieve the desired result, which is that the sinner stops committing his sin. It may be that you need to, at some point, inform the ruler (for example in a Muslim country) about this matter (depending on the person and the seriousness of his sin) so that the sinner can be detained.

Shaykh Muḥammad ibn 'Uthaymeen

A person who reads the Qur'an but cannot understand its meanings is also rewarded

Q. I am consistent in reciting the Qur'an. However, I do not understand its meanings. So will Allah reward me for the recitation?

A. The Noble Qur'an is blessed, as Allah, the Exalted, said:

﴿كِتَٰبٌ أَنزَلْنَٰهُ إِلَيْكَ مُبَٰرَكٌ لِّيَدَّبَّرُوٓا۟ ءَايَٰتِهِۦ وَلِيَتَذَكَّرَ أُو۟لُوا۟ ٱلْأَلْبَٰبِ ٢٩﴾

(ص : ٢٩)

"This is a book which We have sent down to you, full of blessings, that they may ponder over its verses, and that men of understanding may remember." *(Qur'an 38: 29)*

So a person is rewarded for reciting it, whether he can understand it or not. But a believer should not read the Qur'an without understanding its meanings. Say a person wanted to learn medicine for example and studied medical books, it is not possible for him to benefit from them until he understands what is contained in them and understands the meanings of it. In fact, he will take full care and try hard to understand the meanings so that he can implement them.

So what do you think regarding the Book of Allah, the Glorified and Exalted? This book is a cure for what is in the chests and an exhortation for the people. So how can a person read it without pondering over it and not understanding its meanings? It is for this reason that the Companions (may Allah be pleased with them all) used not to pass ten verses except that they learnt what they contained of meanings and acted by them.

So a person is rewarded for reciting the Qur'an whether he understood it or not. But one should be keen and exert effort to understand its meanings, which should be obtained from reliable scholars. This can be done by way of books of *tafseer* such as *tafseers* of Ibn Jareer, Ibn Katheer and others. And Allah knows best.

Shaykh Muḥammad ibn 'Uthaymeen

It is not permissible to throw anything that contains the Names of Allah

Q. We use magazines and newspapers that contain the Names of Allah and then throw them away in the rubbish. So what is the ruling?

A. It is not permissible to throw away anything that has verses of the Qur'an on it or the ḥadiths of the Messenger (ﷺ) in such places where they will be abused and mistreated. The words of Allah are great and thus it is obligatory to respect them, which is why a sexual defiled person is not allowed to read it. Similarly, a person who does not have *wuḍoo'* is not allowed to touch a copy of the Qur'an according to the opinion of many people of knowledge. Infact, most of them say this. So such newspapers or magazines should be totally burnt or shredded and ripped using the latest machines that do not leave a thing after it.

Shaykh Muḥammad ibn 'Uthaymeen

Example of an invalid will

Q. My father wrote in his will that the farm he possessed is to be given to his son only knowing that he has four daughters also apart from this son. So is this allowed? And if this farm were to be divided between all the daughters and the son, how should it be done?

A. Allah, the Glorified and Exalted, explained in His Book how the division of a dead person's property is to be done. He said:

﴿يُوصِيكُمُ ٱللَّهُ فِىٓ أَوْلَٰدِكُمْ ۖ لِلذَّكَرِ مِثْلُ حَظِّ ٱلْأُنثَيَيْنِ ... ﴿١١﴾﴾

(النساء: ١١)

"Allah commands you as regards your children's inheritance: to the male, a portion equal to that of two females..." *(Qur'an 4: 11)*

The Messenger of Allah (ﷺ) said:

> "Verily, Allah has given (in His orders concerning inheritance) the inheritors their rights. So it is not allowed to give anything extra to the inheritors from the will."

So based on this, the will of this father to give the farm to his son only is invalid and it is not permissible to be acted upon. Exception to this is if all the inheritors are happy with that and agree to act upon the will, then there is no problem.

However, if the inheritors do not agree and are not pleased, then the farm should be returned and considered as part of the wealth the father left behind and then all this wealth should be divided according to how Allah, the Glorified and Almighty, ordered. So it should be divided among all the inheritors.

Thus in this case, if the dead person does not have inheritors other than the son and four daughters, then his wealth is to be divided among them by giving the male a share equal to that of two females. The price of the farm would have to be estimated for this to be achieved (as well as anything else he left behind). Everything should be divided into shares and a female gets one share and a male gets two shares (i.e. a male gets twice that of a female based on the verse mentioned above).

Shaykh Muḥammad ibn 'Uthaymeen

The attendance of religious gatherings by women

Q. Is it permissible for a woman to attend religious gatherings and lessons on Islamic jurisprudence (*fiqh*) in the mosques?

A. Yes, a woman is allowed to attend religious gatherings. It is the same whether they are gatherings for jurisprudence (*fiqh*) or belief or *tawheed*. However, this is on the condition that she should not apply perfume or adornments, and should be far away from the men and mixing with them. This is because the Messenger of Allah (ﷺ) said:

> "Best of the rows for women are the last ones and the worst are the front rows."

This is because the front rows are closer to the men than the last ones thus making the last ones better than the front ones.

Shaykh Muḥammad ibn 'Uthaymeen

Ruling on committing suicide

Q. What is the ruling concerning suicide?

A. Committing suicide for whatever reason is *ḥaraam* and among the great sins. It is included in the general meaning of the saying of Allah, the Exalted:

﴿وَمَن يَقْتُلْ مُؤْمِنًا مُّتَعَمِّدًا فَجَزَآؤُهُ جَهَنَّمُ خَٰلِدًا فِيهَا وَغَضِبَ ٱللَّهُ عَلَيْهِ وَلَعَنَهُ وَأَعَدَّ لَهُ عَذَابًا عَظِيمًا ﴿٩٣﴾﴾

(النساء: ٩٣)

> *"And whoever kills a believer intentionally, his recompense is hell to abide therein. And the wrath and curse of Allah are upon him and a great punishment is prepared for him."* *(Qur'an 4: 93)*

It is established in the ḥadith that the Messenger of Allah (ﷺ) said whoever kills himself with something will be punished with it in the Hell fire forever. One who kills himself usually does so because of difficulties and hardships that he is facing either from Allah (i.e. His decrees) or from the people. You find that he is unable to cope with that. He is in reality like a person seeking refuge from the fire with the fire. So he, by committing suicide, has moved from what is bad to what is worse. If he had patience, Allah would have helped him bear the difficulties and hardships. As it is said, it is impossible for a certain situation (of a person) to continue forever (i.e. his difficulties and hardships would have ended and not continued forever, and so there was no need to commit suicide).

Shaykh Muḥammad ibn 'Uthaymeen

Permissible work for women

Q. What is the area in which it is allowed for women to work without it being contradictory to the teaching of Islam?

A. The area in which a woman can work is what is specific to women such as in teaching girls or working in her house sewing clothes for women and so on. As for working in areas that are specific to men, it is not allowed for her because it requires that she mixes with men. A woman is a great *fitnah* and men need to be careful of her. It should be known that the Messenger of Allah (ﷺ) said:

> "I have not left behind me a greater *fitnah* on men than women. The first *fitnah* of the children of Israel was with women."

So a man should keep his women relatives far away from places of *fitnah* or that cause *fitnah*.

Shaykh Muḥammad ibn 'Uthaymeen

What to do with newspapers that contain the Qur'an or Names of Allah after reading them

Q. What should we do with the newspapers (or other similar things that contain verses of the Qur'an or the Names of Allah) after reading them?

A. There is no doubt that the newspapers that contain the Names of Allah or verses from the Qur'an and ḥadiths, are not to be mistreated and thrown away. It is extremely regretful that some people use the newspapers as tablecloths, which is due to their ignorance. If a person can burn these newspapers (which contain the Names of Allah or verses and ḥadiths) then it is best. Otherwise, you should put them all together in a bag or tie them up and put them in a safe place in the house aside from rubbish. (But if they do not contain verses or Names of Allah or ḥadiths, then there is no problem in throwing them away with normal rubbish).

Shaykh Muḥammad bin 'Uthaymeen

Having sexual intercourse with a pregnant wife

Q. Is it permissible to have sexual intercourse with a pregnant wife? Has anything come in the Qur'an or ḥadiths that show it is allowed or disallowed?

A. It is allowed for a man to have sexual intercourse with his wife when she is pregnant because Allah, the Glorified and Almighty, said:

﴿نِسَآؤُكُمْ حَرْثٌ لَّكُمْ فَأْتُوا حَرْثَكُمْ أَنَّىٰ شِئْتُمْ ... ﴿٢٢٣﴾﴾ (البقرة: ٢٢٣)

"Your wives are a tilth for you, so go to your tilth when or how you will." *(Qur'an 2: 223)*

Also, Allah, the Exalted, said:

﴿ وَٱلَّذِينَ هُمْ لِفُرُوجِهِمْ حَـٰفِظُونَ ۝٥ إِلَّا عَلَىٰٓ أَزْوَٰجِهِمْ أَوْ مَا مَلَكَتْ أَيْمَـٰنُهُمْ فَإِنَّهُمْ غَيْرُ مَلُومِينَ ۝٦ ﴾ (المؤمنون: ٥-٦)

"*And those who guard their chastity [i.e. do not commit illegal sexual acts], except from their wives or [the slaves] that their right hands possess, for [in such a case], they are free from blame.*" *(Qur'an 23: 5-6)*

So, He, the Exalted, generalized when He said "their wives" because the basis is that a man is allowed to enjoy his wife in all situations except what has come in the Qur'an and Sunnah of situations when he should not come near the woman (i.e. not have sexual relations with her). So based on this, there is no need for proof regarding the permissibility of having sexual intercourse with his pregnant wife since that is the basis.

It is not allowed for a man to have sexual intercourse with his wife when she is in her menses. However, he can enjoy her in any other way he wishes. Similarly, it is not allowed to have sexual intercourse with the wife in her anus because it is a place of dirt and filth. Also, when a woman is in her post-natal bleeding period, a man is prohibited from having sexual intercourse with her. But when she becomes pure from the blood (both menstrual and post-natal bleeding), he is allowed to have sexual intercourse with her, even if the case is that she has become pure before the normal period of forty days of post-natal bleeding.

Shaykh Muḥammad ibn 'Uthaymeen

My mother is deviant and when I advise her, she becomes angry with me

Q. I see that my mother is not on the straight path. Every time I advise her, she becomes angry with me, and many days pass when she does not talk to me (due to the anger caused by my advices). So how can I advise her without her being angry with me and without Allah being angry with me? Or should I leave her without advising so that I gain the pleasure of my mother and Allah?

A. You should keep advising your mother and explain to her the sin she is committing and the punishment that she could face due to it. If she does not listen, inform her husband or her father or guardian so that they can advise her.

If what she is committing is from the great sins, then you should shun her, and her *du'aa's* (invocations) against you or whatever she says about you regarding disobedience or breaking ties with her etc., will not harm you. You are only doing this for Allah and forbidding the wrong that you see. However, if her sin is among the small sins, then you should not sever relations with her.

Shaykh 'Abdullah ibn Jibreen

A couple playing or enjoying outdoors should be done in secrecy

Q. The ḥadith wherein is mentioned that the Messenger of Allah (ﷺ) and the mother of the believers 'Aa'ishah (رضي الله عنها) had a running race, does it show that it is allowed for women to take part in sports? Please clear this issue for me.

A. This competition that took place between the Messenger of Allah (ﷺ) and 'Aa'ishah (رضي الله عنها) was in a specific situation. It appears to have been in the night after the people had gone to sleep when the competition took place. And it was either in the mosque or near it or perhaps on the outskirts of the city. It may be that the intention behind the competition was to increase and perfect the companionship, love and bond between the couple. So based on this, the ḥadith can be used for other such situations only.

Thus it is allowed for a man to do with his wife what is mentioned in the ḥadith on condition that it is done in secrecy and there is guarantee that it will not lead to *fitnah*.

As for outdoor sports, whether they are amusements or competitions or other such things, then these cannot be deduced from this incident and it should be restricted to the case between a husband and wife according to what we have described above. And Allah knows best.

Shaykh 'Abdullah ibn Jibreen

It is not allowed to prevent pregnancy except due to a necessity

> Q. I am a thirty-seven year old woman who has diabetics. In my last pregnancy, my illness gave me a lot of problems thus I took insulin injections. The delivery was a cesarean and so I had a loop put in. So is this permissible or is it *ḥaraam*? I already have eight children. May Allah give you success and reward you.

A. It is not allowed to have treatment to prevent pregnancy, both permanently or temporarily, except due to necessity. If well known and competent doctors say that the pregnancy will increase the illness or they have a strong belief that it will lead to death, then it is allowed but on condition that the husband is consulted and he agrees whether for the permanent prevention or the temporary solution.

Then, whenever the danger has subsided, the woman should be returned to the normal situation (i.e. if a loop was put in for example, then it should be removed). Among the things that would be considered as a necessity are a woman's illness or her body being weak.

Shaykh 'Abdullah ibn Jibreen

The property and *maḥr* (dowry) of a woman

Q. Is it permissible for a husband to take the wealth of his wife and add it to his wealth if the wife has agreed to that and is pleased? Or do the children have to agree as well?

A. There is no doubt that the wife is more deserving of her *maḥr* and her wealth that she possesses, either through earning (taking into account its conditions), or gifts, or inheritance or any other means. It is her property and she, alone, has the right to do with it what she likes. However, if she has agreed for it or part of it to be taken by the husband, it is allowed for her to do that and it then, becomes permissible for the husband to take. Allah, the Exalted, said:

﴿وَءَاتُوا۟ ٱلنِّسَآءَ صَدُقَـٰتِهِنَّ نِحْلَةً ۚ فَإِن طِبْنَ لَكُمْ عَن شَىْءٍ مِّنْهُ نَفْسًا فَكُلُوهُ هَنِيٓـًٔا مَّرِيٓـًٔا ﴿٤﴾﴾ (النساء : ٤)

"And give to the women their maḥr with a good heart. But if they of their own good pleasure remit any part of it to you, take it and enjoy it without fear of any harm."
(Qur'an 4: 4)

So the condition for this is that she must give it of her own free will. There is no need to ask the children or anyone else if the wife is sensible and wise. But it is not allowed for the wife to boast about the wealth or to make it as a favor to the husband. Similarly, it is not allowed for the husband to ill-treat her or harm her if she does not give the money. It is her property and she is most deserving of it. And Allah knows best.

Shaykh 'Abdullah ibn Jibreen

Looking at photos of women in magazines or movies

Q. Is it permissible to look at photos of naked women in magazines or watching them in movies?

A. It is not allowed to look at naked women's photos. Similarly, it is not allowed to purchase these films or the magazines that contain such photos. Rather, it is obligatory to burn them so that evil and obscenity, as well as all means that lead to it do not spread.

Shaykh 'Abdullah ibn Jibreen

Ruling regarding listening to songs and watching lewd TV serials

Q. What is the ruling regarding listening to music and songs? Also, watching TV serials in which women are shown adorned and beautified?

A. Listening to music and songs is *haraam* and there is no doubt in that. Reports have come from the Companions (may Allah be pleased with all of them) and the *tabi'een* (followers of the Companions) that songs lead to hypocrisy in the heart. Listening to songs is among the idle talks and having reliance upon them. Allah, the Exalted, said:

﴿وَمِنَ ٱلنَّاسِ مَن يَشْتَرِى لَهْوَ ٱلْحَدِيثِ لِيُضِلَّ عَن سَبِيلِ ٱللَّهِ بِغَيْرِ عِلْمٍ وَيَتَّخِذَهَا هُزُوًا أُو۟لَـٰٓئِكَ لَهُمْ عَذَابٌ مُّهِينٌ ۝٦﴾ (لقمان : ٦)

"*And of mankind is he who purchases idle talks to mislead [people] from the path of Allah without knowledge, and takes [the verses of Allah and His path] by way of mockery. For such there will be a humiliating torment [in the Hell-fire].*" *(Qur'an 31: 6)*

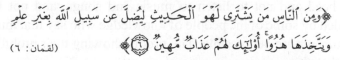

Ibn Ma'sood (ﷺ) said in his explanation of the meaning of this verse: "By Allah apart from Whom there is no other god worthy of worship, what is referred to here is songs." The explanation given by a Companion is considered authoritative. It comes in the third level when explaining the Qur'an since the levels are: explanation of the Qur'an using the Qur'an, then explanation of the Qur'an using the Sunnah, and then explanation of the Qur'an using the sayings of the Companions.

Some scholars are of the opinion that what a Companion says as an explanation of a verse is considered to be the saying of the Messenger of Allah (ﷺ). However, the correct opinion in this matter is not this but rather that a Companion's explanation (of the Qur'an) is the closest to the truth when compared with other scholars' explanations (of the Qur'an).

Also, listening to music and songs comes under what the Messenger of Allah (ﷺ) warned against when he said:

> "From among my followers there will be some people who will consider illegal sexual intercourse, the wearing of silk, the drinking of alcoholic drinks and the use of musical instruments, as lawful."

Imam Bukhari has reported this ḥadith on the authority of Abu Malik al-Ash'ari or Abu 'Aamir al-Ash'ari.

So, based on this, I would like to advise my Muslim brothers to take heed and not to listen to music and songs, and not to be deluded by some of the people of knowledge who say that musical instruments are permissible. The proofs showing their prohibition and that they are *ḥaraam* are clear cut.

As for watching TV serials that have women in them, it is *ḥaraam* since they lead to *fiṭnah*, and watching women and these shows both have a negative and harmful effect. Even if the shows did not contain women and the person watching did not see any women, or a woman did not see any man, even then, they are harmful since their goal is evil. They want to ruin the behavior of the society and their manners.

I ask Allah, the Exalted, to protect the Muslims from their evil and to guide the leaders of the Muslims' affairs to that which contains their benefit. And Allah knows best.

Shaykh Muḥammad ibn 'Uthaymeen

It is not permissible for a woman to shake hands with a man even if she is wearing gloves

Q. Is it permissible to pray in front of a natural landscape? And is a woman sinning if she shakes hands with a man when she is wearing gloves?

A. It is not permissible for a woman to shake hands with a strange non-*maḥram* man even with gloves or from under the sleeve or the outer garments since all that is considered to be shaking hands. As for the prayer mentioned in the question, it is not allowed if the picture is of something that will distract the person praying (and of course it cannot contain anything with a soul since that in itself is prohibited). However, if it is something normal (like a landscape), there is no problem in that.

Shaykh 'Abdullah ibn Jibreen

Mixing between men and women occurring in hospitals

Q. I work in a hospital. The nature of my work is such that I have to always mix with strange women for whom I am not a *maḥram* and also I have to talk to them. So what is the ruling regarding this? And what is the ruling concerning shaking hand with a woman, especially during the month of Ramaḍaan?

A. It is not permissible to mix with women since it has danger associated with it especially if they are adorned and not covered properly. It is obligatory to you to stay away from mixing and seek another job that is safe and does not involve mixing (with women). There are numerous jobs, thanks to Allah.

Similarly, it is *ḥaraam* to shake hands with a woman for whom you are not a *maḥram* because that will lead to *fiṭnah* and arouse desires. The hand of the Messenger of Allah (ﷺ) never touched a woman for whom he was not a *maḥram*. When he took oaths from them, he did so by speech.

Shaykh 'Abdullah ibn Jibreen

It is not permissible to take money from husband's pocket

Q. I am a married woman. I have a house, children and of course a husband, thanks to Allah. I pray, fast and perform all other things that Allah has made obligatory to me. I have a simple question that I hope you can answer. What I do is that from the spending money of the house, I save some without the knowledge of my husband. Similarly, I take money from his pockets without him knowing. But thanks to Allah, I do not spend this money in what may make Allah angry with me but I save it because I fear what may happen in the future to us and to my children. So, is there anything in this that may be a sin upon me, because I fear Allah and His punishment?

A. In my opinion, it is not allowed for you to take from his pocket without him knowing with the intention of saving the money as long as he is not stingy in spending upon you and the children. Similarly, I see that it is not allowed for you to ask your husband for expenses (money) as long as you still have money left over from what you saved from the previous times when he gave money to you. It is the husband who saves the money for the future and guards it.

So, based on this, you should return the saved money to him or inform him of that or seek his agreement for what you already have since the money is basically his money that was kept from him without his knowledge.

Shaykh 'Abdullah ibn Jibreen

It is not permissible to grow the nails long

Q. Is the growing of the nails for the purpose of beauty *ḥaraam*?

A. It is not permissible to grow the nails long. In fact, there is an order to clip them every week or, at most, every forty days.

Shaykh 'Abdullah ibn Jibreen

It is not permissible to keep voluntary fasts before making up for the missed ones

Q. If a woman has some fasts left which she has not observed in the month of Ramaḍaan and still has not made up for them, is it allowed for her to observe voluntary fasts, such as the fast on the day of *'Arafah*?

A. It is obligatory to hasten to make up for the fasts missed during Ramaḍaan, as performing the voluntary fasts before making up for the obligatory fasts is not correct. If a person fasts, say for example, the day of *'Arafah* or any other day with the intention of voluntary fast, it does not reduce the number of fasts that are to be made up for. However, if the fasts are kept with the intention that it is part of the debt from Ramaḍaan, that is correct and that will be rewarded if Allah, the Exalted, wills.

Shaykh 'Abdullah ibn Jibreen

A woman serving her father-in-law

Q. I am a woman who serves my father-in-law since he is a man who has nobody else but my husband. So do I have the right to wash him and take care of him?

A. As for you taking care of your father-in-law, it is something that you should be thanked for because you are doing good to this old person and you are also doing good to your husband (by taking care of his father). You are allowed to wash him except his *'awrah* (between the navel and the knee). As for the *'awrah*, if he can wash it himself, that is good but it is not allowed for you to do that. However, if he cannot, there is no problem in you washing him on condition that you wear gloves so that you do not actually touch his *'awrah*. Similarly, you should also close your eyes and not look at his *'awrah* because it is not allowed for you to look at anyone's *'awrah* except your husband's.

Shaykh Muḥammad ibn 'Uthaymeen

Cheating in subjects other than Islamic

Q. What is the ruling concerning cheating in an English language course or subjects such as maths and so on?

A. It is not allowed to cheat in any subject, no matter what the subject is, because the purpose of the examination is to test the student and estimate his level in that subject. Also, cheating has other things associated with it, such as laziness, deceiving and putting forward a weak student over a strong student.
The Messenger of Allah (ﷺ) said:

"Whoever cheats is not from us."

The word cheating here is used in its general implication and covers all forms for cheating. And Allah knows best.

Shaykh 'Abdullah ibn Jibreen

A woman cutting her hair

Q. What is the ruling concerning a woman cutting her hair?

A. In the Ḥanbali *madhhab*, it is considered *makrooh* (disliked) for a woman to cut her hair. But if she cuts it in such a way that it resembles men's hair, then it is *ḥaraam* because the Messenger of Allah (ﷺ) said:

"Allah curses the women who try to resemble men."

Similarly, if she cuts it in such a way that it resembles the hair of *kaafir* women, then again it is *ḥaraam* because it is not allowed to resemble the disbelievers, as the Messenger of Allah (ﷺ) said:

"Whoever imitates a people is of them."

But if after the cut, it does not resemble men's hairstyle nor *kaafir* womens' hair, then its ruling is *makrooh* according to the Ḥanbali scholars, may Allah have mercy upon him.

Shaykh Muḥammad ibn 'Uthaymeen

Does the severity of an illness wipe out sins?

Q. Do the pains of death wipe out sins? And similarly, does an illness wipe out sins? I hope you can benefit.

A. Yes, whatever befalls a person, such as an illness, or misfortune, grief, worry or even the pricking of a thorn will wipe out some sins. Moreover, if a person also has patience and hopes for reward from Allah, there will be reward for this along with the wiping of some sins for the pain he faced with patience. There is no difference in this between what happens at the time of death and what happens before that. So the misfortunes are a means of sins being wiped out with respect to a believer. The basis for this is the saying of Allah, the Exalted:

﴿وَمَآ أَصَٰبَكُم مِّن مُّصِيبَةٍ فَبِمَا كَسَبَتۡ أَيۡدِيكُمۡ وَيَعۡفُواْ عَن كَثِيرٖ ٣٠﴾ (الشورى : ٣٠)

"And whatever of misfortune befalls you, it is because of what your hands have earned. And He pardons much."
(Qur'an 42: 30)

So, if this is due to what we have done (of sins), then it shows that it is an atonement for what we have done and earned. Similarly, the Messenger of Allah (may the peace and blessings of Allah be upon him) informed that there is not a grief or sorrow or trouble, even the pricking of a thorn, except that Allah will wipe out some sins because of it.

Shaykh Muḥammad ibn 'Uthaymeen

Using eggs, honey and milk as a cure for freckles and pimples is permissible

Q. Some of my friends use eggs, honey and milk to treat freckles and pimples, so is this permissible?

A. It is known that these things (eggs, honey and milk) are part of our food which Allah, the Almighty and Glorified, has created for the nourishment of our body. So if a person needs these things for another purpose that is not impure, such as treatment, there is no problem in that because of the saying of Allah, the Exalted:

﴿هُوَ ٱلَّذِي خَلَقَ لَكُم مَّا فِي ٱلۡأَرۡضِ جَمِيعٗا ... ٢٩﴾

(البقرة : ٢٩)

"He [i.e. Allah] is the One who created for you all that is on the earth." *(Qur'an 2: 29)*

So, when Allah said "for you", it includes any type of benefit as long as it is not considered *ḥaraam* in the Shari'ah.

As for using it for beautification, there are other things, apart from these, that give beauty and using them is better. Know that there is nothing wrong in beautification, for Allah, the Glorified, is Beautiful and loves beauty. However, one should not be extravagant and should not go to extremes in this, so that it becomes the main concern or the only concern of a person. By doing this, a person will neglect many other beneficial things for his religion and his worldly life. Doing this would be considered extravagance that Allah does not like.

Shaykh Muḥammad ibn 'Uthaymeen

Ruling concerning clapping and whistling

Q. What is the ruling concerning what some people do in parties such as clapping and whistling?

A. Its ruling is that it seems to have been taken from the disbelievers for which reason a Muslim should not do it. If something pleases or delights you, say *Allahu Akbar* or *Subḥanallah*. However, this should not be done in a group as is done by some people. Rather, it should be said within oneself. As for saying *Subḥanallah* or *Allahu Akbar* in a group, I do not know of any basis for this act. (Similarly, women should not raise their voices if there are non-*maḥram* men near them).

Shaykh Muḥammad ibn 'Uthaymeen

Making fun of teachers and calling them names

Q. Some students make fun of the teachers and give them names, either funny names or insulting names. They say that they do not mean that but rather they are only joking. So is this permissible?

A. A Muslim should control his tongue from what may hurt other Muslims or degrade them. There is a ḥadith that says:

> "Do not harm the Muslims and do not try to uncover their secrets."

And Allah, the Exalted, said:

﴿وَيۡلٞ لِّكُلِّ هُمَزَةٖ لُّمَزَةٍ ۝١﴾ (الهُمَزة: ١)

"*Woe to every slanderer and backbiter.*"

(Qur'an 104: 1)

He, the Exalted, also said:

﴿هَمَّازٖ مَّشَّآءِۭ بِنَمِيمٖ ۝١١﴾ (القلَم: ١١)

"*A slanderer, going about with his calumnies.*"

(Qur'an 68: 11)

And He, the Exalted, said:

﴿... وَلَا تَنَابَزُواْ بِٱلۡأَلۡقَٰبِۖ ... ۝١١﴾ (الحُجرَات: ١١)

"*And do not call one another with names.*"

(Qur'an 49: 11)

So, we see that degrading and hurting a Muslim is *ḥaraam*.

Shaykh 'Abdullah ibn Jibreen

It is not permissible for a teacher to lower the grade (or marks) of a student

> Q. Some teachers lower the grade of a student than what they deserve when marking and assign them a grade based on their emotions. So what does the Shari'ah have to say about this matter?

A. It is *ḥaraam* to a teacher to do injustice to a student or to prevent him from getting what he deserves or even to give him more marks than he deserves for whatever reason. The teacher should be just and behave equally among students and give them what they deserve.

Shaykh 'Abdullah ibn Jibreen

It may be that you dislike something and Allah brings a great deal of good through it

Q. I started to work in a company five years ago and since I joined, I have not been satisfied with it and would like to change my job because I am unable to fulfill my duties properly. Before I thought about changing jobs, I prayed the *Istikhaarah* (pray, seeking the guidance of Allah to opt or do the right) prayer hoping that my decision will be correct. Then my heart opened up and I decided to leave the job. Whenever I try to leave the job, I find that all other opportunities close on me and the situation comes back to the way it was (i.e. I am still in this company). Since that time, I have been trying to leave my work but am unable to. My question is: is it permissible to pray the *istikhaarah* prayer for this purpose? And if it is prescribed and permissible, then what is Allah's wisdom in me still being in this job since five years even though I dislike it and am unable to change it. Please guide mc, may Allah reward you with good.

A. Do not dislike your stay in this job, even if it is a long time because it may be better than other jobs. Along with this, you should continue your efforts to fulfill your work requirements and if you fall short, then you are not to blame. And there is no problem in searching for another job. Never give up hope of Allah's Mercy. Do not feel that the response to your supplication is slow or not coming, persist in it, and it may be good for you.

The *istikhaarah* prayer is a Sunnah and a virtuous act. It maybe that in Allah's knowledge, it is better for you to stay in this current job rather than something else, even though you dislike it.

Shaykh 'Abdullah ibn Jibreen

A woman secretly taking money from her husband to pay off his debt

Q. A woman used to save her husband's money from what he gave her for expenses of the house in order to pay off a debt that he had towards her brother. She did this without his knowledge. Then one day she told him suddenly, but then the husband was happy with what she did. Later on, the husband started to doubt his wife and would not trust her anymore, even though she is a very religious woman and her intention was good. There are some people around the husband who have complicated the issue and have made the husband doubt her because of what she did. Now this woman wants to know if the act she did was a sin or not?

A. This woman did a good thing as well as a bad thing. She did good in that she was keen to free her husband from his debt and thus she wanted good for him. Also, maybe her intention benefited her brother too by giving him his right (i.e. the money) as quickly as possible because maybe her husband may have delayed the payment of the debt even though he could pay it off earlier. She also wanted that her brother's money paid back to him as quickly as possible since he may be in need of it. Thus she took this step.

However, at the same time, she did a bad thing that resembles cheating and misappropriated the money and also hid some of the money which she used to take for house expenses and thus she was a liar in this respect. So we advise the husband to pardon his wife and think good of her. He should also return his trust in her and be at peace with her once again.

Shaykh 'Abdullah ibn Jibreen

Ruling concerning selling gold that has drawings and pictures

Q. What is the ruling concerning selling gold that has drawings and pictures, such as a butterfly or the head of a snake or something like that?

A. It is *ḥaraam* to wear, buy or sell jewelry that is made out in the shape of animals (or that has animals on it). It is even *ḥaraam* to possess it because it is obligatory for a Muslim to erase and efface it. This is based on a ḥadith in *Ṣaḥeeḥ Muslim* on the authority of Abu Hayyaaj who said that 'Ali ibn Abi Ṭaalib (رضي الله عنه) told him: "Should I not send you on a mission on which the Messenger of Allah (ﷺ) sent me? He sent me not to leave a photo except that I erase and efface it, and to not leave a raised grave except to flatten it." It is also proven from the Messenger of Allah (ﷺ) that he said:

"The angels do not enter a house that has pictures."

Imams Bukhari and Muslim reported this ḥadith on the authority of Ibn 'Abbaas. So based on this, it is obligatory to a Muslim to keep away from using such jewelry, or buying and selling it.

Shaykh Muḥammad ibn 'Uthaymeen

GLOSSARY

Adhaan	أذان :	Call to prayer
Allahu Akbar	اللّٰه أكبر :	Allah is All-Great
Al-Aḍḥaa	الأضحى :	The Feast of Sacrifice
Al-Faatiḥah	الفاتحة :	The opening soorah (chapter) of the Qur'an
Al-Fiṭr	الفِطْر :	The Feast of Breakfast at the end of Ramaḍaan
Al-Masjid al-Ḥaraam	المسجد الحرام :	The Holy Mosque in Makkah
Al-Masjid al-Aqṣa	المسجد الأقصى :	The Holy Mosque in Jerusalem
A'oodhu	أعوذ :	I seek refuge
'Arafah	عَرفة :	A plain with a hill in the sacred Ḥajj area
Ar-rajeem	الرَّجيم :	An attribute of Satan, the stoned, the accursed
'Aṣr	عَصْر :	Afternoon prayer, afternoon
Aṣ-Ṣaḥaabah	الصَّحابة :	The Prophet's companions (May Allah be pleased with them)
'Awrah	عَوْرة :	Parts of the body that must be covered: a) for men: from the navel to the knees,

		b) for women: all parts of the body except the face and the hands
Bid'ah	بِدْعَة :	Heresy, reprehensible innovation in religion
Dinaar	دينار :	A unit of currency in some Arab countries
Du'aa'	دُعَاء :	Supplication, invocation
'Eid	عِيد :	Feast
Fajr	فَجْر :	Dawn, Dawn prayer
Farḍ	فَرْض :	Obligatory, duty, must be done
Fatḥ	فَتْح :	Conquest, opening
Fatwaa	فَتْوى :	(Pl.: Fataawa) Religious ruling or verdict
Fiqh	فِقْه :	Science or knowledge of Islamic laws, jurisprudence, understanding and application of Islamic shari'ah (laws)
Fitnah	فِتْنَة :	Trial, tribulation, affliction, conflict
Ḥadith	حَدِيث :	Prophetic saying (and/or act), the second source of Islamic law after the Glorious Qur'an
Ḥajj	الحَجّ :	Pilgrimage, a pillar of Islam
Ḥalaal (or Ḥalal)	حَلال :	Lawful, allowed, permitted by Islamic law (shari'ah)
Ḥasan	حَسَن :	Good ḥadith (an Islamic term)

Ḥijaab	حِجاب :	Islamic dress-code and related attitudes for Muslim women
Al-*Ḥoor al-'een* (or Hour al-'iyn)	الحُور العين :	Houris, beautiful heavenly virgins of Paradise
Iḥraam	إِحْرَام :	Intention for performing the pilgrimage (Ḥajj) or 'Umrah (minor Ḥajj) and wearing the prescribed dress
Ijtihaad	إجتهاد :	Juristic reasoning to deduct rulings or verdints in Islam
Iqaamah	إقامة :	Second call (similar to adhaan) for establishing actual prayer (Ṣalaah)
I'tikaaf	إِعْتِكَاف :	Seclusion in a mosque to worship Allah (the All-Glorious)
'Ishaa'	عِشَاء :	Night obligatory (Farḍ) prayer, night-time
Istiḥaaḍah	إِسْتِحَاضَة :	Non-menstrual bleeding or irregular vaginal bleeding
Istikhaarah	إِسْتِخَارَة :	A two-rak'ah prayer seeking the guidance of Allah (ﷻ) to do something or not (or to leave it)
Istisqaa'	إِسْتِسْقَاء :	A two-rak'ah prayer invoking Allah (ﷻ) for rain in seasons of drought
Janaabah	جَنابة :	Major ritual impurity due to sexual intercourse or sexual pleasure

Jilbaab	جِلباب :	Women's dress, gown, garment
Junub (Junob)	جُنُب :	Ritually impure (to perform prayer)
Kaafir	كَافِر :	Unbeliever, disbeliever
Ka'bah	الكَعْبَة :	The Holy House in Makkah, the cubic structure in the middle of the Holy Mosque in Makkah
Kaffaarah	كفّارة :	An expiation, an act of expiation
Madhhab	مَذْهَبْ :	A school of juristic thought
Maghrib (Maghreb)	مَغْرِب :	Sunset prayer, sunset, also North African countries
Mahr	مَهْرْ :	Dowry
Mahram	مَحْرَم :	An unmarriageable close relative
Makrooh	مكروه :	Disliked, undesirable, abominable
Masjid	مَسْجِدْ :	Mosque
Minbar	مِنْبَر :	Pulpit
Miswaak (Siwaak)	مسواك (سواك) :	A small or short stick with a softened tip used for brushing or cleaning the teeth
Mithqaal	مِثْقال :	One mithqaal is equal to 4.68 grams
Mujahideen	مُجاهِدين :	Fighters in the cause of Allah (ﷻ), holy fighters (sing.: Mujahid)

Muṣḥaf	مُصْحَفْ :	A copy or a volume of the Qur'an
Mustaḥaaḍah	مُسْتَحاضَة :	A woman having a bleeding or a flow of blood after her days of menstruation
Nafl	نَفْل :	Sunnah (prayer or fasting), optional, supererogatory
Niṣaab	نِصَاب :	The minimum limit above which a wealth or property or trade (business) is subject to tax and Zakah (poor-due), also: quorum
Qamees	قميص :	Shirt, upper garment
Qiblah	قِبْلَة :	The direction of Ka'bah, the direction faced when praying
Qiraaṭ	قيراط :	A dry or square measure, one Qiraaṭ = 175 sqaure metre (of land) or *one Kerat* = 0.195 gram.
Qunoot	قُنُوتْ :	Submissive obedience and devotion, specially during Ṣalaah (prayer), invocation, devoted silence, worship...
Rak'ah	رَكْعَة :	A unit of prayer
Ramaḍaan	رَمَضَان :	The month of fasting, the ninth Hijri month of Islamic calendar
Rukoo'	رُكوع :	Bowing, bowing in prayer
Saheeh	صحيح :	Authentic ḥadith, correct

Salaam	سلام :	Peace, greeting, saying as-salaam 'alaykum (peace be upon you)
Shaafi'iyyah	الشافعية :	A school of juristic thought named after al-Imaam al-Shaafi'ie [may Allah (ﷻ) have mercy on him]
Shayṭaan	الشّيطان :	Satan, the Devil
Shirk	شِرْك :	Polytheism, associating partners or others or anything with Allah (the All-Glorious in worhip
Subḥanallah	سُبْحان الله :	Glory be to Allah
Suḥoor	سُحُور :	Pre-dawn meal before starting everyda's fasting in Ramaḍaan
Sujood	سُجود :	Prostrating in prayer, prostration
Sunan	سُنَن :	Traditions of the Prophet (ﷺ) that we follow, ways of the Prophet (bpuh) – (Sing.: Sunnah)
Sutrah	سُتْرَة :	An object to be put in front of a person when praying but not in congregational prayer (Ṣalaat al-jamaa'ah) in the mosque
Taabi'een	التابعين :	(Sing.: Taabi'ee) persons who met or accompanied one or more of the companions of the Prophet (bpuh), followers of the companions of the Prophet (may Allah be pleased with them all)

Ta'leeq	تعليق :	Not connecting a ḥadith to the Prophet (bpuh) in the chain of narration
Tafseer	تفسير :	Exegesis, explanation of the Qur'an
Ṭahaarah	طَهَارة :	Purity, religiously pure particularly for prayers, physical and spiritual purity
Tahajjud	تَهَجُّد :	Voluntary prayer at night
Taḥiyyatul-Masjid	تَحِيَّةُ المسْجِد :	Two-rak'ah prayer offered immediately when one enters a mosque.
Tajweed	تَجْوِيدْ :	Correct recitation of the Qur'an following precise rules of pronunciation and articulation
Takbeer	تكْبير :	Saying "Allahu Akbar" (Allah is the All-Great) marking the commencement of prayer
Talbiyah	تلبيَة :	Saying "Labbeika Allahumma Labbeik" (meaning: here I am or here we are at Your Sevice complying with Your Order) as a ritual recitation said [repeatedly] when going to Ḥajj or 'Umrah
Taraweeḥ	تراويح :	Ramaḍaan nights prayers, offered after 'Ishaa' prayer in congregation
Tarteel	تَرْتِيلْ :	Rhythmic tone recitation of the Qur'an

Tasbeeḥ	تسبيح :	Saying "Subhanallah" – meaning: glorifying Allah the All-Great
Taṭahhur	تطَهُّر :	Purifying oneself from impurity by having a bath after "janabah"
Ṭawaaf	طَوَاف :	Circumambulating the Ka'bah, going around the Ka'bah (circumambulation)
Tawḥeed	تَوْحِيد :	Monotheism, belief in the Oneness of Allah (ﷻ)
Tilaawah	تلاوة :	Recitation, reading
Tayammum	تيَمُّمْ :	Dry ablution, earth ablution (in the absence of water)
'Umrah	عُمْرَة :	Lesser or minor pilgrimage performed any time of the year
Witr	وِتْر :	Night supererogatory prayer of odd number of rak'aat, i.e.: 1, 3, 5, 7... etc. mostly offered after 'Ishaa' prayer or before sleeping
Wuḍoo'	وُضوءْ :	Ablution, ritual ablution
Zakah	زكاة :	Poor-due, purifying tax payment (2.5%) incumbent on every Muslim. It renders his wealth or property pure and legitimate. One of the five pillars of Islam.
Ẓuhr	ظُهْر :	Midday, mid-day prayer

TRANSLITERATION CHART

أ	a
آ . ى	aa
ب	b
ت	t
ة	h or t (when followed by another Arabic word)
ث	th
ج	j
ح	ḥ
خ	kh
د	d
ذ	dh
ر	r
ز	z
س	s
ش	sh
ص	ṣ
ض	ḍ
ط	ṭ

ظ	ẓ
ع	ʻ
غ	gh
ف	f
ق	q
ك	k
ل	l
م	m
ن	n
هـ — ه — ـه	h
و	w
و (as vowel)	oo
ي	y
ي (as vowel)	ee
ء	ʼ (Omitted in initial position)

ــَ	Fatḥah	a
ــِ	Kasra	i
ــُ	Ḍammah	u
ــّ	Shaddah	Double letter
ــْ	Sukoon	Absence of vowel

SYMBOLS DIRECTORY

(سبحانه وتعالى) : *Subḥaanahu wa Ta'aala* — "The Exalted."

(صلى الله عليه وسلم) : *Ṣalla-Allahu 'Alayhi wa Sallam* —
"Blessings and Peace be upon him."

(عليه السلام) : *'Alayhis-Salaam* — "May Peace be upon him."

(رضي الله عنه) : *Raḍi-Allahu 'Anhu* — "May Allah be pleased with him."

(رضي الله عنها) : *Raḍi-Allahu 'Anha* — "May Allah be pleased with her."

NOTES

NOTES

NOTES